The Revolutionary Party

CONTRIBUTIONS IN SOCIOLOGY

Series Editor: DON MARTINDALE

Small Town and the Nation: The Conflict of Local and Translocal Forces
Don Martindale and R. Galen Hanson

The Social Shaping of Science: Institutions, Ideology, and Careers in Science
Roger G. Krohn

Commitment to Deviance: The Nonprofessional Criminal in the Community
Robert A. Stebbins

Capitalists Without Capitalism: The Jains of India and the Quakers of the West
Balwant Nevaskar

Black Belonging: A Study of the Social Correlates of Work Relations Among Negroes
Jack C. Ross and Raymond H. Wheeler

The School Managers: Power and Conflict in American Public Education
Donald J. McCarty and Charles E. Ramsey

The Social Dimensions of Mental Illness, Alcoholism, and Drug Dependence
Don Martindale and Edith Martindale

***Those* People: The Subculture of a Housing Project**
Colette Pétonnet (Rita Smidt, Translator)

Sociology in Israel
Leonard Weller

THE REVOLUTIONARY PARTY

Essays in the Sociology of Politics

Feliks Gross

Contributions in Sociology, Number 12

GREENWOOD PRESS

Westport, Connecticut · London, England

Library of Congress Cataloging in Publication Data

Gross, Feliks, 1906-
  The revolutionary party.

  (Contributions in sociology, no. 12)
  Includes bibliographical references.
  1. Political parties—History—Addresses, essays,
lectures. 2. Revolutions—History—Addresses, essays,
lectures. 3. Secret societies—History—Addresses,
essays, lectures. I. Title.
JF2011.G76   329'.02   72-806
ISBN 0-8371-6376-5

Library of Congress Catalog Card Number: 72-806

ISBN: 0-8371-6376-5

First published in 1974

Greenwood Press, a division of Williamhouse-Regency Inc.
51 Riverside Avenue, Westport, Connecticut 06880

Manufactured in the United States of America

Here is the most essential difference between Rome and England: the result of civil wars in Rome has been slavery, the fruit of turmoils in England—liberty.　　Voltaire, *Philosophical Letters* (1733)

This is the course of all revolutions: the people revolts but does not know where to stop. It runs to extremes, unaware that the answer is in the middle. . . . All human sentiments are weakened and eventually extinguished, when carried to the extremes. Man, in his attempt to be always free, grows tired of liberty.
Vincenzo Cuoco, Historical Essay on
Revolution of 1799 in Naples (1801)

Fourth Stage:

When the disorder is at its height, weariness brings a desire to return to order and discipline; a despotism of a single man appears less objectionable than the despotism of the people. Whoever dares to seize power is certain to be accepted. Then a bold and ambitious man, a Cromwell or a Bonaparte, emerges from the crowd; armed with a strong will, and backed by a public demand, he snatches power from the mob and gathers it in his own hands. As military force alone can destroy the power of the people, a military despotism is built up on ruins of democratic anarchy.　　Henri de Saint-Simon, *The Reorganization*
of the European Community (1814)

But what do people mean when they proclaim that liberty is the palm, and the prize, and the crown, seeing that it is an idea of which there are two hundred definitions, and that this wealth of interpretation has caused more bloodshed than anything, except theology? It is democracy as in France, or federalism as in America, or the national independence which bounds the Italian view, or the reign of the fittest which is the ideal of Germans?　　Lord Acton, *Inaugural Lecture on the*
Study of History (1895)

Nec totam liberatatem, nec totam servitutem pati passumus.
Tacitus

Contents

Illustrations

Acknowledgments

Most of the essays in this volume first appeared in journals and reviews. With a few exceptions, substantial parts were completely rewritten, with new—sometimes quite extensive—sections and materials added.

May I express here my thanks for permission to reprint the following:

"Beginnings of Major Patterns of Political Parties" and "Sociological Analysis of Political Parties," published in *Il Politico* (Rivista di Scienze Politiche, University of Pavia) 30, no. 3 (1965) and 32, no. 4 (1967).

"Notes on Command and Consensus Structures," *La Revista Mexicana de Sociología* (University of Mexico) 25, no. 2 (1963).

"The Sociology of International Relations, Research and Study," *International Social Science Journal* (UNESCO) 12, no. 2 (1960).

"Independence and Interdependence and the Field of Sociology of International Relations," *Revue Internationale de Sociologie* (Rome) 7, no. 1 (1971).

"Some Sociological Considerations on Underground Movements," *Polish Revue* (New York) 2, no. 2-3 (1956).

This last essay appeared later in my *Seizure of Political Power* (Philosophical Library, 1957), but it has been almost entirely rewritten, and sections were added.

"Political Assassination," *Sociologia Internationalis* (Berlin) 10, no. 2 (1972). This article too is a shorter version of a research paper entitled "Political Violence and Terror" which appeared before *Assassination and Violence*, Volume VIII of a Report to the National

Commission on Causes and Prevention of Violence (Government Printing Office, Washington, D.C., October 1969), pp. 421-476. Comparative materials and a model have been added.

"On Clothing Attire and Symbols" was printed first in Polish in *Tematy* (no. 31-32, 1969), a voluminous quarterly published in Wilton, Connecticut, and it was later translated by Maria de Gorgey. The translated essay has been rewritten and substantially enlarged, with some of my unpublished studies incorporated. The Polish Institute of Arts and Sciences in America was generous and helpful in supplying the initial translation.

"Types of Political Parties" appeared in the appendix of my *World Politics and Tension Areas* (New York University Press, 1966), pp. 297-307, and parts of this essay were reprinted (models reproduced).

Professors Hans Trefousse and Robert East read the manuscript. I am indebted for their criticism and constructive comments.

Teaching and daily academic work impose on us time schedules that cannot be changed. For those who teach, carry on research, and write at the same time, careful apportioning of time is essential. The long hours spent commuting cannot be spared. The New York IRT subway seldom gets a word of praise, but it deserves a kind word. At the night hours the none-too-comfortable cars of the Seventh Avenue Flatbush train turn into reading rooms for Brooklyn College evening students and teachers. At nine, ten, half-past eleven at night, those of us who teach evening and graduate classes rush down into the vast tunnel of the Flatbush subway terminal. We hurry into the cars. The motor is running, brakemen still wait for the late passengers. The doors close automatically, and the train starts rolling with a terrible, oppressive noise. Students open their books and continue to study. Teachers grade and correct papers, some read books, others tense and tired correct galley proofs, read manuscripts.

Brooklyn at night is not a safe place. You cannot board the train safely at certain stops. You can at Flatbush, at Nevins. But crime and danger is not the full story. The human jungle is only a part of the landscape of the great borough of Brooklyn and this civil and enlightened republic, New York City. I carried out my research of this book in the great libraries of New York and Rome. But I wish here to pay my respect to my working companions of the subway cars on the IRT Seventh Avenue train.

Introduction

Although social movements and groups akin to parties appeared in antiquity and medieval times, political clubs made their entrance in times of the Enlightenment. But they were unlike modern parties, especially the disciplined socialist and communist parties of the working class or those of the extreme right, the Fascists and the Nazis of continental Europe. Social and economic inequality, the urge for power, political interests, and differences in religious outlook, ideas, and values divided mankind into political camps even in times of the early urban civilizations. However, political parties as we see them today are a late nineteenth- and twentieth-century phenomenon, and have not always been a welcome one. In antiquity factions were looked upon by some historians with mistrust and suspicion. In medieval Italy two powerful social and political groups—the Guelphs and the Ghibellines—were recorded by a perceptive chronicler as a scourge and disaster. English and American political philosophers and the French of the Enlightenment considered factions, even parties, as contradictory to a free society, a corruption of politics. In times of the French Revolution, political clubs mushroomed. But attitudes changed, revolutionaries were hesitant. Political associations were intermittently prohibited and permitted. In some countries, for example, Italy, the critical, negative attitude toward political parties continued even to the latter part of the nineteenth century. Keen observers quite early saw dangers of total power claimed later by modern continental parties of the extreme right and left.

British and American political parties were quite different from the extreme Continental parties. True, European political philosophers of the eighteenth and nineteenth centuries admired the British parliamentary and the American constitutional governments. True, moderate parties of the left, center, and right—liberals, conservatives, and even democratic socialists—viewed democratic politics of those nations as a model. But Continental parties of a parliamentary democracy faced formidable enemies, parties organized for aggressive political attack. The British and the American did not contend with this type of political pressure and aggression. They grew in a different class structure, in different social and political conditions, and were rooted in quite different political institutions, values, and religious traditions. Political parties are, after all, primarily (of course not solely) organizations geared toward achievement or conquest, the consolidation of political power. The nature of political power in a constitutional democracy is quite different from that in an autocracy or dictatorship. Ostrogorski with his classic study of English and American political parties influenced our perception of parties elsewhere. But certain types of parties in continental Europe, especially the social democratic, peasant parties, communist, and fascist, were quite unlike the British and American counterparts. Their origin and roots were not in the Anglo-American tradition, but in part, at least, in centralistic organizations of the French Revolutions, to mention a prominent model—the Jacobin clubs and also similar patterns that appeared later. Thus various models appeared: the centralistic and vanguardist of professional revolutionaries—small parties, "microparties" of unusual dynamism; "military-command parties," with their political, uniformed militias; underground "small-unit" or cell parties; loosely organized parties of peasants, loyal to a native chieftain who spoke their political language and appealed to their values. The model party of democratic socialist parties, the German Social Democracy (SPD), efficient, broad with its cultural sister organizations, control of trade unions, centrally led and controlled, was widely imitated. This party reflected the smoothly working bureaucratic machinery of the German Reich and something of a Jacobin efficient, centralistic structure.

Let me suggest here a short hypothesis and a premise. A sociological study of political parties, especially those of radical and rapid change, or of aggressive militancy, whether of the right or of the left, encompasses: (1) ideology (the objectives the party attempts to attain); (2) structure (the pattern of its organization); (3) pattern of actions (strategy and tactics). The dynamic nature, and thus effectiveness, of a party of radical change, of political attack, which disregards or acts outside of a parliamentary system, frequently depends on the nature of its structure and its type of tactics. All three elements (variables) are interrelated; their separation reflects only a method of analysis, a matter of logical convenience. Furthermore, the party should be studied within its sociological context, the social-economic conditions in which a party operates. This is of course elementary and seminal.

Let us narrow the problem to structure and tactics. Not the numbers of membership solely, not the passive voters, but the structure of organization and choice of tactics of a party may constitute its strength and success. Certain types of structures, in definite social-political conditions, secure strategic elements of surprise, attack, coordinated action, and efficiency. The various types of party organizations are—to an extent—"neutral." They have been used by those who fought against tyranny and foreign conquest, but also by others, whose intent was to destroy democratic institutions and seize power.

Our times are still times of political crusades. Small, dedicated microparties combined with military units appear in various parts of the globe, with their tactics of violence and flags of liberated humanity. "Liberation" may mean today dictatorship, a tyranny, as well as a free democracy. Symbols are eroded and are used as appeals for never-arriving millenia. Nations today are conquered by foreign and native political parties, by foreign and native military organizations. A violent conquest by a native party or army of their own nation, in the name of "fatherland," "people," or "liberation," may lead, and in fact sometimes has led, to a rule as much or more brutal, exploitative, even cruel, as a foreign one.

* * *

At the turn of the century a revolutionary party had a clear meaning: it was a party of basic and rapid social and political change, a party with a great promise and vision of social justice, economic democracy, and political freedom. Revolutionaries differed in their ideologies, roads they chose, and images they painted of the future society. But they were parties of the hope of freedom and emancipation. There was one final image of a creative social revolution, revolution of freedom, a beginning of a millennium.

The term *revolution* is changing its meaning—so does the revolutionary party. The twentieth-century political revolutions often lead, and may lead in the future, to imposition of tyranny. The revolutionary parties, once destructive of tyrannies and autocracy, have become in the twentieth century a major threat to unstable but democratic governments. The Fascists and the Nazis borrowed the party structure and modes of actions from a model that was once advanced to fight tyrannies. Theirs too was a revolutionary movement, although hostile to freedom and equality. The mushrooming terrorist groups, from Quebec to Uruguay, whatever noble beliefs they may hold, are movements of organized minorities, aimed toward establishing minority and elitist governments.

Revolution, a violent and rapid political change, led some nations to freedom and democracy, others to enlightened—even egalitarian— despotism, still others to tyranny. Great revolutions, as the French and Russian were, had their dialectics, the opposites of extreme freedom and dictatorship. They originated not one, but several social political trends, some of them dialectically opposed, even contradictory.

Machiavelli, in his commentaries to Titus Livius, saw it early, in times of the Renaissance. Voltaire, in *Philosophical Letters*, makes a comparison between Roman, French, and English civil wars. The Roman—he writes—led to autocracy, the English to institutions of freedom.

The political obstacles to necessary social change may be of such a nature that only a violent revolution will open up the roads. The French Revolution was of such nature, argued Saint-Simon. At certain stages of development, a profound, a "revolutionary" social change may be a necessity, but its success does not always depend on violence. To the contrary, working democratic institutions may supply the necessary mechanism for careful selection of intelligent alternatives, for the establishment of priorities. Violent, political revolution resulting in seizure of political power may not bring about desirable changes in social-economic institutions, human behavior, and values. Military revolutions in South America may serve as examples.

Today *revolution* has many meanings. It may mean profound social transformation, rational, enlightened, and free of violence; it may also mean tactics of violence applied by militant microparties, just a technique, a process of violence which carries new elites. *Revolution* also means the disintegration of society, institutions, and values, a kind of a void that does not last. It is a process of social and economic disintegration moving toward reintegration. For some the word itself, its connotation has a magic appeal of hope and heroism; to others, it speaks only of terror.

* * *

In this introduction I attempt to survey major themes and findings of the entire volume, present a kind of guide for the book. This volume is a collection of essays, related in a general way, with a theme common to the entire volume. Most essays were, however, written as separate studies, with the exception of the second and third, at different times. In consequence, some minor repetitions appear in this collection and were not deleted.

The first two essays discuss, in a historical, comparative perspective, the emergence of modern political parties and of the centralistic patterns of revolutionary parties. Chapter 2, "Origins of the Centralistic and Revolutionary Party," discusses the differences between Anglo-American and continental European party models, specifically the centralistic, militant "command parties," which appeared in our times. "Dynamics of a Political Party" (Chapter 3) points to three variables—ideology (value-goals), structure, and pattern of actions (strategy and tactics)— as seminal variables. The major theme, however, is the structure of parties. All three essays are closely tied. The latter two closely follow my lecture on this subject at the University of Milan, where I had the privilege to lecture, at the invitation of the distinguished Italian sociologist and philosopher of law, Professor Renato Treves, and my course in the Department of Political Science, University of Rome, in a program directed by Professor Franco Ferrarotti, while I was a Fulbright lecturer at this University in 1964/65. Both essays appeared in *The Politico* of the University of Pavia. For inclusion in this volume, they have been enlarged and rewritten.

Chapter 4, "The Underground Movements," analyses a specific social-political scenario, secret political movements under foreign conquest, and underground activities against democracy. A short version of this chapter appeared in *Revista Mexicana de Sociología* and in *Polish Revue*, and was later included as a chapter of my book *Seizure of Political Power*. Here again the essay has been entirely rewritten and substantially enlarged.

Terror and assassination belong to the political tactics of violence. Chapter 5, which discusses this subject, is based on my work with the National Commission on Causes and Prevention of Violence, and has appeared in an extensive version in the eight-volume staff report, *Assassination and Violence*, edited by J. F. Kirkham, S. G. Levy, and W. J. Crotty (Washington, D.C.: Government Printing Office, 1970). However, I have included new material and have also used data from other parts of this report. This shorter version appeared in *Sociologia Internationalis* (Berlin).

Militant political parties of our times have developed tactical patterns and techniques of manipulation of multitudes, which contradict the nature of democratic political processes. Man learned early to control his fellow man and maintain subordination by symbols and rituals, even symbols as simple as colors of superordination on the Roman toga. In our times new techniques have appeared. Projection or displacement of military behavior (as well as uniforms) into social movements has permitted party command to manipulate vast multitudes. Potentially volatile crowds have been integrated into disciplined political regiments. Projection of religious behavior into politics secured religious worship of the top party commander, producing modern Caesaristic cults of party leaders. These phenomena are discussed in Chapter 6, "Random Notes on Dress, Rituals, Symbols, and Myth Making," which was first published in Polish in a special issue of the quarterly *Tematy*. For inclusion here the essay has been substantially enlarged. My observations on rituals, symbols, and mass manipulation go back to the early thirties, when as a traveler through Germany, I was struck by the sudden changes of that country, the changed loyalties of even some prominent scholars, and the powerful appeal of political symbolism and ritualism. My interest continued, and I noticed later the variety of "projective" and symbolic techniques (manipulation by parties of a quite different political identity) in other nations. Politics had displaced religion; it had become a new chiliastic creed in our times.

Strong appeal to emotions, hatred, and clear identification of an "arch enemy" are elements of an excitatory political pattern practiced by a variety of totalitarian parties. In the Anglo-American tradition, the political pattern is inhibitory, discouraging appeal to violence and extreme forms of hatred. Electoral appeals are dominated by pragmatic, businesslike platforms and an ideological appeal of a general, philosophical nature. Political symbolism and ritualism of political parties (not of the Parliament and Crown) is restrained and generally free of excessive hostility.

The ideal type model of command and consensus (to which I refer in my discussion of party structure) is discussed in a short chapter, "Notes on Command and Consensus Structures," which first appeared in *Revista Mexicana de Sociologia* 25 (1963) and was reprinted in the *Indian Journal of Social Research* 14 (1963). The next-to-last chapter, "Approaches to a Sociology of International Relations," points to the sociology of international relations and to the major task: the elimination of violence between nations. An understanding of the sociological nature of conflict and cooperation may contribute to our outlook and assist in making more rational policies. Chapter 9, "Independence and Interdependence," which is something of an addendum, was an introductory address at the section of international sociology at the XXII Congress (1969) of the International Institute of Sociology in Rome, and appeared first in the *Revue Internationale de Sociologie*. The second section of the chapter, "Sociology of International Relations," was published in the *International Social Science Journal of UNESCO*.

Widespread tactics of violence and secret, terroristic political micro-parties have appeared in many corners of our globe. Some were the consequence of suffering, social ills and extreme forms of oppression, others were geared toward future dictatorship and totalitarian rule. The study of the sociological nature of political parties is not solely of academic interest.

I

Early Concepts
of a Political Party:
The Changing Social Images

1. THE BEGINNINGS

Political parties of today are perhaps one of the most powerful forces
of social and political change. Here is a creative and destructive elementary force, which builds and ruins, a force which deals with a major
commodity, major energy: political power, and which can be used for
a variety of objectives: to build a democracy or destroy it and build an
autocracy instead.

When did political parties appear? Are they an entirely new, nine-
teenth- or twentieth-century phenomenon? The answer is not simple.
No doubt, the appearance of organized political mass parties in the
nineteenth century marks a beginning of a historical and political period.
But social institutions grow slowly and are more often than not a result
of a long and cumulative process. Later, we shall follow the emergence
of two different major sociological patterns of political parties—those
in England and America and, in the eighteenth and nineteenth centuries,
those in continental Europe. But the process of growth and change of
political parties during the nineteenth and twentieth centuries does not
suffice to trace the very beginnings of social movements directed toward
different or conflicting social goals. The early origins are more distant
in time.

Something similar to parties or movements probably existed in the
early stages of urban society and organized states, when social stratification and inequality appeared. A party meant then an informal
grouping of a leader and followers who had similar economic interests,

1

political goals, or religious beliefs. A commodity for which many compete may of course result in divisions and formation of groups. In the ancient cities man attempted to dominate others, for his own sake and welfare. He exploited others, to spare himself effort and to secure economic and political power. Political power, which secures both freedom and domination over others for those in the saddle, is a scarce and respected commodity. The drive of social groups toward domination and subordination of sections of population appeared early in the forms of slavery and class stratification. Opposition to such domination and struggle for economic betterment and political rights of the ruled at times resulted in social movements, at least in the Greek and Roman city-states.

But again, this is only a part of the story. Plurality and diversity of values and goals, diversity in perception and loyalties also appeared early, or relatively early, in the city-states of the Mediterranean. Parties of a kind were formed in city-states of the Mediterranean when people related differently to a changing situation, such as a threat of foreign invasion, or on the other hand, alliances and peace-making. Diversity of religious orientations appeared among the Israelites, and the prophets and their followers were among the early forces in social movements. Divergent religious interpretations might sometimes, but not necessarily always, have corresponded to economic or political interests. Man's relation to the supernatural is by itself a powerful motivating force, especially at that time.

These social movements were, however, loose, informal groupings of leaders and followers, sometimes, of multitudes. When such movements were structured, institutionalized, they appeared in the form of religious sects or military organizations.

Ancient republican Rome had political parties, of course, but they were not akin to political organizations of modern times. A "party" was a simple group of friends and clients. Friendship was the basic party bond and *amicitia* the fitting term. Since friendship was strong and alive among men, a candidate expected backing and support from his *amici* and *clienti*, the dependents or followers. The latter flocked daily at the master's house to pay respect or to get the customary assistance. Friendship, *amicitia*, implied the exchange of mutual favors and help.[1]

Amicitia was a rather personal relationship between men, a relationship of equality and based on mutual sentiment and loyalty. Favors were exchanged among friends as an expression of mutual trust, loyalty, and, above all, sentiments. In the ideal type, friendship is primarily nonmaterialistic. Material gifts and political favors are a consequence of an emotional and spiritual relationship. Contrariwise, clientelism involves voluntary subordination of clients to the master. This, of course, is not a personal relationship of equals. The master and client are bound by sentiments of fidelity and favors; assistance and support are a consequence and reward of the latter. Friendship or fidelity are different attitudes, values, or relationships than modern party discipline.

Even today in Italian villages and small towns, some of those ancient and traditional attitudes in politics have survived and must have continued throughout the long evolution of political parties. The party leader who runs for an office of a *sindaco*, a village mayor, expects support from his extended family, his numerous *cuggini* (cousins), *compadri* (friends), and followers, who were called in ancient times *clienti*. The candidate knows their children, knows their troubles; he inquires, he tries to help. The reward for his effort is fidelity, a personal loyalty. When the *sindaco* changes the party colors, *cuggini, compadri,* and present-day *clienti* vote for him anyway. Deep in the hills of Abruzzi or Frosinone, a party member opposed to a *sindaco* will tell you today about the mutual exchange of favors of a *cricca,* the ruling clique, which—he will argue—is bound by mutual interest. (The American party system has of course also traditions of clientelism, cliques, and a spoils system. But still, there is a definite, an organized, and, frequently, an efficient party machine. But let us return to ancient Rome.)

With the growth of the empire, these groupings were extended, they were no longer solely personal in nature, as they used to be in republican times. The "party" now had a longer duration, even some kind of a program. They are now called *factio*, sometimes *pars* (a part), or *partes.* For the poet Plantus (second to third century B.C.), the term *factio* still meant a group of friends. But slowly it acquired the evil connotation of a group of men in high position scheming together for their own good.

The Roman historian Sallust (first century B.C.) tells us that *amicitia* means friendship among good men and *factio* among bad. The term from which our *faction* and *party* originated begins to have a negative, pejorative meaning. Sallust uses *factio* for a clique of nobles. Cicero (first century B.C.) speaks already about two major parties, one of the nobles, the other of the people, the "populists." Unlike Sallust—writes historian L. R. Taylor—Cicero calls them *classes*, indicating two major ones: *optimates* and *populares.*[2] In moments of acute struggle or crises, sections of the legions supplied the organized, disciplined structure of capture and consolidation of power.

2. THE BLUES AND THE GREENS—
POLITICAL PARTIES OF THE
ROMAN CIRCUS

A powerful social movement appeared, however, during the declining years of the Roman Empire. This movement rose to unusual significance and grew in power during the fifth and sixth centuries A.D. Here were "political parties" of a kind, of course, in terms of this historical period. These powerful "factions" originated from what we would call in the nineteenth century jockey clubs, or harness racing clubs. By the fourth and fifth centuries the racing clubs of Rome, *factiones*, already had a political significance and circus activities were associated with social and political demands. Centuries later political factions were associated at first with religious movements, and later they grew from philosophical clubs.

The chariots—harness racing of the times—was a popular "passive" sport in Rome, later in Constantinople. It was passive since it was a sport of crowds of onlookers; it provided an outlet for emotions rather than exercise of muscles of individuals. Since the cost of chariot racing was exorbitant, the *factiones* were formed to finance the circus show. Thus, the very term for political faction originates with those racing clubs (*factiones*). Each *factio* maintained and paid for its horse farms, stables, equipment, jockeys, trainers (*magistri*), charioteers, veterinarians, tailors— to mention only some of the numerous personnel, in Roman way, carefully and precisely identified and structured. The club paid also a cheerleader and his band, *iubilatores*, whose cries and exhortations encouraged the charioteers and excited the crowds of onlookers. *Factiones* competed in those famous races in the race track of the time, the Circus of Rome, and later in the Hippodrome of Constantinople.

Rome had four major racing clubs: the Whites (*factio albata*), the Greens (*factio prasina*), and on the other hand the Blues (*factio veneta*) and the Reds (*factio russata*). The season began in January. Twenty-two races were run in one day, interrupted by such exciting events as fights of men against wild beasts, tightrope walking, and wrestling—enough to totally absorb and channel the emotions of multitudes.

Those racing clubs had thousands of fans, or factionists, who were far more dedicated and pugnacious than their modern descendants, the enthusiastic fans of Dodgers, Yankees, Mets, or Red Socks. This sport of

the onlookers, this "passive sport," also played a far more important
role in the life of the city and nation than it does in our times. From
the records of chroniclers and historians, from the glorification of
gladiators and charioteers on colorful mosaics (e.g., in the Museum of
Villa Borghese in Rome), we can guess today their role in this ancient
civilization. The famous Roman historian Suetonious in his short account
on the reign of Emperor Domitian singles out as one of his major contributions the addition of two new chariot racing teams, the Golds and
the Purples.

Initially, emotions and interests of a volatile and idling populace
were channeled from politics into circus, from the business of exercise
of political power into the tense climate of games. But the excitement
of the circus led to frequent and violent fights between the racing fans,
the factionists, identified by colors. As in politics, polarization intensified the competitive and frequently hostile sentiment. The contrasting
colors of the factions intensified the opposition as they did and do in
war. The racing clubs were eventually reduced to two major factions,
the Blues and Greens. Sport and racing could not be the only cause of
those struggles, although they moved the conflict, fed hostilities, and
prompted and precipitated brawls and fights. There were probably
political, social and economic differences between the Greens and the
Blues. With time, the Greens found support among sections of the
populace, which might be called small bourgeoisie and "proletariat"
traders, craftsmen, and sailors. The Blues had the sympathies of the
landed elite whom we would today call an upper class, perhaps aristocracy,
and their followers.

When the center of power moved from Rome to Constantinople, so
did the enthusiasm for racing with its brawls between the Green and
Blue factions. Tensions increased, and so did polarization between those
two powerful "political-sport parties." These colors were "functional"
symbols, used to emphasize the difference, thereby keeping people
apart in competition and conflict. This difference in color extended to
style of clothing, and appeared not only during the races but even in
daily street life. Procopius of Caesarea, a prominent historian of this
period (sixth century A.D.), reported:

> The factionists above all introduced a new style of hairdo. They cut
> their hair in a different way than the Romans. Factionists grew
> whiskers and beards, as long as possible, Persian style, and instead of
> removing hair from their temples, they let them hang long and

spread, like the Massagets. For this reason this style was called a fashion of the Hunns.

They dressed in an unusually careful manner and beyond their means. They wore tunics with sleeves very tight at their wrists and then enlarging to an incredible size. That way, when they threw the arms screaming and inciting in theaters and circuses, this part of their dress was lifted suddenly and gave the impression of a powerful body. . . .

They have adopted coats, trousers and many types of shoes according to the fashion of the Hunns, and identified by Hunnic names.

Procopius tells us that many carried weapons.

At the time of Justinian, streets in Constantinople were unsafe, and as Procopius relates, no one even knew why people were assassinated. Now the streets belonged to the factions. In the dark of the streets, the Greens assassinated the Blues, but soon they murdered also those who had no adversity to them.

The city was terrorized by the bands of Blues and Greens. There was no need to hide the crimes, continued Procopius, since the factionists were not afraid of punishment. In fact they did emulate in perpetration of crime just for the sake of a show of force and courage, to demonstrate their prowess, skill in killing a man with a single coup of a dagger. The factionists did not hesitate to kill an accidental passerby.

Eventually, this conflict between the Blues and Greens developed into a powerful revolutionary mob action, threatening the power of the emperor. Pretenders to the imperial office now attempted to win support of factions. However, a bloody massacre in the Hyppodrome of Constantinople, in which both the Blues and Greens were slaughtered by legions of Justinian, followed by execution of pretenders, put an end to the growing tension and unrest. Chroniclers relate that 30,000 were killed, but statistics of those times were not very precise.

The Blues and Greens have had a long story. Their beginnings can be traced as early as the first Roman emperors, and they were still active in the ninth century A.D. But by the twelfth century, chroniclers mention them as past history.[3] Thus the time span of those circus parties was close to a millennium. The significance of factions as a political force seems to have increased by the fifth and sixth centuries, when Emperor Theodorius favored the Greens.

The history of Blues and Greens gives us distant glimpses in political psychology. For so many scholars today, socioeconomic determinism has displaced the belief of medieval historians in a direct intervention of Providence or Satan in a historical destiny of man and nations. The great unknown social forces are always at work, of course. But history of mankind is made of a complex process, in which individuals and strong emotions shared by groups and multitudes may at times decide. There is this emotional, psychological strain which appeared in this powerful movement of Blues and Greens, at least in their beginnings. Those circus parties were fed on tensions and emotions generated in the arena, and later the goals and actions were attached to or projected into politics. Then of course, tensions escalated, now moved by powerful interests of social classes.

This emotional, "circoid" nature of intense conflict, even protracted rioting, rebellion, is not banished solely to the distant past. In September 1969, the town of Caserta in Italy witnessed a true soccer revolution, in which thousands of "factionists" of a local team occupied and burned the railroad station, built barricades in the streets, and fought police. The riots were a response to a decision of the football league: the local soccer team, *Casernana*, was not promoted to League B, and was kept in lower class C. In May 1964, when in Lima, Peru, the referee nullified a goal won by the Peruvians against an Argentine team, the goodnatured fans changed into a mob.

In September 1962, Gabonese and Senegalese were slain and wounded in a "soccer war" which erupted after a victory of a team of Congo over a team of Gabon. Several Gabonese were killed, thirty wounded, and riots lasted several days.

Incidents of senseless killings in the streets of Constantinople are not only a distant historical case. Today, New York could probably offer some comparative data of violence, though distant in time. In May 1969, 2,000-3,000 young people, mostly students, invaded Zap, a small community in North Dakota. The business section, a block-long main street of this village, was completely destroyed in a joyful enterprise.[4]

The ancient records of Constantinople and today's news from Lima, Congo, Zap, and Caserna may suggest that violent behavior, release of hostilities is natural to man, while it is usually controlled by external or internal discipline rooted in our values.

Perhaps in this history of Blues and Greens we can see some of the deep-seated psychological needs, which suddenly surfaced as social behavior, and which are necessary to bring about a powerful social political movement (such as socioeconomic processes, ethnic and national conflicts, value conflicts, struggle for power).

In the story of Greens and Blues, we can also see the significance of stress, of emphasis on difference in building of the political parties, and of manipulation of hostilities. Hatred is a powerful political drive. True, hatred, hostilities, have their roots above all in deprivation and frustration of man, but in some cases hatred is also a "cause" in itself. Hating is a part of human nature of so many. In our times some nations were artificially divided on a parallel and incited to fight. And they did. To institutionalize hostility, symbolic difference must be emphasized and manipulated. In the case of Blues and Greens, (1) the attention was centrally focused in the Hippodrome; (2) all other interest was temporarily suppressed by the show; (3) emotions were intensified and easily manipulated; (4) the onlooker self-identified with the color of his faction; (5) antagonism was displayed toward individuals of contrasting color (opposed faction) so that the "enemy" was identified as a clear target of action; and (6) aggression was released toward a target identified by color.

The Nazi Parteitag bears certain limited similarities. The great party stadium of Nuremberg, like the Hippodrome of Constantinople, lent itself to manipulation of masses by means of exhortation, music, and lights. Hitler and his elite supplied the focus. The multitudes were excited by direct appeal to hostilities, not by means of games. Hitler's cohorts were structured and disciplined, unlike those in the Hippodrome. But here and there, intense hostilities were set free; they were associated with an "enemy," who was "developed" by manipulators (in the German case) in an elaborate way into a target of aggression.

3. GHIBELLINES AND GUELPHS

Political movements also appeared, of course, in medieval cities, sometimes as popular movements, usually with religious tendencies. Religion supplied the ideological focus and rationale. Those who favored secular power and those who favored ecclesiastical domination mutually formed their "parties" or even organized armed camps. Supporters of contending families banded together. Family or dynastic loyalty was their ideology, fidelity the dominant value.

In medieval theory, to quote Gierke, "Church and State were two coordinate powers," but they were also distinct, independent: on one hand, *sacerdotium,* on the other, *imperium.* This order, according to this theory, was originated by the Lord, for the distinct but coordinate powers had their unity in the hands of God. This unity was twofold and was a consequence of the two aspects of the Christian community. The unity, however, was a desired goal and only a political ideal.

Two major power centers guide the political history of medieval times: the secular and the ecclesiastical. The paramount influence of the papacy and of the imperial crown affected the entire social and political life and conditions of Western Europe. The realities of this politics were supported by and took also an impetus from medieval political theory, which supplied adequate political philosophy (we may say today rationalization) for the two competing centers and in consequence, political movements. The two orders, spiritual and temporal, were in a continuous competition for power, sometimes for supremacy. This competition moved at times into bloody conflicts.

The Ghibelline and Guelph parties, whose history spans the late medieval period, are the two major actors of this drama of the medieval political theater. The Ghibellines carry the banners of Roman emperors in this struggle and fight for secular power and imperial supremacy in Italy. The Guelphs support the papacy against the secular supremacy of the emperor.

The two great parties of medieval times appeared by the end of the twelfth century in Italy. (These two appellations originated from corrupted German family names.) The Ghibellines and Guelphs were political movements from the beginning. Their goals, throughout the thirteenth century, were clear. The Ghibellines were the party of *imperium,* of temporal power of the emperor and aristocratic domination of the cities, while the Guelphs supported the supreme power of the papacy, at the same time defending the popular government, the democratic municipal institutions of the times. The Roman republican traditions, not yet fully extinguished, survived in custom and in a modest form. The cities saw in papacy an ally against the Roman emperors.

Guelphs were at the time also an early augury of a party of the nascent Italian nationalism opposed to the German princes. Both social movements also had a class identification. The Ghibellines were a party of the aristocracy, the Guelphs of the popular classes of the cities. The craftsmen, the artisans, belonged to the guilds, while the nobility and clergy formed separate estates. Divisions were clear, established and safeguarded by means of law and public institutions. But estates and guilds of those corporate states reflected only in fact the class character of the medieval society. The Florentine aristocrats of the time owned large, landed estates; the nobles lived also in cities and had their urban residences. They inhabited the same streets in close neighborhoods, and their urban strongholds could be recognized by the towers.

Florence of the twelfth and thirteenth centuries was a commercial, financial, and industrial center. Three major classes or social strata could be identified in the thirteenth century: The *grandi*, the aristocracy. Their profession was a military one; their income came from estates. By and large, they were Ghibellines. Below were the popular classes, *i popolani*, mostly Guelphs. With time, new divisions split the *popolani* into two subclasses. The members of the powerful and rich "greater guilds" belonged to a kind of upper bourgeoisie and were called *popolo grasso*, "fat people." Below, the *popolo minuto*, "minor" or "small" people, belonged to the less prosperous "lesser guilds." The "small people" had far less access to political power than the *grassi*, the fat ones. Below the grassi and minuti were the *ciompi*, the "wooden shoes," as they were called. *Ciompi* were the working classes who did not enjoy any privileges of free associations. They did not form guilds, and their conditions of work were hard, far more so than those of the legally protected guilds.

In spite of this medieval structure, within the context of time, Florence enjoyed a surprising share, if only a share, of freedom. Serfdom was abolished in Bologna as early as 1256. The abolition of serfdom was, of course, an extended process rather than a single act. Florence followed Bologna, and by 1289 serfdom legally ceased to exist in the Florentine republic, almost six hundred years prior to abolition of serfdom in Russia and about five and a half centuries before the emancipation in most of the central European states.

The sharp dividing line between the Ghibelline *grandi* aristocracy and Guelph *popolani* led to frequent clashes and feuds. This was the conflict between partisans of temporal and ecclesiastic power, but at the same time it was also a class struggle with a national overtone. It was a struggle between the partisans of an aristocratic domination and defenders of a democratic (in terms of time) and independent municipal government.

Machiavelli, in his *History of Florence* (*Istorie Fiorentine*, Book III, Chapter 1) wrote about this class conflict in a brutally clear and simple manner: "A serious and quite natural hostility which arises between the nobles and the popular classes is a consequence of the will and wish of the first to command while others are not willing to obey. Those are the reasons of all evils which are born in the city. This diversity of sentiments, tendencies, is the cause of all evils which disturb the Republic."[5]

The political struggles of Florence were ruthless, and total defeat, even extermination, of enemies was desired more often than compromise. Conflicts were cumulative and intensive: social, political, international. They led to a kind of "ethnic" tension and brawls between inhabitants of two republics when Guelph Florentines met with Ghibelline Pisans in Rome in the thirteenth century.

Victors had little mercy for the defeated, who were killed, banished, or, if lucky, escaped to exile. Their property was confiscated. Already at that time, Guelphs settled in France as political exiles.

The Guelphs, with all their popular and democratic sentiments, were no friends of freedom of conscience. Paradoxically the Ghibellines harbored heretics and dissidents. In those intolerant centuries, they did have some tolerance for religious and philosophical difference.

Where the populist Guelphs won, the proud towers of aristocratic mansions were cut down to a proper size of seventy-five feet, and bricks were used to strengthen the walls of the city. When, in turn, the Guelphs were defeated, their houses were torn down and their property confiscated. There was a fury in this method. The Ghibelline ruthless and cruel terror was answered by a Guelph terror against the Ghibelline heretics and schismatics. The thirteenth-century religious "storm troopers," called the Society of Captains of the Holy Mary, were dedicated to the extermination of heretics. Their leader, Friar Pietro of Verona, who led expeditions against religious dissidents, was rewarded with a high rank of Inquisitor of Tuscany and Lombardy. Eventually killed by people tired of his persecutions, the tormentor became a martyr saint—St. Peter, martyr of Verona.

Indeed, both parties were instruments of persecutions. After the victory of the Guelph party, a list was made of those who suffered from the persecution of brutal and cruel Ghibellines. The property of the latter was confiscated. The confiscated capital (called *il monte*) was now divided into three parts: one to repay indemnity of Ghibelline crime to Guelph victims, second for the commune, third for the Guelph party.

Now the Guelph party was structured and organized. Six party governors were elected: three from Guelph Knights and three from popular classes. Two councils were in control of the treasury: the privy council of fourteen and a general council of sixty members. First, they met in a church (Santa Maria Sopra Porta) but soon they had their own party headquarters. Their major goal was persecution of the political enemies, the Ghibellines. Quite efficient in their pious work, they soon had achieved political power. Historian Villari writes: "Excluding all political opponents from public post, sentencing them to exile, and confiscating their goods, these functionaries rose to increasing power and injured the republic they served."

The populists were not satisfied by simply ousting the nobles, continues Villari; they wanted their lives, and this was accomplished by bloodshed and revolutions.

Machiavelli's comparative method employs contrast rather than analogy. In comparing the class conflicts in Rome and Florence, his account of the Roman past might not be entirely accurate. By use of comparison and contrast, however, the issues of Florence are sharply drawn:

> In Rome [writes Machiavelli, in *Florentine Histories*], the hostilities at their very inception were solved by law, in Florence by exile and death of many citizens. The struggles of Rome increased the military virtues, while those in Florence were wasted; the feuds of Rome led from equality of citizen to the greatest inequality; those in Florence from inequality to a wonderful [*mirabile*] equality. This difference in effects was caused by difference in goals. The people of Rome desired to share the supreme power with nobles, those of Florence wanted to be alone in government and exclude the nobles.

Thus political conflicts, and those violent *mutamenti*, changes as they were called, led at the end to a tyranny of a powerful family, an enlightened one but still tyrannical.

Thus, Florence had political parties, and the name *Parte Guelpha*, Guelph party, was in use in the fourteenth century. It was an institution, corresponding in form to laws and customs of its time.

The function was rather simple: create a party fund and persecute adversaries (Ghibellines). The Guelph party also had its governance: *Lo Statuto Della Parte Guelpha*. This governance of 1335 is probably the oldest known party bylaws. The Ghibellines also had a well-developed ideology. Dante's treaty on monarchy, *De Monarchia*, was a capital text. Dante was a Ghibelline and a "White."

In the twelfth and thirteenth centuries, Florence had parties of a kind, institutionalized at least in part, with some kind of ideologies. With time, the nature, the ideology of Ghibellines and Guelphs changed. At the beginning of the fourteenth century, Ghibellines were not what they used to be. New factions of Whites and Blacks emerged. The Whites supported the secular power.

The story of the Ghibelline and Guelph parties spans one and a half centuries of the late medieval times and early Renaissance. Their major theme was the struggle between ecclesiastic and secular power.

Power distribution and power relations of medieval times produced a variety of patterns of political conduct. A political situation usually suggests a limited number of possible responses, which we today call "options." Thus, in addition to ruthless conflicts and complete submission, other types of conduct and answers appeared, sometimes akin to modern techniques or tactics. Compromise is, of course, an ancient and essential device, seminal in politics, but political games and infiltration can also be traced to thirteenth-century Italy.

Thus, the citizens of the Republic of Todi, a medieval city-state, finally eased the ruthless and brutal struggles between the Ghibellines and Guelphs by an ingenious compromise. In order to achieve the desired *concordia,* they decided to elect a government composed of eight *priori*—four of them Ghibellines and four Guelphs. This *concordia* lasted only seven years (1330-1337), however.

Il Pope Boniface VIII (1294) also knew how to infiltrate parties and play shrewd political games. In Todi he infiltrated or won over the antipapal Ghibelline party, which turned propapal but kept its proimperial and antipapal name. When the once imperial and antipapal party became propapal, the papal Guelphs also reversed themselves becoming antipapal but retaining their propapal name.

By now the term "party" or "faction" was associated with this cruel past. The "acoustic image," as an early semanticist would say, had its full of negative content, of pejorative meaning. It meant a political evil, and more about this will be said later. Of course, Ghibellines and Guelphs are not parties of modern times, but they carry the seeds, the elements on which modern parties grow.

The Reformation a few generations later was not only a religious revolution; it was also a social and political revolution. Thus, the religious movements, whether in Bohemia or England, were at the same time social, political, and philosophical. They assumed the social bonds of religious congregations and of military ranks. Religion and politics, sects and "parties," of this time were fused. These early movements were a consequence of the very nature of man—his economic or class interest, his drive for power, his inquiring mind, personal loyalties, religious zeal, and ethical commitments—as well as of the imperative to respond to changing situations. This type of social movement was, however, different from the modern democratic mass parties or those totalitarian or semitotalitarian highly disciplined organizations that are guided and commanded by their central committees, submissive to their superelites and leader, and integrated by an elaborate political ideology.

4. THE LEVELLERS

The early forerunners of modern movements also made their entrance in times of Reformation as they did in Italian cities in times of Renaissance. The sentiments and values they expressed point to the continuity of our civilization and to moral heritage.

About 1646, during the Civil War in England, a sect appeared, which had already a rudimentary organization of a political party. The Levellers, as they were called, practiced democracy in their own movement, a democratically elected House and democracy of the local government were essential tenets of their platform. They were among the early religious-political movements that elevated religious toleration to the fundamental principle and a political program. The Levellers, as well as their more radical brethren, the Diggers, were egalitarians.

The Leveller views and ideology could be traced to Anabaptists, the early pacifist forefathers, who rejected war and military taxes, as well as capital punishment. They did not take oath nor did they have any paid ministry. The leader of the German peasant war of 1525, Thomas Munzer, and his followers were close to the Anabaptist creed.

The Levellers were a revolutionary party in the original meaning of this term, a party of an enlightened, humane, and fundamental social change. "The Levellers anticipated our fathers in most of the social and political reforms of the next three hundred years," wrote H. W. Brailsford in his fascinating study of this movement. Until Cromwell crushed them, continues Brailsford, they carried the initiative in the crucial years of interregnum and would have done for the peasants what the French Revolution accomplished one and a half century later.[6]

Their Royalist adversaries saw them as an ugly and despicable lot. The contemporary weekly *Mercurius Politicus* (16. November, 1647) wrote about agitators:

> By the name of Levellers, a most apt title for such a despicable and desperate knot to be known by, the endeavor to cast down and level the enclosures of nobility, gentry and propriety, to make us all even, so that every Jack shall vie with a gentleman and every gentleman be made a Jack.

This progressive movement had a substantial support from the middle class, craftsmen, and farmers. There were among them well-to-do merchants as well as weavers and lead-miners.

The Puritans based their creed and orthodoxy strongly on the tenets of the Old Testament. The Anabaptists and the Levellers looked instead toward the early, egalitarian Christian church and ethics of the New Testament.

In those times, the spoken word spread, above all, from the pulpit and the academic lectern. The dialogue was cultivated in the tavern. The religious dissent grew often in university halls as had happened in Prague where Jan Huss lectured. The sermons from the pulpit of the churches were listened to by multitudes and with the exception of those times of dissent, accepted obediently. The university halls had a selected though small audience.

It was the tavern which became a political meeting point, a kind of political club. The Levellers' headquarters were located in certain inns, and there they had their meetings. In the urban centers, pamphlets were also circulated, but they did not reach the large masses of uneducated and illiterate.

Each district in London elected its party representatives called "London Agents." Each member paid his dues to the party treasurer. The Levellers had also their headquarters, their "party organ," a weekly news, and a party color (sea green).

They had their peaceful tactics (petitioning the parliament), and when their actions failed to give results, they tried to win the army. Thousands of women signed a petition on behalf of Leveller prisoners and carried it to the House of Parliament, displaying sea green ribbon on their dresses. At times it was an influential, even a powerful, movement.

Thus, the Levellers had their ideology, rudiments of an organizational structure, and their patterns of political action.

In their platforms of 1648, they asked for an active and passive parliamentary franchise for all men of twenty-one years of age and older. The supreme authority had to be given to the representatives chosen by this electorate, to the House of Commons. They called for abolition of the death penalty except for murder and treason, vast enlightened reforms of the judicial system, separation of the legislative and executive powers, and extension of civil rights. Indeed, they were centuries ahead.

Their major merit was, however, the elevation of religious toleration to a fundamental principle. The idea and practice of toleration can be found in the Greek and Roman civilization. Even a short-lived edict of toleration was proclaimed in Milan (312 A.D.) in the times of Constantine. We may find lonely and courageous philosophers of religious toleration during the Renaissance, for example, when Pico de la Mirandola appealed to the dignity of man. Sometimes edicts of toleration were signed as a political compromise of contending parties (the Edict of Nantes in France). However, the Levellers were among those early organized movements which elevated the toleration for all as a fundament of a civil society. The Levellers, like the Anabaptists, rejected any coercion in matters of religion.

Brailsford sees in the Levellers the first modern, democratically run political party. Still, the Levellers are a party of the Civil War, a party of their times, when religious differences divided men into political causes. Political philosophy was already separated from religion, but the powerful, historical social movements were still religious or perhaps political-religious, social-religious. And so were the Levellers a party of their times, still anchored in religious divisions which were deep-seated in armies and politics.

Our modern civilization is built on few, very few indeed, core values or fundamental principles. Toleration is paramount among them. Religious toleration led to political toleration and reinforced a general respect for dissent.

The Levellers formed what we may call today, the extreme left, the radical wing of the English Revolution. The extreme left of the English Civil War advocated an uncompromising, unqualified toleration and respect for difference. They practiced what they believed.

The extreme left of the French Revolution practiced and professed intolerance toward ideological dissenters. The extreme left of the Russian Revolution elevated ideological intolerance to a major political principle.

5. SECULARIZATION OF POLITICAL IDEA SYSTEMS

It seems that the ideological premise of the modern political movements appeared with the age of Enlightenment and rationalism, when
scholars and thinkers once again separated political philosophy and
theory from theology and religious interpretations. Thus the process
initiated during the Renaissance was completed. That historical period
coincided with the general weakening of the feudal system and medieval
institutions as well as processes of social emancipation, and above all
the appearance of a relatively substantial educated class of people. Also,
the urban civilization began to dominate the still largely rural society.
With the Enlightenment and rationalism, the idea of a rational and
fundamental change was entertained, different types of society were
studied and compared (the American Indian societies as much as the
English political system), and a search for a new form of government
was again initiated. Religious ideas and *Weltanschauung* were differentiated step by step from political ideologies, and these new ideas
had their appeal to the emerging educated and political class. Scholars
and philosophers, however, who produced the ideas and methods,
seldom suggested political action. America was perhaps an exception.

After the American and French revolutions, political philosophies
in a digested, simplified, and eventually symbolic form reached a large
audience of readers and listeners. Thus the political ideology of mass
parties made a historical entrance. Ideas were combined or translated
into action and became a powerful social force. Indeed, by the end of
the nineteenth century, organized political mass parties, "macroparties," or dynamic, secret, underground "microparties," small
political organizations, became an important, if not the most significant,
social-political force of contemporary civilization.

6. TWO IMAGES

Ancient or medieval political associations, or even those prior to the
French Revolution, differ greatly from the image of European mass
parties of this century. Our contemporary image was shaped by our

audiovisual experience of the interwar period; it was affected by the
mass media of radio and cinema. Through them, our audiovisual
experience became universal. It was not limited, as in times of the
French Revolution, to local events. New York, London, and Paris
saw the details of the Bolshevik action in 1917, saw Lenin and Trotsky,
Kerensky or Stalin. We heard Hitler and Mussolini and the mad
screams of the storm troopers. We saw the marching Fascist militia.
From the abstract concept of a definition, the political party grew into
a visible and audible "thing" that one could almost touch.

The generations of 1918 to 1939 were perhaps the first to see and
hear the party in the cinema; the mass meetings, marches, and exhortations appeared as a functioning whole. The sight of the individual was
lost, the party, step by step, was reified into an "object." Of course, as
early as the times of the French Revolution such images appeared, but
now the behavior, the pattern was standardized, regimented, and
modern mass communication had a powerful impact on our perception
and on the formation of a social phenomenon. The image of the
totalitarian party reached now the distant corners of the world, even
the illiterate. The image of the party, or at least of a certain type of
party, is today distinct; it is a consequence of our "empirical experience": we saw and heard it. Many also have suffered. The party was
the new deity that supplied legitimacy for firing squads and concentration camps. From an abstraction, the party became a reality. Now, the
party was more than a political tendency or philosophical orientation,
or a linkage of a leader and followers. The party emerged as observable,
composed of an ideology, of structure (organization) and a pattern of
actions (strategy and tactics), and played by political actors.

7. SEMANTICS: *PARTY* AND *FACTION*

This type of organization of course did not exist in the eighteenth
century, and the image of a political movement at that time was different. The term *party* had a different meaning, although the prototype,
the ingredients were already there. The sign was the same, the content
still largely different. Let us limit ourself here solely to the sophisticated
eighteenth-century French, who knew and admired the English parliamentary system and English parties.

The bright Encyclopedists perceived *the party* in terms of their times and current sentiments. It seems that its meaning was not yet clearly established, and *party* meant a general political orientation and a loose association of leaders and followers. The difference was drawn between *faction* and *party*. At that time, scholars were not yet entirely clear whether parties and factions were a necessary and healthy expression of social and individual will, or perhaps an "evil" symptom of conspiracies and evidence of personal interest and greed for power. Even thoughtful men were not sure whether a faction was a curse or a blessing. Opinion was divided.

In the original *Encyclopédie ou Dictionnaire Raisonné* (1751-1765) the party is defined as "faction, interest, or power which is considered as opposed to the other" ("parti est une faction, interet ou puissance que l'on considère comme opposé à une autre.").[7] This is a comprehensive definition in terms of the times. It means, in fact, a general orientation of a government or of certain, not necessarily organized, informal groupings. To Voltaire, a party meant an intellectual grouping of a leader and followers, not solely a political one. But the term *faction* had already a different taste. Voltaire defined it for the *Encyclopédie*[8] and gave a shorter version in his *Philosophical Dictionary:*

> The word "faction" comes from the Latin facere; it is employed to signify the state of a soldier at his post, on duty (en faction) squadrons or troops of combattants in the circus; green, blue, red, and white factions.

> The acceptation in which the term is generally used is that of a seditious party in the state. The term party in itself implies nothing that is odious, that of faction is always odious.

> A great man, and even a man possessing only mediocrity of talent, may easily have a party at court, in the army, in the city, or in literature.

> A man may have a party in consequence of his merit, in consequence of the zeal and number of his friends, without being the head of a party.

> Marshal Catinat, although little regarded at court, had a large party in the army without making any effort to obtain it.

> A head of a party is always a head of a faction; such were Cardinal Retz, Henry Duke of Guise, and various others.

A seditious party, while it is yet weak, and has no influence in the government, is only a faction.

Caesar's faction speedily became a dominant party, which swallowed up the republic.

When the emperor Charles VI. disputed the throne of Spain with Philip V. he had a party in that kingdom, and at length he had no more than a faction in it. Yet we may always be allowed to talk of the "party" of Charles VI.

It is different with respect to private persons. Descartes for a long time had a party in France; it would be incorrect to say he had a faction.

Thus we perceive that words in many cases synonymous cease to be so in others.[9]

"Le terme de *parti*," writes Voltaire, "par lui-même n'a rien d'odieux, celui de *faction* l'est toujours." "Faction," says Voltaire in the original *Encyclopédie*, "signifies a seditious party in a state." Thus, he makes a clear distinction between a party and a faction. The former, he argues, is not "repulsive." In his *Republican Ideas*, he seems to favor political parties.[10]

Today the concept of a faction is different. In ideological parties, such as socialist or peasant parties, a faction means an informal grouping of persons of a different orientation than that of other members of the party. For example, we speak about the liberal faction within the Communist party of Czechoslovakia of 1968.

In the model republic of the eighteenth-century world—the United States—the concepts and views on "factions" were quite dissimilar to today's concepts, at least among some of the leading theoreticians and architects of the new constitutional government. Madison, in his famous *Federalist* essay (no. 10), defined the faction thus: "By a faction I understand a number of citizens, whether amounting to a majority or minority of the whole, who are united and actuated by some common impulse of passion, or of interest, adverse to the rights of other citizens, or to the permanent and aggregate interests of the community." Madison uses the term *faction* interchangeably with *party* when he argues that inequality of talent and property breeds the division of society, and "from the influence of these on sentiments and views of the respective proprietors, ensues a division of society into different interests and parties. The latent causes of faction are thus sown in the nature of man."

8. FREEDOM OF POLITICAL ASSOCIATIONS: BEGINNINGS OF A CONTROVERSY

The party entered our history with a bad reputation. This opinion did not change for centuries, almost until the beginning of the nineteenth century.[11] Only briefly in those pristine times of the early Roman Republic was a party tantamount to friendship, *amicitia*. Soon, it changed to *factio*, an evil compact of the powerful and rich. In medieval times this reputation did not improve. When the two great parties of Guelphs and Ghibellines appeared in Italy in the thirteenth century, the chronicler Malaspina wrote, "two horrible women appeared in the skies of Tuscany, and covered the land like two hideous clouds" moving in a continuous struggle.[12] The Renaissance historian Agnolo Guicciardini called them the "most bloody factions of Guelphs and Ghibellines." They well deserved this description, according to stories of their deeds recorded by this gifted sixteenth-century writer.[13]

The party as a kind of faction, an organized and ideological group advancing particular interests and ideas, was also looked upon with mistrust by eighteenth-century, progressive, enlightened men of politics. "Anti-faction," "anti-party," even "anti-association" views and sentiments were expressed in writings, assemblies, and appeared in laws.[14]

Modern democratic and constitutional concepts are rooted largely in the seventeenth- and eighteenth-century theories of social contract. The social contract theory is in fact a consensus theory. Members of a political society enter into a compact, form an assembly, discuss issues, vote, and the majority view is accepted by the minority. Such is this idealistic model. The minority may disagree, but since the origin of civil government is of a contractual nature, a minority eventually assents to the majority view and a consensus follows. Difference of opinions, differences of interests are adjusted by mechanisms of compromise and consensus, believed the eighteenth- and nineteenth-century philosophers, and political polarity should not dominate the process of decision making. This common-sense philosophy guided by the principle of fairness (the term in English suffers when translated into

other European languages) dominates the pragmatic approach to
democracy today. The *London Economist,* in an editorial (October 24,
1970) defining the working of a democracy, put it well: "The Western
idea of democracy, as it has taken root in Western Europe and North
America, is based on two main propositions. The first is that the great
decisions of government should be acceptable to, and in some checkable
way approved by the majority of those whom the government governs.
The other is that there should be a corrective machinery—parliament,
courts, a press and television open to opposing views—through which a
minority can set about the business of getting the majority's support
or actually converting itself into the new majority."

Democracy works through agreement reached in an argument
between the majority and the minority. This is not a tyranny of
majority over the minority. The working of this political dialectics is
made possible by the classic English two-party system. Early, however,
in the seventeenth and eighteenth centuries, those basic ideas, appeared
in theories of social contract, and with them appeared a sensitivity to a
divided, polarized society, one divided in many different groups and
unable to work together. Such a division is what one seventeenth-
century philosopher, Locke, saw in factions or parties. The sensitivity
to this problem and the foresight in anticipating divided and unwork-
able parliaments—of which Europe has produced so many—is rather
remarkable. On political society and majority rule in the assembly,
Locke, a teacher of English and American statesmen and philosophers,
in his *Second Treatise on Civil Government* wrote that

> the variety of opinions and contrariety of interests which unavoidably
> happen in all collections of men, 'tis next impossible ever to be had.
> And therefore if coming into society be upon such terms, it will
> be only like Cato coming into theatre, *tantum ut exiret.* Such a
> constitution as this would make the mighty *Leviathan* of a shorter
> duration than the feeblest creatures.

> . . . For where the majority cannot conclude the rest, there they can-
> not act as one body, and consequently will be immediately dissolved
> again.—

> . . . And thus, that which begins and actually constitutes any political
> society is nothing but the consent of any number of freemen capable
> of a majority, to unite and incorporate into such society. And this
> is that, and that only, which did or could give beginning to any
> lawful government in the world."

Still, England in times of Locke had *sui generis* parties, to mention only the Whigs.

Separated by water and time from Locke's England, two generations later Madison wrote (Federalist No. 10):

There are again two methods of removing the causes of faction: the one, by destroying the liberty which is essential to its existence; the other, by giving to every citizen the same opinions, the same passions, and the same interests.

It could never be more truly said than of the first remedy, that it was worse than the disease. . . .

Liberty is to faction what air is to fire, an ailment without which it instantly expires. But it could be no less folly to abolish liberty, which is essential to political life, because it nourishes faction, than it would be to wish the annihilation of air, which is essential to animal life, because it imparts to fire its destructive agency.

The second expedient is as impracticable as the first would be unwise. As long as the reason of man continues fallible, and he is at liberty to exercise it, different opinions will be formed. As long as the connection subsists between his reason and his self-love, his opinions and his passions will have a reciprocal influence on each other; and the former will be objects to which the latter will attach themselves. The diversity in the faculties of men, from which the rights of property originate, is not less an insuperable obstacle to a uniformity of interests. The protection of these faculties is the first object of government. From the protection of different and unequal faculties of acquiring property, the possession of different degrees and kind of property immediately results; and from the influence of these on sentiments and views of the respective proprietors, ensues a division of the society into different interests and parties.

The latent causes of faction are thus sown in the nature of man; . . .

Madison complained about the "mischief of factions." He wrote about parties and "methods of caring" as one writes about a disease. The divisions of opinions and political orientations did, however, exist; parties were slowly emerging, in spite of suspicions and mistrust.

In terms of eighteenth-century perceptions and concepts, the party also represents a "particular will," a will of a specific, distinct group and

of interests opposed to the general will. Rousseau was an advocate of
"general will," unfettered by a "particular" one. The "particular" will
at that time was an expression of the special interests of organized feudal
corporations and guilds.[15] With his opposition to the particular will,
Rousseau was interpreted recently as an early philosopher of modern
totalitarianism. Chapman, however, is quite convincing in his argument
that this is largely a result of misinterpretation of his writings.[16]
Rousseau—his advocates argue—was opposed to free political associations in terms of his times, meaning by the latter the then contemporary feudal groupings of special interest and privilege.[17] Whatever the
defense of Rousseau, the fact is that his philosophy of contract, freedom,
and equality was used by a ruthless dictatorship; it was the ideology of
the Jacobin clubs in the late period of terror. What a philosopher intends
and what his philosophy does are two different things. Let us, however,
keep in mind that this happened in the eighteenth, not in the twentieth
century, and that it was not a simple matter to reconcile the two concepts of general and particular wills. In theory at least, they did appear
as contradictions. The dialectics of many conflicting or opposing
interests, appearing in a complex society, did not necessarily fit into a
logical theory of a perfect general will. Here, in France, in times of a
quest for a perfect society, theory dominated over experience. In
Anglo-American practice, it is experience which dictated the rules of
political theory. But the proverbial Gallic clarity prevails again in
Montesquieu, who in his *Persian Letters* discovers that dissent and
protest, even sedition, is the mother of liberty. In this delightful volume,
a Persian traveler writes to his friend from distant France about his
visit to a library and about the histories of various nations codified in
orderly arranged tomes. His guide, a savant, tells him: "The historians
of England have found that freedom originates incessantly from the fire
of discord and sedition. The king is always tottering on a firm and
unshakable throne; this is an impatient nation, wise even in its rage and
fury, (without a precedence until now), a mistress of the seas, which
combines trade and commerce with an empire."[18] Hence, discord and
difference is not necessarily a mother of political weakness. But the
dilemma of factions and parties continued.

   The consequences of this dilemma were noticeable during the French
Revolution, and it is my impression that whatever the interpretation
and the issue of Rousseau's theory, the problem of freedom of political
association remained open and at times controversial throughout the
French Revolution. It was a time when the government and those in

power learned how to prohibit and destroy free political associations. This was a technique of consolidation of power after its seizure.

Political discussions were not solely theoretical. Legislative assemblies and governments at that time reflected strong "anti-association" views by voting for antifactional and anti-associational laws. Thus, the classic document of the Revolution, the Declaration of the Rights of Man, promulgates freedom of opinion and expression of thought, but does not specify freedom of association.[19] The Constitution of 1791 proclaims only freedom of assembly, while a special law of 13-19 November 1790 states expressly the principle of freedom of association ("L'Assemblé . . . declare, que les citoyens ont le droit de s'assembler paisiblement et sans armes et de former entre eux de sociétés libres."). It is also possible that the revolutionary legislators at that time did not make as yet clear distinctions between reunion and association or between permanent and transient groupings.[20]

Were the clubs of the times of the Revolution regarded as associations or as meetings and assemblies? During the entire period of the Revolution, the legislators were changing views and laws, while the political clubs flourished. At one time, political associations were prohibited, another time permitted for a while. Again, while the political situation changed and the power of the ruling groups was threatened, or the very existence of the republic endangered, political associations were again prohibited. The change in attitude toward political parties and free associations reflected acute political struggles and conflicting interests, as well as ancient theoretical disputes.

Thus the law of Le Chapellier of 14 June 1791 prohibited professional associations and feudal corporations while it permitted meetings and assemblies. This seems to reaffirm Rousseau's philosophy. Marat criticized this law. He saw in it a limitation of political activities of the working people. Already at this session, a demand was made to extend this law to all political activities.[21] Again, in September 1791, Le Chapellier, in the name of a constitutional committee, declared that clubs which were useful at the beginning of the Revolution now became useless and that the affiliation of clubs of various cities carried political dangers. It is precisely the affiliation of local committees with a national organization that forms the fundamental, even elementary, horizontal structure of the modern political party organization. But again, the Constitution of 1793 seems to have modified the earlier tendency, adverse to freedom of political associations. This constitution reaffirms the right to form "popular" associations ("droit de se réunir en sociétés populaires"), tantamount also to the right of initiating political societies. When the Terror came to its ending stage, on 23 August 1795, the Convention dissolved all the assemblies known as "clubs" or "popular societies." The Constitution of the III Year (1795) imposed again limitations on "particular societies." Now they were not permitted to correspond, affiliate, or to combine local associations into federations.[22]

This controversy has a far deeper meaning. First of all, it harbors the basic problem of power and freedom. The changing laws during the French Revolution on the issue of freedom of political association was only an external reflexion of shifting distribution of power, growing insecurity, political disintegration, and, at the end, the quest for total power. Here, the tendency of political and bureaucratic routine—one could even call it habit—to prohibit others to associate, to profess differing ideas, grew after all from an old tradition of institutional behavior, which the church had established in the religious and other fields.

9. EARLY TENDENCIES TOWARD A MONOPARTY

The tendency toward total power and a "monoparty" appeared early in revolutionary programs. During the last days of the French Revolution, the Conspiracy of the Equals, headed by Babeuf, attempted to overthrow the government and restore the Constitution of 1793 (see Chapter 2, section 5). The program of the Equals has been called by historians an early socialist document. The Equals, however, opposing the monopoly of political power of the ruling group, advocated dictatorship of their own party. Thus in their Act of Insurrection, the committee aimed an armed uprising against the ruling group: "a conspiratorial faction (as the Committee called the government in power) has usurped the sovereignty by substituting its particular will for the general will ("en substituant sa volonté particulière à la volonté générale"). The secret party of Equals further accused the government of "populicide" in making "every thought, every act a national crime."[23] Their arguments mirror Rousseau's terminology and dilemmas of particular will, factions, and parties.

A generation later, when the Russian political liberals, known as Decembrists, outlined constitutions and frames for a future free society, the problem of freedom of political association and parties was not yet fully and definitely resolved among Continental revolutionaries. One of the Russian's leaders, Muravieff, argued for freedom of political association, while Pestel, perhaps the ablest of this group, argued in his *Russian Justice* for prohibiting all political societies.[24] Thus, totalitarian ideas were born in the quest for freedom.

The institutions and parties of democracy and of totalitarianism were born at the same time and in the same labors of European history. Both grew from seeds of a revolution. The controversy of ends and means, the search for a perfect state, a political Eldorado, supplied an appeal of totalitarian parties, which suggested dictatorship and eradication of difference by force as a short cut in a historical itinerary. Democratic parties did not promise a perfect solution but advocated political pluralism and freedom of political associations. Thus, the two patterns reflect also differing political ideals: the perfectionist and the melioristic one. The latter, pragmatic, largely of Anglo-American making, promises a better society eventually and favors a mistrust toward perfect, social solutions of a utopian nature. The latter, largely of Continental origin, was prominent in French, German, and later in Russian political theory and thinking, promises a perfect, just, and happy society, a perfect solution, which is near, just within the life span of the generation.

Thus, the concept and the organization of modern political parties grew slowly. In the eighteenth century, when political groupings made their appearance, feelings and attitudes were divided. Mistrust seems to have prevailed against organized, strong political parties representing definite interests and unchanging opinions. Political philosophers saw them as corruptive of a free and democratic political society. In the latter part of the nineteenth century, the models of modern ideological parties were already well developed. In their structure, pattern of actions, and ideology they carry the historical inheritance of political systems and institutional prototypes. The early concepts of the political party or faction reflected modes of thought, values, and perceptions of the eighteenth century. The values and ideology of philosophers affected their own perception of social conditions and political relations. Moreover, the concepts of the eighteenth century have to be related to social and political conditions, views and values of those times. But once an attitude and a theory appeared, it had a tendency to affect the future.

NOTES

1. Lilly Ross Taylor, *Party Politics in the Age of Caesar* (Berkeley: University of California Press, Sather Classical Lectures, 1949), p. 6. Professor Taylor's book is an excellent and detailed analysis of Roman political parties and struggles.

2. Ibid., pp. 9-10.

3. Edward Gibbon, *The Decline and Fall of the Roman Empire* (New York: Modern Library, n.d.), II: 141ff. Gibbon used extensively the *Secret History* (*Anekdota*) of Procopious from Cesarea, whose account on the rule of Emperor Justinian gives interesting details on major factions. Although authenticity of his text was challenged by some, nevertheless historians and political philosophers of such stature as Gibbon and Montesquieu have based their work on his information. His criticism of Justinian and Theodora is severe, but his descriptions are vivid and have a sense of authentic observations. This writer used Procopious's *Secret History* in this section next to other sources: Procopio Di Cesarea, *La Storia Arcana* (reprint ed., Roma: Fratelli Polombi, 1944). Furthermore, see Gaius Suetonius Tranquillus, *The Twelve Caesars* (Penguin Classics, 1965), p. 299; Jérome Carcopino, *Daily Life in Ancient Rome* (New Haven: Yale University Press, 1958), pp. 212-47; Jack Lindsay, *The Ancient World, Manners and Morals* (New York: Putnam's Sons, 1968), pp. 283ff; L. Friedländer, *Darstellungen aus der Sitten Geschichte Roms*, 10th ed. (Leipzig, 1921-23), II: 32ff.

K. Bluntschli a hundred years ago noticed this significance of identification by colors in differentiating groups and parties. See Bluntschli's short discussion of the Blues and Greens in his *Character und Geist der Politischen Parteien* (Nördlingen, 1869), pp. 14ff.

4. On soccer revolt in Caserta, see *Corriere Della Sera* (Milan), Sept. 9, 10, 1969; *Il Tempo* (Rome), Sept. 10, 1969; on Gabonese "Soccer War," *The New York Times*, Sept. 25, 1962; on soccer riots in Lima, Peru, *The New York Times*, May 25, 1964; student folly in Zap, N.D., *The New York Times*, May 11, 1969.

5. Niccolo Machiavelli, *Istorie Fiorentine*, in Collected Works, *Tutte Le Opere* (Florenz: G. Barbera, 1928). The following are all highly informative: Pasquale Villari, *The Two First Centuries of Florentine History* (London: Fisher Unwin, 1908), especially chap. IV, pp. 173-239, "State of thè Parties," p. 546ff. Oscar Browning, *Guelphs and Ghibellines* (London: Methuen, 1891). E. Emerton, ed., *Humanism and Tyranny* (Cambridge: Harvard University Press, 1925), pp. 255-84, "Bartolus on Guelphs and Ghibellines." On social stratification in Florenz, see Edcumbe Staley, *The Guilds of Florence* (1906; reprint ed., New York: Benjamin Blom, 1967), pp. 33-74. For general background, Hélène Nolthenius, *In That Dawn, The Thirteenth Century Italy* (London: Darton, Longman, & Todd, 1958), chapter 3, "The Cities," chapter 4, "The People." Leonardo Olschi, *The Genius of Italy* (New York: Oxford University Press, 1948), chapter VI, "Guelph Theocracy and Ghibellin Worldliness." (This writer used a German edition, *Italiens Genius und Geschichte* (Darmstadt: Gentner Verlag, 1958), chapter VI, "Guelphische Theokratie und Ghibellinische Weltlichkeit," chapter VI, "Dante und sein Kreis.") And of course, Jacob Burkhardt, *The Civilization of Renaissance in Italy*, Vol. 1, Part 1, "The State as a Work of Art" (New York: Harper Brothers, 1958), and Alberto Tenneroni, *Vicende Storiche di Todi delle Origini ai Giorni d'Oggi* (Todi, 1955), p. 67.

On theories of *sacerdotium* and *imperium* and unity of two coordinate powers, see Otto Gierke, *Political Theories of the Middle Age* (Boston: Beacon Press, 1958), pp. 16ff.

6. This section on the Levellers is based primarily on H. W. Brailsford's extensive and splendid study, which the London *New Statesman* called an "imperishable work of passion, scholarship and art. . . . a glorious book." H. W. Brailsford, *The Levellers and the English Revolution* (Stanford: Stanford University Press, 1961), pp. 10ff., 31ff., 150ff., especially chapters 2, "Pulpits and Taverns," 15, "The Levellers Party," 19, "Toleration," and 26, "The Levellers Platform."

The major theme of this essay and space do not permit me to deal extensively with the religious, social, and political peasant wars of the Reformation.

Frederick Engels, *The Peasant War in Germany* (Moscow: Foreign Language Publishing House, 1956) gives a penetrating and classic sociological analysis of those movements.

A recently published history of Anabaptism: Claus-Peter Clasen, *Anabaptism, A Social History 1525-1628* (Ithaca: Cornell University Press, 1972), gives a comprehensive account of the movement in Switzerland, Austria, Moravia, and south and central Germany.

7. *Encyclopédie ou Dictionnaire Raisonné des Sciences, des Art et des Métiers par une société de gens de lettres. En ordre et publié par M. Diderot . . . par M. d'Alembert* (Paris, 1751, 1765). The 1765 edition which appeared in Neuchatel was available to this writer.

8. Text from *Encyclopédie* (1765):

"FACTION, s. f. (*Politiq. et Gram.*) Le mot *faction* venant du latin *facere*, on l'employe pour signifier l'état d'un soldat à son poste en *faction*, les quadrilles ou les troupes des combattans dans le cirque, les *factions* vertes, bleues, rouges et blanches. *Voyez* FACTION, (*Hist. anc.*) La principale acception de ce terme signifie *un parti séditieux dans un état*. Le terme de *parti* par lui-meme n'a rien d'odieux, celui de *faction* l'est toujours. Un grand homme et un médiocre peuvent avoir aisément un parti à la cour, dans l'armée, à la ville, dans la littérature. On peut avoir un partiparson mérité, par la chaleur et le nombre de ses amis, sans etre chef de parti. Le maréchal de Catinat, peu considéré à la cour, s'étoit fait un grand parti dans l'armée, sans y prétendre. Un chef de parti est toujours un chef de *faction:* tels ont été le cardinal de Retz, Henri duc de Guise, et tant d'autres.

"Un parti séditieux, quand il est encore foible, quand il ne partage pas tout l'état, n'est qu'une *faction*. La *faction* de César devint bientôt un parti dominant qui engloutit la république. Quand l'empereur Charles VI. disputoit l'Espagne à Philippe V. il avoit un parti dans ce royaume, et enfin il n'y eut plus qu'une *faction*; cependant on peut dire toujours *le parti de Charles VI*. Il n'en est pas ainsi des hommes privés. Descartes eut long-temps un parti en France, on ne peut dire qu'il eut une *faction*. C'est ainsi qu'il y a des mots synonymes en plusieurs cas, qui cessent de l'être dans d'autres. *Article de M. De Voltaire*.

"FACTIONS, (*Hist. anc.*) c'est le nom que les Romains donnoient aux differentes troupes ou quadrilles de combattans qui couroient sur des chars dans les jeux du cirque. *Voyez* Cirque. Il y en avoit quatre principales, distinguées par autant de couleurs, le vert, le bleu, le rouge, et le blanc; d'ou on les appelloit *la faction bleue, la faction rouge*, etc. L'empereur Domitien y en ajouta deux autres, la pourpre et la dorée; dénomination prise de l'étoffe ou de l'ornement des casaques qu'elles portoient: mais elles ne subsistèrent pas plus d'un siècle. Le nombre des *factions* fut réduit aux quatre anciennes dans les spectacles. La faveur des empereurs et celle du peuple se partageoient entre les *factions*, chacune avoit ses partisans. Caligula fut pour la *faction* verte, et Vitellius pour la bleue. Il résulta quelquefois de grands désordres de l'intéret trop vif que les spectateurs prirent à leurs *factions*. Sous Justinien, une guerre sanglante n'eut pas plus fait de ravage; il y eut quarante mille hommes de tués pour les *factions* vertes et bleues.

Ce terrible évènement fit supprimer le nom de *faction* dans les jeux du cirque."
   9. M. de Voltaire, *Philosophical Dictionary* (Boston: Josiah P. Mendum, 1856), p. 319.
   10. For an excellent study of the beginnings of the concept of the party, see Mario A. Cattaneo, *Il Partito Politico nel Pensiero del Illuminismo e della Rivoluzione Francese* (Università di Milano, Publicazione della Facolta di Giurisprudenza, Serie II. Studi di Filosofia del Diritto, N. 8, 1964.) For a discussion of the definition in the *Encyclopédie* by Voltaire, see pp. 36ff.
   11. The attitudes varied, of course. In the United States and in Great Britain political parties became recognized institutions, an essential part of the subtle, electoral, democratic mechanism. Political views on parties differed between groups and individuals. Still, it is significant that as late as in times of Cavour, during the second half of the nineteenth century, an Italian statesman and writer, Marco Minghetti, defended the need for political parties, arguing that parties are a "central fact" in a parliamentary state, that on them depends political freedom. But Saragat, in a candid introduction, argues: "Minghetti saw the antinomy germain in the very existence of the party; they are necessary as institutions of liberty, but the totalitarian tendency of parties is at the same time destructive of freedom." Here Saragat, the democrat and antifascist, speaks from his long experience. Marco Minghetti, *I Partiti Politici*, introduction by Giuseppe Saragat (Rome: Atlantica, 1945), pp. iii-vii.
   12. Hélène Nolthenius, *In That Dawn*, p. 42, p. 228, n. 33, quoted from *Rerum Italicorum Scriptores* (Milan: Editore Muratori, 1723-1751), VIII, 787.
   13. [Agnolo] Guicciardini, *History of Italy* (first published in Florence, 1561; American edition, New York: Washington Square Press, 1964), pp. 120, 356.
   14. Cattaneo, *Il Partito Politico*, p. 10, and Sergio Cotta, "La nascita dell'idea di partito nel Secolo XVIII," *Il Mulino*, 1959 (quoted by Cattaneo), point to the eighteenth-century criticism of political parties. Cotta quotes Hobbes' views, who argued that the sovereign should dissolve political parties since parties affect political unity. Even Locke did not see their positive values.
   15. J. Torrade, in "Le groupe de pression du commerce à la fin de l'Ancien Régime et sous l'Assemblée Constituante," *Bulletin de la Société d'Histoire Moderne et Contemporaine*, 4th ser., 60-63, pp. 23-27, suggests such early types of pressure groups of commercial interests under the old regime which continued during the early days of the Revolution. To these groups belonged a few merchant deputies in the Constituent Assembly.
   16. John W. Chapman, *Rousseau: Totalitarian or Liberal* (New York: Columbia University Press, 1956), pp. vii, 80.
   17. For a passionate and able defense of Rousseau, see ibid., esp. chapter 7, "Totalitarian Implications Limited." Cattaneo, *Il Partito Politico*, pp. 17, 21ff., critically presents Rousseau's views on parties. The issue, however, is not clear. Even Chapman admits elements of totalitarianism in Rousseau's philosophy.
   18. Montesquieu (Charles, Louis de Secondat), *Lettres Persanes* (New York: Putnam, 1907), letter XCVIII (CXXXVI), p. 216. On Montesquieu's views and significance of his argument on this issue of difference of political views and political parties, see also Cattaneo, *Il Partito Politico*, pp. 18, 19 and Cotta, *La nascita* quoted by Cattaneo), pp. 482-83.
   19. Janet explains that the Constituent Assembly did not proclaim freedom of associations, since it could see only reestablishment of industrial guilds and religious congregations. Paul Janet, *Histoire de la science politique dans ses rapports avec la morale*, 3d ed. (Paris, 1887), p. xlix, quoted by Cattaneo, *Il Partito Politico*, p. 64.

20. Bastid suggests that the French Revolutionary legislation did not have a clear distinction between assembly and association. Cattaneo, *Il Partito Politico*, p. 65.

21. Ibid., pp. 66-68.

22. Ibid., pp. 70-73.

23. [Filippo] Buonarotti, *Conspiration pour l'Egalité dite de Babeuf* (1828; reprint ed., Paris: Editions Sociales, 1957), II: 164-66.

24. See Feliks Gross, *Seizure of Political Power* (New York: Philosophical Library, 1957), p. 69. See Renato Treves, *Spirito Critico e Spirito Dogmatico* (Università Di Milano, Instituto Editoriale Cisalpino, 1954), especially the Introduction and chap. 1, in which Professor Treves discusses the "spirit of criticism" and its significance in times of crisis and advent of the "regimes of the masses." Professor Guido Calogero in *Filosofia del Dialogo* (Milan: Communità, 1962) advanced in the same spirit the idea of the "dialogue" of intellectual toleration and spirit of criticism.

II

Origins of the Centralistic and Revolutionary Party

. . . Robespierre *au fond* was by no means a republican . . . he enslaved and used in his service the *Social Contract* (Rousseau's ed.), this code of all our mystifications about the representative and parliamentary government. He was convinced, with certainty, that democracy is impossible in France. . . . He wanted again the greatest concentration of power. . . . *Lord, deliver us from Jacobinism* (Dieu, délivrez nous du Jacobinism).

> P. J. Proudhon, April 11, 1851
> (from a letter to the French historian J. Michelet)

Before we attack the despotism of princes, let us begin by fighting despotism among soldiers of liberty.

> P. J. Proudhon, July 23, 1855
> (from a letter to the Russian philosopher and socialist A. Herzen)

1. DIFFERENCES BETWEEN ANGLO-AMERICAN AND CONTINENTAL EUROPEAN PATTERNS

Keen observers of American and British political systems have realized the historical significance of political parties. The "official" political science of the nineteenth century, however, favored a juridical, philosophical, and historical approach and not a sociological one. It was De Tocqueville who, after his American journey, indicated the need of a new political science for the "entirely new world." ("Il faut une science politique nouvelle à un monde tout nouveau"). Ostrogorski tried to answer De Tocqueville's challenge in his *Democracy and Organization of Political Parties.* It took fifteen years to write this voluminous work based on extensive research, both historical and empirical. Ostrogorski traveled in England and in the United States, interviewed political leaders, and observed political meetings. His intention was to study political forces, not political forms. By the latter he meant juridical, formal institutions. The advent of democracies, wrote Ostrogorski, destroyed the ancient structure of society— the class hierarchy—and also weakened the mutual dependence and cohesion of classes. The old traditional ties that united the individual and the collectivity, essential in any working political system, were now broken. The answer to this dilemma in terms of a working political system was in the methodical organization of the "electoral masses" in the form of permanent and organized parties. The parties are not part of the institutional-juridical parliamentary structure but part of what he called an "extraparliamentary organization." Ostrogorski seems to have foreseen the basic pattern of future political development in Great Britain and in the United States, and that these two countries would set a worldwide pattern which sooner or later would be followed by other industrially advanced nations.[1]

However, in most of the states of continental Europe different types of political parties developed than those discussed by Ostrogorski in his pioneering work. The nations of continental Europe had different political institutions and different historical traditions. Class structure, economic conditions, and ethnic and religious values differed from those in Great Britain and the United States. Consequently, the pattern of political movements that developed in these two nations differed from those in Europe. This difference appeared especially in the European mass parties of the interwar period. By "continental Europe" we mean here major nation-states such as Russia, the East European nations, prewar Austro-Hungary, Germany, Italy, France, and Spain. The development in Switzerland, Scandinavian nations, and Holland led to different results. For the sake of brevity we shall limit our discussion to the former.

Britain and America and continental Europe represent two major patterns of political parties. Each of these patterns, but especially the continental European, developed not one but several related party models. In a broad approximation, the British-American political parties were a consequence and part of the representative system. Generally they were loosely organized and their functions limited. Continental European parties existed even in the absence of a representative government, many as protest movements against autocracy or monarchy. Continental European parties of social and political protest were far more influenced by the Jacobin models of the French Revolution, which diffused to various types of centralism, than by Anglo-American models. A centralistic command party with a military discipline (discussed in the following chapter), adopted by parties of the extreme left and right during the interwar period, is also an evolution of the Jacobin organization. In addition, until 1939 an "integral" disciplined democratic party was another Continental party model. Such a party, unlike the British-American pattern, penetrates a wide area of the cultural and personal life of its members and includes such ancillary organizations as unions, cooperatives, cultural activities, sports and entertainment, and even book clubs and tourist associations. (Among the British parties, the labor movement has some involvement in these activities.) This model was fully developed toward the end of the nineteenth century by the German Social Democracy and had a worldwide influence.[2]

2. BEGINNINGS OF BRITISH POLITICAL PARTIES

It is difficult to pinpoint a definite historical starting point of political parties since they usually grow slowly and frequently originate from "neutral" social institutions such as clubs and scholarly or literary meetings, which under the impact of political events or a social trauma, such as revolution, change their function. (Such was the case during the American and French revolutions.) Social and political "movements" appear first, and a more definite party organization grows later. Such movements are often called social forces; they comprise rudimentary or transient groups of leaders and followers representing common interests, values, and goals, who are attempting to change or maintain

social, economic, and political conditions or maintain, achieve, and
even conquer power. They perform the functions of future parties or
are tantamount to the latter. In Eastern Europe political parties sometimes grew from a fusion of these nascent social movements and the
evolution of political and cultural associations ("circles"). Likewise,
the party in a definite, organized form grew slowly in Britain and a
two-party system in a modern sense did not appear until late in the
eighteenth century.[3]

The major theme of social protest movements in the eighteenth and
nineteenth centuries was of course the eternal problem of inequality
of men. This protest against the subordination and exploitation of
man by man was expressed in the quest for equality and liberty, quest
for equal access to political power, equal economic share, and, last
but not least, limitation of arbitrary power.

The idea of liberty and equality was a consequence of religious
ethics; it was also a dominant part of contemporary rationalist
philosophy. The ethical motivation is continuously activated by this
hiatus between the ideal and the reality, the contradictions between
imperatives of ethics and on social conditions. The closing of this gap
is the crucial issue. With the Industrial Revolution, interests of large
and underprivileged social classes coincided with this quest for a rational
society free of economic subordination. The misery of the working
class and the quest for improvement of their social and economic
conditions was a powerful appeal.

The prototypes of modern political parties in Europe can be traced
to three major patterns: (a) An early type, such as a small informal
meeting of party elites, notables, and leaders in various clubs. This model
of organization grew into a limited party structure, "top heavy,"
oriented toward notables, leaders, and opinion makers. (b) "Primary"
political associations or clubs, small philosophical circles, dedicated to
the discussion of social and political problems and to the search for
solutions and new forms of a future society. These groups later merged
with the broader movements of social protest. (c) Social protest movements of a large following. Mass movements grew in Great Britain in
times of the Industrial Revolution, but their origin can be traced to
earlier religious protest actions.

The early political meetings connected with elections were more or
less informal and influenced by notables and political elites. The
business of politics and national government was a profession of the
upper classes. A more definite political association appeared in the

latter part of the eighteenth century in defense of political rights. Both the American and French revolutions had considerable influence. Political associations mushroomed in England, and some American political terms such as "caucus" and "committees of correspondence" became popular. The British political parties developed definite political customs and style and functions that were different from those of the Continent. The Maxwell Fyfe Committee, examining the structure of the British Conservative party, suggested its two major functions: "a machine for winning elections and an educative political force."[4] The party structure evolved toward these two major functions and also became a more permanent organization of voters and a communication system between leaders and the electorate.

Generally, parties grew from a rudimentary organization of small elitist clubs and leadership groups. After the Reform of 1832, the party organization expanded in the form of the so-called registration association. However, membership of this association was limited. The great political clubs such as Carlton (founded in 1831) and Reform (1836) were in fact informal liaison organizations of the members of Parliament and leadership. Public opinion was formed in these organizations and from there it sifted down to the rank and file of the voters. This informal aristocratic and elitist leadership was generally accepted. The Reform of 1867 and general franchise was followed by the extension of the party organization and the growth of a modern structure. Now the party organization became representative in form. Local party committees and councils gained influence and national party representation was formed. In 1877 an integration of these local associations was accomplished by the National Liberal Association.[5]

However, there is another original source of political parties, especially of mass parties. As was mentioned before, early protest movements can be traced to the religious movements of the seventeenth and eighteenth centuries and even to much earlier periods when the custom of public and candid expression of differences of opinion and protest against social conditions was established. In these religious movements, leveling and equalitarian tendencies appeared, antecedent of future historical movements of social and political equality. These protest movements reappeared in the eighteenth century in a secular form. Rationalistic philosophy and scientific economy had displaced the religious argumentation or had reinforced the latter. Such protest movement appeared in 1839-1840 in the well-organized Chartist movement.

From these beginnings and from early socialist circles, trade unions, and, later, the Fabian Society, grew the powerful Labour party, which appeared rather late in the history of this advanced industrial nation. Nevertheless, the earlier models of political associations and electoral meetings had a profound influence on structure, political custom, and style. The Chartist movement and the Labour party also mark the beginning of an explicit working-class party. The appearance of this mass party is closely linked with changes in the social and economic relationship in Great Britain and with the continuity of representative institutions.

The British type of party and the American one are respectively clearly anchored in Parliament or Congress and the functions of the party are limited. The party is primarily a vital "liaison organization" between voters and their interests and Parliament or Congress. Power and political decision-making in Great Britain is located in Parliament, not in the party.[6] The British and American parties are part of a particular political culture of these countries and developed in societies separated for centuries from the European continent. Conditions for political growth were more sheltered in England and America than in Europe. While the two nations were not politically or culturally isolated from Europe, they were protected from the violent experiences of European international politics.

3. BEGINNINGS OF AMERICAN POLITICAL PARTIES

Colonial American political development was related to English traditions and experiences. Spontaneous, small, friendly meetings of informal groups which met periodically formed the beginnings of political associations. The American Revolution, however, was a turning point. The function of clubs that met according to their professional affiliation—for example, the Merchants or the Mechanics club—changed spontaneously and became centers of political discussion. At the same time the political movement was reinforced by the new patriotic associations. From these modest and spontaneous beginnings political parties began to grow. Much later the Jacobin movement also had its influence here. The French style invaded even the American political parlance. Good democrats in Boston began to address each other as

"citizen" and ladies as "citizeness," and later even "citess."[7] Candidates
were formally nominated in town and county meetings, but political
tendencies and influences were expressed in informal cliques, circles,
clubs, and meetings, which were part of the urban and rural culture of
eighteenth-century America.

The difference between England and America, however, is to be
found in the early growth of American social movements and in the
class structure of these nascent parties. Unlike England, or even
revolutionary France, the free American farmer at the end of the
eighteenth century was a political and at times a revolutionary element.
The Federalists and Republicans had the making of modern parties,
the former of an elitist one and the latter of a mass party. They had a
rudimentary organization, elaborate ideology, and pattern of actions.
They also had their press and following. In May 1793 Jefferson outlined the class structure of the corresponding political movements:
"The line is now drawn so clearly as to show on one side—1. The fash-
ionable circles of Philadelphia, New York, Boston and Charleston;
natural aristocrats. 2. Merchants trading on British capital. 3. Paper
[money] men. All Tories are found in some one of these three
descriptions. On the other side—1. Merchants trading on their own
capital. 2. Irish merchants. 3. Tradesmen, mechanics, farmers and
every other description of our citizens."[8]

By 1793 Democratic and Republican clubs were organized. They
followed the Jeffersonian antifederalist ideology favoring a free union
of men and appealed to a broad rank and file, especially to farmers and
"mechanics," a general term for skilled craftsmen and technicians. The
clubs grew and expanded. A formal organization with a mother society
in Philadelphia was established. Correspondence and "intervisitations"
were exchanged between the new clubs. The Federalist party also had
its informal organization and influential press. The informal party
network was the network of party leaders, officeholders, correspon-
dents, and beneficiaries.[9] Thus, the prototype of the modern party
made an early beginning in America with a well-developed ideology
of agrarian democracy opposed to centralism, with an appeal to grass-
roots movements and an emphasis on popular control, the elective
principle, and universal suffrage.[10] The original nuclear organization
of American political movements did not survive long. The basic
ideological tendencies of agrarian democracy reappeared, however, in
the Jacksonian democratic movement. The appeal to definite economic
interests of grass roots and pragmatic programs became then a charac-

teristic feature of American ideology.

At this time the national convention system was firmly established, which, to an extent, has determined the American party structure. Similarly, the industrial development and the Civil War decisively affected American political movements. During and after the Civil War, the modern political parties took their definite shape. With the evolution of conventions, "spoils-system," "politicians," and the "political machine" made their appearance. The party became primarily an electoral machine with a pragmatic approach to politics and limited functions. In spite of all its faults and corruptions, the party system has always been anchored in a representative system of government. With the exception of fringe groups and microparties, American political movements never developed into rigid, centralistic, highly disciplined structures.[11]

4. PARTY STRUCTURE AND CONTINUITY. UNIVERSALITY AND COMPATIBILITY OF AMERICAN INSTITUTIONS

American and English political institutions both had continuity and compatibility. The British Parliament and the American Congress had an uninterrupted existence since the turn of the eighteenth century during the entire period of industrial growth and economic transformation. In that crucial historical period political parties developed their modern structure and ideology. The Parliament and the Congress are unusual mechanisms of continuity and change. While both institutions had almost a perfect political stability at this time, both were evolving and the suffrage moved from narrow groups of voters to a general franchise. In Great Britain this evolution was gradual by means of the Reform bills. In the United States the universal suffrage was an ideal goal of the American Revolution and part of the radical ideology. The Civil War, emancipation, and eventually, after a long development, in 1920, the franchise to women were the historical stages of this evolution. While the industrial society and the working class grew in their political significance and the need of social economic reforms became urgent, the representative institutions evolved, and through them protest and discontent could move into constructive change and reform.

Modern political parties appeared in England and America at first as a consequence of representative government and later grew with the growth of an industrial and urban society, which increased class divisions and the concentration of population. On the European continent, the centralistic bureaucratic system of the monarchy was compatible with the hierarchical and aristocratic organization of the Catholic and the Russian churches. Rigid religious dogma had its parallel in the rigidities of political ideologies; religious intolerance was echoed in political intolerance. In contrast, in the United States, religious institutions influential at the time of the Revolution were to a large extent compatible with the emerging political parties. Fundamentally, the United States were built on English institutions and Protestant, sectarian values. These roots today are still vigorous and germane, although symptoms of their weakening have appeared in our midcentury. The elective, representative principle dominates the American Protestant institutions as much as the political one. The government is elected, and so is the governing body of the religious, "sectarian" Protestant congregation. The pastors of numerous Protestant sects or denominations are not appointed by a higher central authority; the decision and power was, and is, in the congregation, not in an hierarchy. The dominant principle of a congregation is the general consensus, not command. With the exception of Puritan or fundamentalist sects, differences in values or judgments are not sins, and the differing sect is neither an opponent nor an enemy. This respect for differences of sectarian intellectual movements was, and is, associated with certain relativism and may contribute to a certain insecurity. Strong Judeo-Catholic values and their absolute nature give a more definite sense of direction.

In addition, the military and bureaucratic structure was weak or limited in numbers and function during the crucial period of American development, and the consensus pattern of society penetrated into the military establishment.

This is, however, only one side of the picture, and our discussion calls for qualification. I do not intend to idealize the American society of those times. It was only "half-free," and while in Europe serfdom had on a whole disappeared by the middle of the nineteenth century, slavery continued in the United States with its corrupting and destructive effects on masters and slaves. The South had an inner moral and political contradiction between the reality of an oppressive and often cruel slavery system and the ideals of freedom and Christianity. Nevertheless, in sections of the country, most of the institutions were compatible. The institutional behavior within the church was not different from a representative government. The Catholic church in America grew differently from its counterpart on the Continent. It was the religion of a minority, and such religious movements differ greatly from those of dominant churches.

A government that was good for the House of the Lord was good for the House of Representatives. The institutional forms were compatible and complementary, and the value structure in religion and politics favored respect for differences in ideas. A general, consistent institutional pattern and behavior are easily assimilated in other fields whenever social action expresses itself in an organized way. Thus, American political parties followed the general pattern of institutional development, which was neither rigid nor centralistic.

Parliamentary institutions of the European continental major states had neither continuity nor a consequential evolutionary pattern. The forces of despotism and old aristocracy were deeply entrenched. The revolutionary changes had their ups and downs. Parliamentary government and representative institutions were destroyed again and again, suspended or limited, and "ancient regimes" or more modern imperial Bonapartist systems restored. Parliaments had an erratic history and in some nations, no continuity, while political movements had already established an ideological, and frequently, an organizational sequence. While the representative institutions were weak or in certain countries (e.g., Russia) almost nonexistent, polarizing political parties of social-political protest and reaction flourished in nineteenth-century Europe in their own way. The secret form of organization became part of the political landscape. Unlike the United States and Great Britain, such parties were neither a consequence nor an extension of a representative, parliamentary government.

5. DEVELOPMENT OF CENTRALISTIC PARTIES IN CONTINENTAL EUROPE

Unlike the established patterns of America, much of continental Europe had a relative continuity and universality of centralistic and hierarchical institutions. The state, dynastic, and church organizations were hierarchical and centralistic in their nature, in a considerable part of Europe. Their bureaucratic and power structures reinforced each other. Political movements of rapid social change in Russia, Germany, and post-revolutionary France faced a centralistic, integrated, and disciplined power structure, unwilling to yield privileges, frequently unaware of the consequences of industrial evolution, and ignoring the rise of new social classes and their misery. How could a loosely organized party of weak discipline win a war against a centralistic and autocratic Russian government and bureaucracy? Or, how could a party representing "subjects" deprived of proper representation lead a legal political attack against a tightly organized bureaucratic monarchy with a strong military establishment? The dominant political institutions and the general political environment determined conditions of organizational efficiency. A degree of centralism in party structure, unlike the United States or England, was essential for the party of mass protest in order to attain the political goals it hoped to achieve. The dominant structure of public institutions and government usually influences forms of organization and social relations in other fields: politics, enterprise, and education. The tendency toward institutional compatibility appeared here, as it did in the United States. While in the latter the continuity and universality of representative institutions favored a loosely organized federalistic form of party organization relatively free of centralistic party orders in municipal, county, and state politics, in continental Europe the general political environment and institutional structure favored the opposite—a centralistic party structure. The centralistic tendency, borrowed from the Jacobins, was in lesser or greater degree assimilated at first by parties of social protest, parties of the left. Subsequently, the developed and extreme centralistic forms were borrowed from this source by mass parties of the radical right such as the Fascists and Nazis, which appeared much later.

6. CLASS AND PARTY STRUCTURE

Unlike the northern states of America and in spite of economic changes, class behavior in daily relations in Europe followed the ancient feudal pattern. Human relations were rooted in a specific class culture.

The class divisions were deep, and the institutions and behavioral patterns of the feudal systems were projected into the new industrial society. These divisions were reflected in the distinct class character of political parties. Slavery and the plantation economy in the South created a specific oppressive system of human exploitation, but the feudal pattern was not massively projected into the North American culture or class structure as was the case in Hispanic America. Indentured servants were a passing and ancillary institution.

The farmer was politically active in America from the time of the Revolution. However, in the crucial period of industrial and economic change, the peasantry of central Europe and Russia was still in bondage. Serfs do not form political parties. Their sporadic revolts were violent but short-lived. Ideology and organization, the two essential components of political continuity, were weak or absent. Peasant revolts were symptomatic of deep discontent, but discontent alone is not enough to produce effective political action. The liberation and emancipation of the peasantry in central eastern Europe came about the middle of the nineteenth century.

The revolutionary or, as in Poland, insurrectionist tendencies and pressures of the cities contributed greatly to this liberation. In France, where the peasantry was emancipated during the Revolution, farmers grew conservative. To a large extent, the rural population of Europe in the middle of the nineteenth century was politically immobile. In contrast, in the early 1870s in America, radical farmers' movements—the Grangers, Greenbacks, and later the Populists—appeared in the political arena as powerful forces of reform and social change. The peasant movements of eastern Europe began at the end of the nineteenth century, and they did not exercise any significant political influence prior to the beginning of the twentieth century. Young America was politically mature when old Europe's democratic politics were in its formative years. Thus, the development of democratic political movements in Europe was primarily an urban phenomenon until almost the end of the nineteenth century.

7. CLUBS AND DISCUSSION GROUPS

Political parties in Europe, and similarly those of England and

America, are the result of a long, evolutionary process. They appear in a modern form as a result of the fusion of several social tendencies and an integration of several groups. This process of the integration of ideas, individuals, and groups was prompted by changes in political and socioeconomic relations. The French Revolution was a precipitant point of the great transformation of European continental society. The components of modern ideological political parties had already appeared at that time and the process of integration and transformation of earlier trends and groups took place. The disintegration of the feudal system was accompanied by the emergence of dynamic social forces and new forms of social organization. One of these was the political party. Leadership and followers are only part of the fabric modern parties are made of. Every social movement, as well as religious ones, has its leaders and its followers. The major components of a modern political party are: a social, economic, and political ideology that suggests the direction of action; a pattern of action, that is, strategy and tactics; and a structure upon which to build party organization. The Jacobins already had these ingredients.

Modern political parties in Europe appeared during the nineteenth-century struggles for democratic representative systems and social reforms, but their goals differed. Part of these movements early adopted an ideology aiming at a fundamental transformation of the political and economic base of society. National liberation from foreign rule became another major theme of European continental parties. Political change based on religious issues was yet another impetus. Thus, socialist, nationalist, political-religious movements and later, at the turn of the century, populist and peasant movements made their historical appearance. The goals of some of these powerful movements went beyond the demands or the frames of politics of a representative government of limited objectives and limited powers. Some of the major political parties continued their support and struggle for representative government considered by the leaders and followers as a safeguard of personal liberty and political rights as well as thus far the only known safe mechanism of humane and orderly social transformation, a civilized system for the conduct of the business of government. As early as the turning days of the French Revolution, some leaders and their party members, among them the late Jacobins, anticipated a transitory stage of dictatorship in order to consolidate power and prepare a new era of integral democracy. Others—radical and ultra-conservative parties—planned to reach their goals without or against the democratic representative principle. Thus, by the middle of the nineteenth century, the life and existence of political movements in major states of continental Europe was not as firmly attached to the representative government as those of England and the United States.

In the life of institutions and social organizations, the early years of a nascent movement affect its future development. The institutions are, of course, a consequence of social conditions and ideological trends. But once an institutional structure and apparatus is formed, once the past becomes custom, tradition, or history, even a legend and myth, a "superstructure" is formed. Sooner or later, it is ossified and may resist basic changes. The formative years of political parties in sections of continental Europe were different from those experienced by British and American ones. Thus, these formative years of political movements affect the evolution of the general pattern of party organization. Of course, there were similarities in the growth of continental European and English as well as American political movements, but there were also substantial differences which had their share in shaping the future social and political picture of Europe. The political parties in Europe also grew from small philosophical or political informal discussion groups, which produced and reduced ideas and philosophies and supplied direction and goals to the nascent social movements of discontent. These ideologies suggested methods of social change and ways of consolidating power.

The evolution of a Jacobin model of party organization was of singular significance. It became an influential pattern for parties advocating rapid social change and revolutionary attack aimed at dictatorial powers. In its extreme expression, this model was used as a strategic means destroying representative government. The history of its beginning was long forgotten or erased when this organizational principle was applied by the twentieth-century movements of the extreme and intolerant right or left.

The founders of the Jacobin movement looked toward a free and democratic republic. They had other intentions than did their future imitators. They called themselves friends of the constitutions. In their hall the American, English, and French flags were displayed as well as busts of Franklin, Rousseau, Mably, and Mirabeau. But, ideas and institutions have their own destiny and are not anchored to the will of their authors.

The Jacobin pattern was not the only type of continental European parties. First of all, there were variations of the Jacobin movements.

Another major model emerged about seventy years after the French
Revolution in Germany, a result of the fusion of a mass movement with
a German pattern of bureaucratic organization. The German Social
Democracy grew into a model democratic mass and class party, a
pattern later imitated all over Europe by labor movements. Firmly
oriented toward the representative system and a democratic process,
the well-disciplined German Social Democracy retained a limited
measure of centralism. The party solidarity expressed itself in efficient
and concerted action.

8. THE FUSION OF MAJOR MODELS

Continental European political parties appeared as a consequence of
basic social, economic, and political changes. The socioeconomic base
should not be overlooked in a study of these movements; however, this
is only part of the history of the complex process of causation and
interdependence. The questions are two: why did political parties of
Europe appear in a specific form, and why did they develop specific
style and structure, ideology, and strategy different from those of
England and America? The patterns can be traced to a number of
original sources, but these beginnings are the consequences of earlier
processes and development. The original sociological roots are very
distant indeed. What is meant by beginnings here is a stage preceding
the appearance of organized political movements.

In this sense some of these sources are: (1) English influence and
receptivity to a representative form of government. Informal meetings
and loose organizations of political tendencies were part of the early
representative system. (2) Similarly, American representative institutions and forms of democratic social movements. (3) The general
pattern of political associations developed during the French Revolution, especially the Jacobin and post-Jacobin centralistic party structure.
(4) Eighteenth- and nineteenth-century secret political societies such
as the Carbonari and the Freemasons which supplied some of the elementary concepts and techniques of future underground organizations.
(5) Religious rituals, manifestations, and even concepts (in a formal
sense) were projected and later integrated into political movements,
shaping the style of activities and party folklore. Symbolism and
certain forms of cults were assimilated. (6) The efficient bureaucratic

government apparatus imitated by disciplined, multifunctional party organization, adopted by the German Social Democracy. (7) Military behavior, structure, and discipline projected into political behavior. This pattern was assimilated by the totalitarian parties of the extreme right—the Fascists and the Nazis. It appeared, however, earlier in the Communist movement in Russia, and in times of political crisis in a specific and reduced form in democratic and republican movements as a defensive measure to safeguard representative institutions. The parties of Europe were a synthetic product, a result of a not always conscious but frequently spontaneous social process of fusion of a variety of patterns and traditions, many of them alien to American and British party organization.

9. BEGINNINGS OF THE JACOBIN MODEL

The French club and circle movement was part of the general trend, part of the history of the Enlightenment and the growth of rationalism. As early as 1724 the members of Club de L'Entresol, presided by Saint Pierre, discussed and expressed their admiration for British political ideals and institutions. This early political association was closed by the king's order in 1731.[12] Various types of discussion, perhaps conversation groups, lodges, and clubs appeared all over Europe especially in times of political and intellectual unrest. They appeared in England and America as well as in Italy and Poland. But, it was the Jacobin group that played the historical role in the development of several patterns of centralistic party structure. The other clubs disappeared in the great river of history or originated different patterns of intellectual or political associations.

Where and when did the Jacobins originate? Some historians of the French Revolution trace their history to 1789 when the Estates General were revived and met in Versailles. The plebeian and ecclesiastic deputies from the Third Estate used to meet in a café to discuss current politics as well as to prepare a general policy for the meetings of the Third Estate. The deputies from Brittany were probably familiar with English parliamentary customs. This informal association was called Club Breton. The club grew rapidly when other radical deputies joined. With the establishment of a constitutional monarchy and a national assembly, deputies moved to Paris. Now the club was large and influential. A large hall was rented and in 1790 The Society of Friends of Constitutions at the Jacobin convent was founded. From this meeting place they were called Jacobins.[13] This name, which originated with this exclusive society, was at first used generally for radical democrats and republicans.

According to another historical interpretation, the original example should be traced to England, where in 1789 a Club of the French Revolution was formed. The organizational techniques of the Jacobins, according to this interpretation, were borrowed there. Branch societies were formed in various cities, which were directly affiliated with the London group, and liaison was maintained by the exchange of correspondence among members and branch clubs. In this way a widespread association formed a concerted union of all the true friends of liberty.[14] The Paris club might have copied the pattern of affiliation and correspondence from London as well as borrowed it from the American committees known in France by that time.[15] It could also have been an independent social innovation. Nevertheless, the Paris club at rue du St. Honoré in the Jacobins convent began by 1790. Until about 1792 this was an association of republicans, democrats, and even constitutional monarchists presided over sometimes by men of aristocratic origin. The society grew rapidly and by 1790 had 1,100 members and about 3,000 persons at their large meetings. By 1791 they already had a network of 406 societies in the provinces, which in turn formed a number of minor associations and sections in the surrounding areas.[16]

Crane Brinton estimates about 6,800 Jacobin societies for all of France, and "guesses" an estimate of 500,000 enrolled Jacobins in times of the Terror and one million as the top limit of the total club membership.[17] We shall accept here his estimates, which are based on extensive research, as a hypothesis. The number of members he suggests is, for eighteenth-century France, a very large one indeed. Although the Jacobins, by the time of Terror, was already an organization of "cadres" banded into clubs, it is difficult to guess how many were convinced, hard-core members of the revolutionary clubs, and how many of them joined in order to survive. In a state ruled by means of organized violence the problem of survival for individuals and families becomes a daily and paramount problem. For those whose nerves cannot stand the pressure, and in most cases this pressure sooner or later affects large sections of the population, the safest place at such time is frequently within the organization of terror that controls the power. Inflated membership thus reflects fear rather than enthusiasm for principles.[18]

10. TRANSFORMATION OF THE CLUBS: CLASS AND PARTY

The transformation of political clubs usually occurs in times of a general crisis and in wartime. It is a transformation that is also symptomatic of the nature of the revolutionary process. At a certain stage, radical symbols, principles, and radical projects appeal to active and energetic minorities. The Jacobin organization changed and expanded during the rapid disintegration of feudal institutions: the destruction of the feudal social structure, the displacement of feudal behavior in daily life, and the decline of its symbolism. The survival of the nation called for a rapid reintegration by means of new institutions, symbols, and symbolic behavior. All this was imposed by extreme forms of coercion, which came to be called the Terror (the term in its new meaning emerged probably at that time). The type of an organization the Jacobins created penetrated the entire society, reaching other groups and small communities, thus integrating the nation in times of dissolution. The Church had this type of an organization, which by the very nature of religious life penetrated into personal and private aspects of life.

At first, the members of this club were men from various social ranks and strata: former aristocrats, intellectuals, lawyers, artisans, scholars, and priests, as well as men without definite occupations. While the organization grew, according to Crane Brinton, the Jacobin clubs became largely bourgeois. His definition of the bourgeoisie embraces, however, sections of the new educated classes, the future intelligentsia, the product of the Enlightenment. This is the class that was destined to play a dynamic role in the future democratic, progressive, and radical movements of Europe. Crane Brinton includes in the bourgeois class lawyers, priests, teachers, artists, liberal professors, businessmen, shopkeepers, and officers. He calls cobblers, locksmiths, masons, and carpenters the working class, and lists peasants separately. Brinton investigated clubs in groups of twelve and forty-two in different periods. According to his data, the twelve clubs of group I (1789-1795) included 62 percent bourgeois, 28 percent working class, and 10 percent peasantry. The twelve clubs of group II (1789-1792), 66 percent bourgeois, 26 percent working class, and 8 percent peasantry; the 42 clubs of group III (1793-1795), 57 percent bourgeois, 32 percent working class, and 11 percent peasantry. "The names of Jacobins," continues Brinton, "are almost never found among poor."

Brinton's estimates indicate that Jacobins, whatever their social class, tended to be a bit more prosperous than their peers. Age varied from 28.3 to 45.4.[19] A statistician may ask, however, in this case for the standard deviation. Differences in age are perhaps relevant here. At a glance only, some of the prominent leaders, to mention Robespierre and St. Just, were young men. To repeat, the bourgeois class, as defined by Brinton, was not a homogenous social stratum. Among its substantial sections were the new educated classes, the nascent intelligentsia.

Crane Brinton seems to overlook the significance of a marginal class, which had already appeared at that time. These were the déclassés, the unfrocked priests, unfinished students (today we call them dropouts), gifted but unsuccessful writers and lawyers, half-educated persons without definite trade and income ready to discuss everything and join whenever change might promise them a future, a new start, or power and status. This was not a new phenomenon. It appeared before and thereafter. It was already described about nineteen hundred years before by Gaius Crispius Sallustius, the Roman historian, in his story of the conspiracy of Catilina, in times of Cicero, when Julius Caesar made his first steps into history. This time it was Napoleon Bonaparte who made his entrance.

11. JACOBIN CENTRALISM

The Jacobin organization grew from a relatively liberal debating organization dedicated to republican and democratic ideology into a rigid, highly efficient, centralistic organization of ideological orthodoxy and intolerance. The Jacobin party at its last stage controlled the collective behavior by means of mass terror.[20] From the beginning, Jacobin members were received upon recommendation and careful scrutiny of their "ideological purity."[21] The method of acceptance of new members suggests the beginnings of a "vanguardist party" of a selected elite, which in this case later grew into a broader party of "cadres" of carefully selected and large membership. Clubs were affiliated. The pattern of affiliation and central control is here in its initial form, although Crane Brinton stresses that, unlike modern totalitarians, the clubs did not have complete control over the French people. The Jacobins created a network of affiliated clubs united by a single, although not monolithic ideology subject to central direction, with a political vision, goals, and tactics—all components of future centralistic parties. This political group imposed on its members and on the country its dominant values in the form of an ideological orthodoxy controlled by means of terror. The commanding few decided what was wrong or right, patriotic or nonpatriotic. Any difference from their views was regarded as treason, and men who differed or opposed were branded as enemies of the people. The Jacobin party itself was integrated not solely by its organization, of course; common ideology and common interests kept the coherence of the political movement.

The all-powerful Paris committee controlled the disciplined provincial clubs. Instructions and proposals as well as agents were sent from Paris to local sections to impose control and political directives and to assist political activities, tighten party discipline, and strengthen links with Paris. For the first time in history, a party gained decisive control over a nation's press.

After the fall of the monarchy, the Jacobins controlled political power in France, imposing the will of the Paris ruling group over the entire country. They displayed mutual solidarity and support of their members and ruling cliques. In times of disorganization, they maintained an iron link with various sections and thus continued the centralistic tendency. Although a centralistic model had been used long before by the French crown, French historian Aulard suggests that the Jacobins established in the general mind the passion for centralism.[22]

Before the Jacobins, Europe had had experience with a variety of religious terrors and physical elimination of dissenters for the sake of religious purity and the maintenance of a single religious organization. The long-lasting Inquisition need only be mentioned as a major example of organized terror. The organizational models and ideological concepts detached from an ancient or declining idea system are sometimes unconsciously displaced into emergent social relations and processes. In a process of transformation of idea systems, forms (concepts) and behavioral patterns are displaced and supplied with a new ideological content. Thus, the concept of "one true religion" is displaced and appears as "the one and only true political ideology." While the values and ideological content of political actors change, their thought models and behavioral patterns may continue.

The Jacobin experience in coercion was one of the unintended byproducts of a misinterpreted rationalism, for it was an attempt to impose a new, rational, and logical form of society with disregard of the fact that a society is the product of a long historical process. Values and institutions as well as human behavior cannot be changed solely by proclamation of new principles. Manipulation of organized fear may change behavior but may only little affect the dominant, internalized values of the subjects. A democratic and rapid social change requires much more complex policies than fear.

During times of war and inner disintegration, however, the Jacobins maintained the unity of the country; and the question could be asked whether during this historical stage of the French Revolution another type of organizational structure could have developed as rapidly and operated as effectively as a centralistic one based on and integrated by a powerful ideological appeal. A nation is integrated by means of a variety of social institutions and relations into one, however complex, working system. In a political and social revolution, as the French was, the traditional linkages between men disintegrate rapidly, as do the symbolism and rituals which are among the "social tools" by which a society operates. The Jacobin clubs penetrated the disintegrating French society, and reintegrated the nation in times when the old institutions and social relations were in a state of dissolution. This sociological function cannot be overlooked. The Jacobin clubs—very numerous indeed, as Crane Brinton's data indicate and under continuous pressure from Paris—were prompted into efficiency and discipline by permanent fear of terror. Thus the clubs projected a new social structure onto a society bereft of the old one.

12. THE JACOBIN MODEL CONTINUES: THE CONSPIRACY OF EQUALS

With the end of the Jacobin rule, the centralistic party organization did not disappear. A new party called the Conspiracy for Equality, headed by Graccus Babeuf, evolved from the Association of Pantheon. This was a revolutionary movement aimed at overthrowing the republican government. The Equals accused the government of usurpation and betrayal of principles of equality. They advocated a wide economic democracy and appealed to the new industrial classes. In spite of the broad ideology and radical rhetoric, the beginnings of a single party theory and of a police state can be traced to this movement.

The Equals, a secret, underground organization, planned a seizure of power and the establishment of a social and economic democracy. This goal, according to the theorists of this group, could be achieved by establishing a dictatorial government, although members of this conspiracy professed an ideal of perfect democracy. Fragments of one project, the "Decree on Police," give us a foretaste of an authoritarian police state. The state—according to this decree—would decide what is "useful work." Even a scientist would be required to have a "certificat du civisme," a confirmation that his discipline is regarded as useful.[23] The theory and ideology of the Equals already contained the contradictions that appeared later in the authoritarian tendencies of socialism.

A political democracy, however, leads in its logical consequence to economic democracy. Since France's social problems were not answered by the Revolution, the Equals searched for the answer in integral democracy. However, a rational democratic society had to be achieved by what amounted to a dictatorship of a selected few. Thus, a contradiction between means and ends was associated with a dichotomy between ideal vision and real politics. This dichotomy was by no means new in the history of Western ideas.

A directing secret committee (directoire secret de salut public), headed by Graccus Babeuf, was established in 1795. It in turn organized a centralistic, secret (today called underground) network which closely followed the Jacobin mode. The directing committee elected twelve principal, secret revolutionary agents. To every agent a section of the city of Paris was assigned as an area of operation. The entire network was built from the top down—from the central committee to the grass roots. Later, "military agents" were added in the metropolitan police and army units.[24] In fact, the first symptoms of insurrection appeared in the police. The Equals had their influence among the Grenadiers who formed the guard of the legislature. These were the keys to the strategic centers, to the instruments of political power. On the local level, the organization was developed through "intermediary agents" in charge of smaller units. Only principal agents had personal contact with the central committee. Agents organized meetings, distributed the literature, conducted discussions, and reported to the committee. The nature of the centralistic government of France favored a strategy of a massive political action in the capital city. Capture of Paris and establishment of a dictatorship could have been a decisive strike and could bring half of a victory. But the insurrection failed. The end of this party also marks a period of intensive consolidation of power in the hands of the new political classes.

With the Conspiracy of Equals, the vanguardist principle—the concept of a small and centralistic party led by a professional revolutionary elite under an authoritarian leadership and tight party discipline—made its appearance for the second time. The structure was again developed in a somewhat Utopian way in the next generation of revolutionaries.

13. BLANQUISM AND
TWENTIETH-CENTURY PARTIES

The French Revolution did not solve the social problems of France. With the Industrial Revolution, the problems of the working class appeared, and new socialist movements spearheaded reform and social change. At this time, two tendencies had already appeared among socialists and reformers: one was democratic and libertarian, the other authoritarian and aiming at a centralistic organization, even dictatorship, during a nondefinite "transitional period." The hiatus between these two tendencies grew with time, and differences between the democratic, liberal orientation and the centralistic, authoritarian one became more profound with every political generation. These differences were eventually to be reflected in the various types and autonomous structures of the German democratic and socialist working class movement under the leadership of Ferdinand Lassalle.

In France the traditions of a centrally organized political party continued and were advanced by Auguste Blanqui. Half a century after the French Revolution, he suggested a political party structured for capturing power through direct action. In his younger years, Blanqui did not hope for a peaceful social change which would result in emancipation and improvement of economic conditions of the workers in a predominantly agrarian and conservative France.[25] Blanquism, as his theory came to be called, suggested a highly disciplined, centrally organized revolutionary party and direct action.

A link can be traced between the disciplined and authoritarian Jacobins and the conspiracy of Equals of the French Revolution on the one hand and the Blanquist party patterns on the other. Blanqui, too, was probably influenced by Philip Buonarotti, one of the leading personalities of Babeuf's Conspiracy for Equality, who emigrated to Brussels and was later prominent in the Carbonari movements. The

Carbonari form a link between centrally organized political movements
of the French Revolution and modern revolutionary parties. This group
was a clandestine, political lodge, which appeared in times of the Holy
Alliance and was directed against the renascent royalism and tyranny,
resisting the restoration. They were democratic in terms of their times.
Blanqui joined the Carbonari at the age of seventeen.[26] His design of a
small-group, tightly integrated organization, consisting of many separate
but secret branches, may have originated with his experience among them.

It would be, however, a grave mistake to link all revolutionary movements and all models of revolutionary parties to Blanqui. In fact,
Blanqui had many and powerful adversaries in the democratic radical
movements, as well as in revolutionary parties, who rejected his Jacobin
party models and Jacobin ideas of a political dictatorship. His was a
party of a minority.

The tendency toward centralization appears frequently in social
groups in processes of aggression and in defense situations. A century
ago it was noticed and discussed by Herbert Spencer. Revolutionary
parties of the time, geared toward political attack, were sooner or later
affected by this tendency. This does not make their members and even
their party a Blanquist one. Warnings against political Jacobinism,
Blanquism, and emphasis of goals of political freedom were frequent
among some of the major revolutionary movements of the last two
centuries.

14. THE REVOLUTIONARY PARTY
DIFFUSED TO RUSSIA

The theoretical discussion of party structure appeared in the early
Russian revolutionary movements of agrarian socialists, known as
Populists (Narodniki), during the second half, especially in the last
quarter, of the nineteenth century. The Populists were revolutionary
agrarian socialists of various shades advocating a sort of economic and
political democracy. The problem of party organization, of adjusting
the structure to changing political conditions and party tactics were of
paramount significance. Peter Lavrov, theoretician of the Populists and
an early and prominent Russian sociologist, wrote an essay on political
parties, and political leaders and other theoreticians argued the issues of

a federalistic pattern composed of autonomous groups and of centralistic organization.[27]

Ideas of a vanguardist party appeared early in the theories of the radical Frenchman, L. A. Blanqui. Discussions on this type of a party had probably taken place in Russia sometime in the early 1870s as a consequence of the political situation and the political experience of the Populists at that time.[28]

We shall discuss later the sociological nature of a vanguardist model (see Chapter 3, section 5). Here we want to emphasize again that this model is a party of a dedicated and professional few, of a political elite, under strong leadership. Such a party neither intends nor attempts to recruit a mass following. It advances a social myth that the party has the legitimacy to represent the people or certain classes and acts in the name of the entire people or respective classes. Such a party usually claims that it represents the supreme good and ultimate political truth. In consequence of its legitimacy and creed of supreme good and ultimate truth, the party arrogates the right to impose its will, the will of a minority, on the entire nation and repress by force any dissenters or opposers as enemies of the people.

In 1875, an argument in favor of a vanguardist party with a centralistic structure appeared in an article by a Russian writer and revolutionary, Peter Tkachev ("Organization of Revolutionary Forces") in an obscure emigré publication *Nabat* published in London.[29] It is Tkachev, who, with Lenin is frequently credited for advancing the vanguardist model. Tkachev suggested a small, centrally organized party of professional revolutionaries who would seize power in a moment of a spontaneous revolution or unrest and establish some kind of a dictatorship or permanent rule. A few years later (1882) theories of a permanent terror appeared in a pamphlet by Nicholas Morozov. The Populists were centrally organized; their party was a kind of a vanguardist one; individual terror was their tactics. But the extreme forms of centralism and an idea of a dictatorship of a political vanguard or elite met with strong criticism. Some of the Populists saw early dangers of what is called today authoritarianism or totalitarianism. Letters and articles against "Jacobinism," as such tendencies were called at that time, appeared in the underground and emigré papers.

From Tkachev a historical link leads to Lenin's famous 1902 essay, *What Has To Be Done* (see Chapter 3). Thus Lenin's model of the Bolshevik party had its umbilical cord attached to Tkachev's theory and model. Tkachev in turn was probably influenced by Blanqui, and

Blanqui by the French conspirators Buonarotti and Babeuf, who originate ideologically from the late Jacobins. This seems to be the historical lineage of the model. The vanguardist model is one of the variants of a centralistic revolutionary party. The Jacobin attitude toward politics and party structure was discussed among Russian Populists during the last quarter of the past century. It was at this time that terror from spontaneous isolated action was evolving into a "stystem" (a term used by the Populists), for terroristic struggle required an adequate party structure. A disciplined, centralistic party of small groups of trusted revolutionaries was adopted by the Populists and later by the Social Revolutionaries (SR). This type of party may have influenced Lenin's thinking (he approved this structure and saw in it an antecedent of his model). But the Populist leadership was not authoritarian; furthermore, the Populists and Social Revolutionaries rejected and opposed the Jacobin attitudes, party model, and their ideas of a dictatorship. Their parties were revolutionary, centralistic ones, rooted in the small unit system (see Chapter 3, section 5), but it did not have the quality of a vanguardist party, which is characterized by absolute power of the leadership, portending future dictatorial powers.[30]

Institutional patterns, however, have an existence and an appeal of their own. They can be detached from their original social base and adopted by the leadership of political movements and adjusted to different social objectives. And this was part of the history of totalitarian parties, which borrowed models from movements dedicated to ideas of social and political equality and freedom, using their political instrument as the means to impose dictatorship. A powerful, centralistic party, even if not large, represents an uneven, formidable match vis-à-vis loosely organized, nonintegrated political movements or vis-à-vis a passive populace. Such parties are capable of imposing their will over large territories or upon a passive population.

15. MILITARIZATION OF CENTRALISTIC PARTIES: ITALY AND GERMANY

After World War I, the centralistic structure was widely adopted by mass parties of extreme orientations. Mussolini, familiar with problems of party organization, applied the principle of an elite party with cadres on a wide scale in his Fascist movement. In addition, the Fascists and Nazis projected military structure, behavior, and insignia (uniforms and ranks) into military structure. They tightened party discipline in a military fashion. Thus, a new type of powerful military command party emerged at the beginning of the postwar period, and these were the parties that shaped the destiny of Europe. (Military detachments of the party organization in its nuclear form had appeared long before in underground movements and in times of revolutions. The structure of this model is discussed in Chapter 3, section 5.)

During World War I in Germany, military discipline was imposed as a kind of general behavioral pattern, and the entire population became adjusted to military structure and behavior. As a consequence, after the war the military pattern was spontaneously adopted by parties of the extreme. Uniformed political regiments of the extreme right, called Stahlhelm, SS, and SA, appeared, while the defense of the republic forced the other parties to organize similar organizations. Thus, political armies made their historical appearance.

Their power was of such a nature that all other parties had to adjust their policies and strategies to the initiative of the former, which were by no means parliamentary parties in the British or American sense. These parties also used the techniques of control by symbolism and political rituals.

An early and visionary draft of a model which in its structure resembled a fascist militia or a private political army although with leftist and socialistic ideology (a kind of a socialist "science-fiction") was outlined in France in a forgotten document. The plan of a military arm of a party or a projection of the military organization into a political party was made again by L. A. Blanqui in his instruction for an armed uprising.[32] The reader may remember, however, that Blanqui wrote in the times of Napoleon III, who came to power in France by means of a military revolution and imposed a monarchy. Blanqui's proposal appeared at a time when the Russian Czars exercised absolute power over tens of subject nations, and Prince Bismarck was changing Germany from a loose confederation into a centralistic state. How to oppose or how to change autocratic regimes? This was the problem. Blanqui, no doubt, represented an extreme alternative of violence, for more democratic answers were being advanced by powerful social movements.

"The army," wrote Blanqui more than half a century before Mussolini's *squadristi* made their appearance, "has two great advantages over the people: the rifle [*chassepot*] and organization." The latter, he continued, is "immense and irresistible." What is the essential and, thus far, absent condition of victory in a revolution? *Organization*, answers Blanqui. The army—in his view—supplies the model. What follows is a detailed outline of a militarized revolutionary party, of cadres, divided into companies, companies into platoons (*pelotons*), and platoons are in turn divided into sections, all headed by their officers and noncoms. Such a militarized and armed party—a replica of an army—based on strict command and obedience would present a formidable force. "Rester en ordre, observer la silence (sauf le cri de Vive la République poussé seulement à signal donné . . . signal des chefs)" "Keep the order, observe silence (with the exception of the exclamation 'Long Live the Republic' cried only in response to a signal of chiefs)" reads the instruction.[33] No discussion, no voting or opposing; orders are given by political commanders and must be obeyed.

Here is a model of a militarized command party, a party organized on the model of an army. Two generations later, the fascist militia, Hitler's storm troopers, were organized in a party which carried the semblance of Blanqui's model. However, the storm troopers commanded by their political officers and noncoms no longer cried "Vive la République"; their appeal was "Death to the Republic."

Blanqui in his youthful years advanced a strategy of a Parisian insurrection and dictatorship. His strategy, of course, followed the Jacobin theory closely. Since a revolution in France was doomed to fail at that time because the peasantry was not inclined to support a radical change of intellectuals led by workers, Blanqui suggested that the proper strategy was a local insurrection in Paris led by a small but determined group of revolutionaries and establishment of a dominance or dictatorship of this Parisian "Vanguard." But twenty years later, Blanqui could no longer believe in the success of a victory of a small, revolutionary Vanguardist party. In consequence, he advanced or rather dreamed up a plan of a militarized, centrally controlled mass party. Thus, he moves from the theory and practice of small, vanguardist centralistic party to an utopia of a large militarized mass party, structured and led like a regular army.

Blanqui's last model was applied with success—not to overthrow a tyranny or a monarchy, but to overthrow a republic (Germany) and a nascent democracy (Italy). The same centralistic model can be applied against a variety of political systems, against autocracy or a representative democracy. But let us stress here again, Blanqui's model, written longhand, remained in archives, unknown until 1930.

16. POLITICAL FOLKLORE: RELIGION
AND REVOLUTIONARY LITURGY

Political folklore did not originate with the revolutionary movements
of the Continent. At the time of the American Revolution, popular
political songs, flags, slogans, and even art appeared, forming the beginning of a political folklore. This was added to by the several patriotic
societies that sprang up after the Revolution, one of which was the
Tammany societies (also known as the Columbian Order in New York
City). Taking its name from that of a Delaware Indian chief, its rites
and ceremonies were based on pseudo-Indian forms. American political
folklore later developed into cheerful full bloom at the 1840 national
convention. While the associations and clubs of English tradition were
aristocratic in nature and were thus exclusive (e.g., the hereditary order
of Cincinnati of the officers of the Revolution), the Tammany organization stressed the democratic character of its membership; its goal
was "to connect, in indissoluble bonds of friendship, brethren of known
attachment to the political rights of human nature and the liberties of
the country." It was originated as a secret society and initiation rites
were also practiced. Furthermore, its organization was quite unusual; it
was divided into thirteen tribes corresponding to the number of the
states. Tribes carried names of animals: fox, wolf, eagle, etc. Indian
appellations stressed the American character of the association. Its
members met for suppers and festive gatherings. Tammany rituals,
songs, and even organization reflect already folkloristic qualities. It is
a kind of political folk culture originated by its members. The first
Tammany society was organized in Philadelphia in 1772; the famous
one in New York City was initiated later, in 1789, by an Irish
upholsterer.[34]

Tammany was a forerunner of the "lodge," a kind of a fraternal
organization popular in the United States by the nineteenth century
and even today. The lodge organizations, although it may have its roots
in ancient guilds and masonic lodges, became a typical American
primary ("face to face") association; there are, for example, the nonpolitical Elks, Shriners, Rotarians, and Lions and the quite political
Grangers and Ku Klux Klan. All of them have a lodge organization,
rituals, songs, some kind of initiation rites. Here, however, political
rituals and symbols were separated from religion and, in accordance

with popular attitudes, remained cheerful and free of antagonistic charge (with some exceptions, of course, for example, the KKK). A sense of humor prevailed, and the elephant and the donkey (borrowed from a popular cartoon after the Civil War) were adopted as political symbols. The political folklore of the French Revolution was far more elaborate, although its beginnings can perhaps be traced to the American Revolution; and while the American political folklore was dominated by humor, the French Revolutionary folklore and symbolism were characterized by pathos.

The efforts in France to secularize public life and to limit the influence of the church generated a new, political religion. The old religious forms were projected into new idea systems; old concepts were replaced in a process of "ritualistic substitution"—that is, the integration of an old ritual, which functioned within an original religious or political system, into a nascent and different religious or ideological movement, which "substitutes" for (displaces) the former one. Rituals usually correspond to certain psychological needs or perform a certain sociological function, such as the reintegration or reinforcement of a group. "Symbolic substitution" serves as a tool in displacing the old and reinforcing a new creed.

Thus the cult of Martyrs of Liberty during the French Revolution competed with the cult of saints. Marat was the first martyr to be worshipped. In 1793 the Commune of Ris informed the convention that Brutus was to be adopted as the patron of the comunity in place of Saint Blaise. Later revolutionary triade, or trinity of martyrs, was formed of Marat, Lepeletier, and Chalier.[35] Although this new religious fervor subsided, the general pattern of revolutionary symbolism and ritualism continued with a strong infusion of religious forms, behavioral traits, and concepts, which were easily assimilated since they were grafted onto well-established patterns of religious behavior.

The quasireligious expression of political ideologies is symptomatic of deep sentiments and unconscious emotional needs. Rituals supply formal, socially acceptable channels for the expression of these needs, which are sometimes repressed. A war dance may either intensify and escalate hostilities—an aggressive tendency—into combat, or it may channel them into harmless activities. Rituals are multifunctional and can exercise alternative, even mutually exclusive, functions. A military parade in 1912 in Switzerland might have performed different social functions from a military parade in Berlin at the same time.

The destruction or transformation of institutions, changes in legitimacy of power, and coercive changes in values and in dominant ideologies or religions are often accompanied by abolition of rituals, prohibitions of certain symbolic behavioral patterns, and destruction of symbols (e.g., prohibiting sacrifices to Roman gods and destroying the monuments of pagan deities already at the end of the fourth century). This was, however, not always the case. In the history of revolutionary movements, ritualistic and symbolic substitution plays a major role during rapid consolidation of power.

Rituals are usually deeply embedded in a society. Repeated during the same seasons for centuries, and often for millennia, they become part of the customs that regulate social life. Such seasonal rituals reflect or maintain a regular, necessary rhythm in the yearly cycle of work and activities. Prohibiting such rituals can alienate social classes or groups, which new elites attempt to win. Instead of destroying the rituals, new political or religious leaders use the same days or seasons for the same or similar rituals, equipped, however, with new content and symbols. Thus, established rituals become carriers of new creeds; their forms—the mechanism—remain but the content changes. The melody of the royal anthem in a patriotic celebration carried a republican content and symbols, or, in reverse, the French republican tricolor of the Revolution became the imperial flag of Napoleon Bonaparte. Hitler and his cohorts kept May 1 as a holiday but displaced the socialist content with their own idea system and symbolism. The Continental democratic labor movement also had a minor share of symbolic forms and ritualistic behavior. After all, this symbolism was part of the entire culture; political behavior is only part of it.

A massive projection of religious rituals and worship in political mass movements appeared with the growth of totalitarian tendencies during the interwar period. During the Stalinist period in the Soviet Union, Caesaristic worship of the leaders, especially of Stalin, Lenin, Marx, and Engels, was cultivated and imposed by public administration, the police, and the schools. The October Revolution was celebrated in a manner reminiscent of holy days. The cult of martyrs that arose after Kirov's assassination was similar to Jacobin efforts. The near apotheosis of Stalin was diffused by the Communist party all over the world.

The Nazi and Fascist leaders were probably not familiar with the historical origins of political cults. They adopted the Jacobin model indirectly by imitating the pattern and the political folklore of the historical mass parties of the left and of Italian fascism, assimilating their ritualism and symbolism and developing them into new techniques for mass manipulation. Another cult of martyrs appeared, this time in Germany (Horst Wessel and others), created and manipulated by the party leadership. Advertising techniques supplied patterns for daily sales campaigns of their political objectives. The cinematic techniques of the "colossal" performances on such themes as Roman history supplied an image and model for the manipulative techniques of their propagandists. The Nazi parades, with their Roman insignia and vulgar music, were indeed a replica of the circus, gladiators, and Roman legions—as well as garish movies of the 1920s and 1930s.

Practical psychological experience taught them various kinds of manipulation by means of hatred and hostilities. They learned how to channel discontent and pent-up anger against clear targets: ethnic minorities, "traditional enemies" (*Erbfeinde*), and political institutions of democracy. The latter were called "decadent," and this word symbol legitimized the use of violence in the interest of the "true" and "pure" nation-race. The "propagandists," the new social manipulators, learned how to use political rituals and symbols first to intensify emotional tensions, and second, to release them in the form of violence or other types of hostility.

For the time being, we shall finish discussion on this theme. Here, we have only indicated the manipulative techniques of political collective behavior. (This theme is unfolded further in Chapter VI, "Random Notes on Dress, Rituals, Symbols, and Myth-making.")

17. CONTINENTAL EUROPEAN AND AMERICAN PARTIES COMPARED

During the interwar period, the differences between the European Continental political arena and the Anglo-American were accentuated. The specific socioeconomic and political environment of Europe and different historical conditions, as well as the growth of specific political ideologies, produced particular patterns of political behavior and organizations. The mass parties of Europe grew differently from those of the United States. European mass movements were visionary, while American politics had grown pragmatic. Through elaborate ideologies and vision of a future society, the former appealed to a broad and dy-

namic segment of the social base. The American political movements
had already gone through their visionary period in the eighteenth century.

The differences extend to the structure of the party, to political
behavior, and to modes of operation. Collective political behavior can
be roughly divided into excitatory and inhibitory. The former emphasizes overt patterns such as mass manifestations, mass rituals, use of
exhortation, music, lights, and even architectural devices in the manipulation of the masses. The Fascist and Nazi movements greatly advanced
such manipulative techniques. Physical expressions of emotions under
stress or excitement were channeled and formalized. What is called
"irrational" behavior is usually an external expression of deep-seated
and subconscious psychological needs. The excitatory political behavior
grows especially in times of crisis.

In times of intensive crisis and on special occasions, as elections, such
behavior in a restrained and controlled manner is tolerated also in the
Anglo-American political arena. Here, however, other safe channels are
available for funneling psychological needs. With the exception of minor
fringe groups, party uniforms or frequent party mass meetings and
regimented behavior did not appeal to the British or American voter.
The fact remains that acute crisis produced in Germany strongly
excitatory types of movements such as Nazism, while in similar situations such movements did not succeed in Great Britain. The British
and American political movements had inhibitory tendencies that
discouraged and restrained strong polarization of society, emotional
appeal, and manipulation of crowd behavior.

A number of "mass parties" as well as "microparties" of the Continent were chiliastic in their appeal. Messianistic political movements
unveiled an image of a perfect future society, or perfect, total rule of a
"chosen" nation or a "chosen" class. The Communists, Anarchists,
Syndicalists, Anarcho-Syndicalists, even Social Democrats were "per-
fectionists," believers in a perfect society, ready to promise a perfect
solution in the not-so-distant future. The Nationalists appealed with
an image of a state of one perfect nationhood. Contrariwise, British
socialists, the Labour party, or American liberals or Populists, and the
liberal wing of Democrats had a "melioristic" approach, which had its
appeal rooted in pragmatism—in practical answers to problems and in
far more modest attempts at a better, not a perfect, society. Probably
few among them believed in a perfect man or perfect society.

There is also a basic difference in value-goal orientation. In Anglo-
American political philosophy the individual is the end (a consumatory

value), the state only a means, an instrumental value. İn the Fascist philosophy and also in other movements of the European continent, which were not necessarily extreme, the state or nation is the consumatory goal, the end in itself; individuals are only an "instrumental value," a means, not an end. Mussolini argued that states and nations count in history, not individuals. (European humanistic socialism, however, always stressed man, his freedom, and his welfare as an end, and this general philosophy was reflected in party ideologies and militancy.)

18. NEW SYMPTOMS

Until the early sixties, there was indeed a difference between the basic Anglo-American inhibitory model of political macroparties and various European excitatory party models. This difference was visible; it was striking to an occasional observer, although I doubt whether it can be pinned down in terms of rigorous, statistical methods and definitions. Not all of our life can be captured by our *a priori* methods and definitions. During that decade (1960-1970), however, new social movements of an affluent society appeared in the United States, some with a bizarre origin of quasireligious cults connected with a growing use of drugs and a search for a deeper meaning of life from that offered by traditional behavior and institutions. The civil-rights movement at its beginning followed the nonviolent pattern of American tradition. The Vietnam war created new conditions, however. New antiwar protest movements appeared, and new extreme groups of racial ideologies advocating violence and terror became vocal. Diverse student groups and what can be called microparties, small and by themselves insignificant political groupings, which appeal to marginal classes, merged with marginal social groups in their public manifestations of violent action. (Space and theme do not justify further discussion of this important phenomenon, which on one hand reflects serious and urgent social problems and on the other, psychological urges and ethical sensitivity of a well-fed society. It is a complex phenomenon, which is also symptomatic of psychological and moral ethical needs of our times.) In consequence, violent and excitatory behavior appeared on the streets of American cities. Thus far, this trend has not affected the basic political patterns of the major parties, although change of behavior and attitudes was noticeable among students in the late 1960s.

It may be noteworthy that the organized American working class and farmers neither supported nor sympathized with the violence associated with youthful protests of the status quo. The American worker has achieved, finally, after a long struggle, high wages and relatively short working hours. The United States probably has the highest wage scale and the shortest working week in human history. But a worker still has a workingman ethos and seems to view with suspicion some of the idle, unkempt youths adorned with chains and necklaces and excited by drugs—that's what he seems to perceive on the streets and on television. They have had access to the leading and comfortable colleges; he did not; they somehow have enough money to live doing nothing, or very little. So many of them—he hears or reads—come from the wealthy classes, classes of traditional idlers. A worker, still dependent on his daily work and weekly wage, still earning his money in physical effort, did not trust this new "subclass," rejected their appeal, and at times has shown hostility. The public manifestation of construction workers in New York of spring 1970, supporting President Nixon's foreign policy, was in its slogans and symbolism an expression of opposition to and separation from the new youth protest movements. The general public had neither patience nor interest to consider the nature and deeper root causes of those protests and violence. It rather reacted to visual images and instant impressions.

The social structure of the United States has undergone revolutionary changes since World War II, producing new marginal classes. Masses of rural population have been displaced and have moved to the cities. Inner migrations have created a transient population. The cities, built for an eighteenth- or nineteenth-century image of an agrarian-urban society, have outlived their utility, but there is not imagination enough to build new, uncrowded habitats for those who are affected by this historical technological revolution. Vested interests remained unyielding. New social problems which call for social change have appeared. Few appreciate the magnitude of this change and the subsequent problems, which calls for imaginative and daring policies.

New elitist microparties with an appetite for violence and total power have emerged. Their members, with a strong urge for power and prestige, seem to distrust or even reject the traditional democratic process. With a prophetic urge leaders of these minor movements claim their right to impose their will over large majorities of population. In consequence, new forms of behavior have begun to influence American

political life. For how long? In what direction will these tendencies
move? The new groups appeal far more to sentiments, emotions, and
passions than do the traditional American parties.

By 1971, however, the impetus and drive of those movements began
to decline rapidly. The American commitments in Vietnam had been
greatly reduced, and the tendency to end the war became apparent.
Recession created new problems. The social problems continued and
the need for a protest was slowly channeled into new forms and demands
for constructive and substantial social change. Political violence has
declined but major problems still remain.

Ideologically, the American student movement of radical protest
was committed to ideas of peace, equality, and, in some cases, extreme
individualism. Certain minor groups were willing to approve despotism
for the price of a "left-wing" philosophy and ideology. But tactics are
a different problem. The forms of violence and protest they practiced,
intolerance toward difference of opinion, interruptions of speeches,
disruption of meetings, use of obscenity, cult of youth, emphasis on
action, contempt for history and the works of the past, senseless destruction—all bore striking similarities with fascist tactics. It may be
argued that tactics of violence were adopted by a minority, even an
insignificant one, and the prevailing mood was one of humanity and
sensitivity. Of course, all this is an impression. But even so, the violent
minority for a time set the style; those few, often irresponsible, not
even serious in their expression, were at times the style setters and often
leaders. But with war coming to an end, with progress in the field of
civil rights, the microparties began to rapidly disintegrate, and tactics
of violence slowly to be abandoned by the end of 1971.

19. CENTRALISM AND POLARIZATION

In Europe, the centralistic form of organization and excitatory appeal
reflect the polarization of political parties. American parties integrate
within the party different tendencies, absorbing political tensions within
the party structure. The process of polarization in continental Europe
corresponds to antagonistic ideological and accentuated class divisions
and differences. Pareto noticed in 1920, prior to the period of European
dictatorships, a process of rapid breakdown of central authority accom-

panied by the increase of centrifugal forces. The decision and power shifted, as Pareto saw it, from the government to the parties, unions, and what he called the "class of speculators."[36] The centrifugal process was not solely a result of class division but also of the weakness of political institutions unable to cope with the situation. The very nature of the major Italian political parties had its share in this social transformation which led to fascism.

After World War I, a historical sequence may be traced: (1) The power and decision making shifts from parliaments and governments to the party headquarters; (2) The Continental polar parties of the so-called extreme right and left cut their umbilical cords from the parliaments; (3) A third stage follows in which a monoparty takes over total power. The historical separation of powers (never fully advanced) as well as various forms of diffused power (self-government and autonomy) is displaced by a power center of a single party. In the crucial years of World War II (1941-1944), representative parliamentary government disappeared from the Continent from Gibraltar to Vladivostok with the exception of a few nations on the outskirts of the mainland. Powerful monoparties ruled conquered nations. The opposition was driven underground and the conditions of underground struggle forced upon them a centralistic elitist, or cadres, model. At this time the Continental parties were a different political animal from the British and American parties, as they were described by political scientists and sociologists at the turn of the century.

The end of the ideological world war and the defeat of monoparties of the extreme right marks also a return to the multiparty system in Western Europe and the decline, or at least the reduction, of the excitatory, centralistic military type of political parties. The return to representative government also resurrected parliamentary political parties. After the cruel experience of monoparty rule and some embarrassing experimentation in mass tyranny, Europeans, not without some prodding, returned to autonomous, less rigid forms of social organization. After the death of Stalin, the Communist party underwent important changes. The Caesaristic cult was abolished, display of military might replaced to an extent the ritualistic performances and artificial mass enthusiasm. Even more profound transformations in Yugoslavia, Czechoslovakia, and for a certain time in Poland and Hungary, did not, however, change the very nature of a Communist monoparty, rigidly and centrally controlled. Some of the ritualistic trimmings of early communism were maintained. In China the old Caesaristic model continued with the manipulation of mass behavior, emotional build-up, and cult of the leader as well as escalating hostilities. The well developed centralistic structure of the revolutionary party, originated in times of the French Revolution and transformed by the Bolshevik rule, had become a powerful instrument of the status quo and a means of consolidating power by the new super-elites.

20. DIFFUSION OF PARTY PATTERNS

From these two sources—Europe on the one hand and Great Britain and the United States on the other—the major and quite different patterns of political parties diffused all over the world. Native cultures have absorbed the political models in their own way. They have been adjusted to the needs and functions of changing but still traditional societies.

The world can be divided into political-cultural areas of distinct political institutions, political behavior, and values. In turn, the large culture areas usually contain several subcultures. The extensive Anglo-American area, rooted in predominantly Protestant values, is characterized by the continuity of representative institutions, the absence of a police state in their long history, and rather loosely organized, not rigid, pragmatic political parties inhibitory in behavior, working through a mechanism of compromise. The northwestern fringe area of Europe, embracing Holland and the Scandinavian countries, is closely related to the former and in addition has a successful cooperative movement.

The continent of Europe—of predominantly Catholic and orthodox values—was and still is characterized by parties of well-developed ideologies but with a tendency toward polarization which has sharply declined in certain countries after World War II. In this area, two major patterns of organization appeared: a democratic, efficiently administered party with a rudimentary bureaucratic structure, and on the other hand, centrally organized movements and monoparties. Next to the latter, there were of course, other types of party organizations, to mention only peasant movements of Central and Eastern Europe. These parties usually had a loosely organized network of committees and were strongly oriented toward cooperatives and self-government. They were built around the charismatic personality of a major leader rather than on an extensive philosophy. These parties were pragmatic in their political approach.

The monoparties, however, had to play the major historical role. As much as their growth is closely related to "historical conditions," socioeconomic structure, and change, their centralistic pattern, mode of operation, and forms of political folklore can be traced to the late stage of the Jacobin party organization. The powerful monoparties of our centuries unwittingly borrowed from this major historical model. The early Jacobins, with their symbols of political freedom, were ideologically on the opposite pole of the extreme right, but the forms of organizations and modes of operation of a later Jacobin stage were borrowed by the radical right as one borrows a tool. We may add, however, that "revolutionary situations" favored both: an independent invention of party structure as well as diffusion or assimilation of historical models.

The fate of our ideas and inventions is not decided, may we repeat, by their initiators, fathers, or apostles. Philosophies of freedom have been reinterpreted into an enthusiasm for dictatorship, religions of mercy into intolerance. Religious and political movements so often begin with apostles and end with secretaries and secretariats. Still a short, final note. Let us not confuse the issues: the party and the revolution. The revolutionary party is not tantamount to a revolution, and a party alone does not make the latter. The party at best, may or may not become an instrument of a violent and revolutionary change. It is and was in not a few historical cases a vehicle used by new out-elites to move into power and become in-elites and super-elites.

The two necessary ingredients of a revolution, frequently forgotten by philosophers and historians, are enthusiasm and fear, indeed a powerful fear. It is enthusiasm which so often moves the party and the masses to action; it is fear which moves the very same masses to obedience and submission to the party and its elites. Without enthusiasm, which usually appears first, and fear, which comes next, there is neither a revolutionary drama nor a spontaneous, mass revolution from below. The party moves not only within a socioeconomic environment; it also moves within this subtle, difficult-to-identify or describe psychological "climate" of moods, which are dynamic, sometimes change suddenly, and have their ups and downs.

NOTES

1. M. (Moisei) Ostrogorski, *La Démocratie et l'Organization des Partis Politiques* (Paris, 1903). Calman Lévy Editeurs. This writer has used the French edition. However, in 1964 a new, inexpensive, but abridged English edition appeared: M. Ostrogorski, *Democracy and Organization of Political Parties*, edited by Seymour Martin Lipset (Garden City: Doubleday Company, 1964).

2. Siegmund Neumann, *Modern Political Parties* (Chicago: Chicago University Press, 1956), pp. 403-405, makes a distinction between parties of integration and parties of representation. Neumann and Lipset suggest that parties of integration weaken democracy while parties of representation strengthen it. Seymour Martin Lipset, *Political Man* (Garden City: Doubleday, 1959), p. 86.

This is not always true however. The three major social democratic parties between the wars—the German, the Austrian and the Polish (the Polish Socialist Party, PPS)—were parties of integration, since their activities integrated a variety of functions and groups of the working class movement. At the same time, all three were major democratic forces and were supporting and defending a representative government. All of them had their cultural and educational branch organizations, as well as associated sport and leisure clubs. Last, not least, they were integrated with the trade unions and had direct influence on sections of cooperative movement. All three parties had political militias of varying strength. The destruction of the German Social-Democratic party (SPD) and of the Austrian Socialist party marked the end of the representative government in those countries. The Polish Socialist party (PPS), allied with the Peasant party and the Christian Democratic party, struggled for reestablishment of representative government in Poland.

In countries where the powerful parties of the extreme right were centrally organized, a counterbalance was formed by the "integral" parties of the democratic left and in Germany also by the Catholic party. With the emergence of the military command parties of the right (see below Chapter 3), the defense of representative government called for even stronger organization of the forces of the democratic left. But such polarization led eventually to the destruction of the representative government.

3. R. T. McKenzie, *British Political Parties* (New York: Praeger, 1964), and Sir Lewis Namier, *Monarchy and the Party System* (Oxford, 1952), pp. 1-6, 19.

4. Maxwell Fyfe Report, quoted by McKenzie, *British Political Parties*, p. 185. McKenzie comments that two other functions should be added: the party is a channel of communication between the leader and the rank and file of a mass party, and it also gives an opportunity to those politically active to exercise some influence in the formulation of policies and the selection of the leader.

5. See ibid., pp. 8ff. For a historical survey and analysis of British political parties, see ibid., Ostrogorski, *Partis Politiques*, and a short digest also in Samuel H. Beer, "Great Britain: From Governing Elite to Organized Mass Parties," in *Modern Political Parties*, ed. Sigmund Neumann (Chicago: University of Chicago Press, 1956), pp. 9ff.

6. See McKenzie, *British Political Parties*, esp. his conclusions, p. 635.

7. See J. B. McMaster, *A History of the People of the United States* (1893), II, 94, quoted by Ostrogorski, *Partis Politiques*, I: 114.

8. Quoted by William N. Chambers, *Political Parties in a New Nation: The American Experience, 1776-1809* (New York: Oxford University Press, 1963), p. 75.

9. Ibid., p. 41.

10. Chambers sees in Republican and Democratic clubs early pressure groups

rather than a political party. DeGrazia, however, suggests a prototype, an early
but organized form of mass movement. Chambers, *Political Parties*, pp. 61ff,
Alfred DeGrazia, *Politics and Government* (New York: Collier Books, 1962),
I, 192ff.

11. For a survey of the development and pattern of American parties, see
V. O. Key, *Politics, Parties and Pressure Groups* (New York: Crowell, 1958);
DeGrazia, *Politics;* Ivan Hinderaker, *Party Politics* (New York: Henry Holt &
Co., 1956), pp. 244-69; W. Chambers, *Political Parties;* William Goodman, *The
Two Party System in the United States* (New York: Van Nostrand, 1956); and
Hugh A. Bone, *American Politics and the Party System* (New York: McGraw-
Hill, 1955).

12. Gaetano Salvemini, *La Rivoluzione Francese* (Milano: Feltrinelli, 1964
ed.), p. 37.

13. Ibid., pp. 194 ff. For the history of the Jacobins, see especially Clarence
Crane Brinton, *The Jacobins* (New York: Macmillan, 1930).

14. P. Bessano-Massenet, *Robespierre* (Paris: Plon, 1961), pp. 41ff. Also
quoted by him Cardenal, "La Révolution et Societés Populaires," in *Revue de la
Révolution Française* (Paris, July-September, 1924).

15. On American influence on the French Revolution, see A. Aulard, *Etudes
et Leçons sur la Révolution* (Paris: Alcan, 1921), VIII; 58ff.

16. See Salvemini, *Rivoluzione Francese.*

17. Brinton, *The Jacobins*, pp. 39-43.

18. Alphonse Aulard, "Derniers Jacobins," in *Etudes et Leçons sur la
Révolution* , VIII; 84ff.

19. Brinton, *The Jacobins*, pp. 50-57, 70, Appendix II.

20. For a discussion of various types of Jacobin terror, physical as well as
psychological, see ibid., pp. 111ff.

21. The rules and techniques of acceptance of new members into Jacobin
organization changed according to the temper of the revolution. For a more
detailed discussion and quotation of rules, see ibid., pp. 23ff.

22. Alphonse Aulard, *The French Revolution* (New York: Charles Scribner,
1910).

23. "Fragment d'un Projet de Décret de Police" in [Filippo] Buonarotti,
Conspiration pour l'Egalité dite de Babeuf (1828; reprint ed., Paris: Editions
Sociales, 1957), II: 201.

24. Ibid., I: 98, 99; "Organization des agents principaux au nombre de douze
et des agents intermédiaires. Premières fonctions de chacun d'eux, ibid., II: 182-192.

25. Max Nomad, *Political Heretics* (Ann Arbor: University of Michigan Press,
1963), p. 48; M. Nomad, *Apostles of Revolution* (Boston: Little, Brown and
Company, 1939), p. 32; Alan B. Spitzer, *The Revolutionary Theories of Louis
Auguste Blanqui* (New York: Columbia University Press, 1957).

26. Spitzer, *Revolutionary Theories*, p. 158. The details of the organization,
especially the rituals, are described in Lucien de la Hodde, *History of Secret
Societies* (Philadelphia: Lippincott, 1856), especially chap. 21, pp. 203ff. Both
Nomad and Spitzer question the veracity of sections of this work by Hodde, a
former police agent of a royalist government. Sections on the structure of
organization seem to be accurate; they follow in general the early model of the
Conspiracy of the Equals.

On organizational structure and ideology of the Carbonari, see Gino Bandini,
Giornali e Scritti Politici Clandestini della Carboneria Romagnola (Roma-Milano:
Albrighi, 1938); Angelo Ottolini, *La Carboneria* (Modena: Collezione Storica di
Risorgimento, 1936); Valentino Labate, *Un Decennio di Carboneria in Sicilia*

(1821-1831), documenti (Roma-Milano: Albrighi, 1909); Albert Falcionelli, *Les Sociétés Secrètes Italiennes* (Paris: Payot, 1936).

27. Pyotr N. Lavrov, *Gistoricbiskie Pisma* [Historical writings] (St. Petersburg, 1906, pp. 79-148. English translation in *Source Book of History* (New York: Brooklyn College, 1949), pp. xix-18. Ludwik Kulczycki, *Rewolucja Rosyjska* [The Russian revolution] (Lwow [Lvov], 1911), II discusses the development of the centralistic organization of the Social Revolutionary party of "Narodnaya Volya" (People's Will), whose goal in fact was democratization of the czar's empire. The centralistic pattern was eventually firmly established by 1879 in the party congress of Voronesh. An underground centralistic party was established at that time with a powerful central committee.

28. Blanqui's idea probably had some influence in some of the discussions of the Populists. However, in my readings of their original writings, I did not notice the name or direct presentation of theories of Blanqui. The centralistic structure of a small, vanguardist terroristic organization was argued in terms of the existing social and political situation, by the moderate Stepniak—e.g., see his chapter on terrorism in *Underground Russia* (New York: Lowell, 1882)— as much as the extremist theoretician of terror, Nicholas Morozov (see his *Terroricheskaya Borba* [Terroristic struggle], 1880). It seems to me, however, that the extremists like Morozov and Tkachev were influenced by Blanqui's ideas.

29. Reprinted in Pyotr N. Tkachev, *Isbrannye Sochinnyena Na Sotsialno Politicheskie Temy* (Moscow: Istor-Revolutsiennaya Bibl., 1932-1933), III: 227; his article first appeared in a little known paper called *Nabat* (The Alarm Bell). Kulczycki, *Rewolucja Rosyjska*, II, 213ff.

On professional revolutionaries see Luciano Pellicani, "I Rivoluzionari di Professione," a reprint from *Rivista di Sociologia* 9 (September-December 1971): 1-92.

30. Nineteenth-century theoreticians and historians, some of whom participated in revolutions, in explaining and justifying the choice of a secret, centralistic conspiratorial organization, defend such a structure and tactics of struggle (use of violence) on the basis that they were made necessary by extreme forms of tyranny in times when the "masses" of the peasantry or urban population were passive. This is the argument of the Populists as has been mentioned already. Kulczycki, *Rewolucja Rosyjska*, discusses at length conditions in nineteenth-century Russia and suggests also that the "conspiratorial" movements emerge in conditions of despotism.

Interestingly enough, Giuseppe Ferrari, a nineteenth-century Italian democrat and revolutionary, a historian and political scientist, in his *La Rivoluzione e i Rivoluzionari in Italia* (Milano: Universale-Economica, n.d.), which appeared originally in 1844-1845 (in Part I "Movimento Politico"), advances a similar viewpoint and theory. Vincenzo Cuoco, a generation earlier, in *Saggio Storico Sulla Rivoluzione Di Napoli* (1801; reprint ed., Milano: Universale-Economica, n.d.), points to the fact that the Napolitan Revolution against autocracy and the Inquisition was not a popular one nor was it carried by the people, since the latter were passive or hostile to the French and the French army carried the revolutionary changes. This revolution of enlightenment was made by small groups, sympathizers of the American Revolution and of the Jacobins, supported primarily by the French. This was a revolution of small political elites. He called it a "passive revolution," since the people of Naples were "passive" and did not support the revolutionary movement.

31. Bourgin, who published this document, evaluating the circumstances and content, placed it sometime between 1869 and 1870. Georges Bourgin, "Blanquis

Anweisungen für den Strassenkampf," *Archiv für die Geschichte des Sozialismus und der Arbeiter-Bewegung,* XV (1930), 270-272.

32. L. A. Blanqui, "Instructions pour une prise d'armes," reprinted in ibid., pp. 272-300.

33. Ibid.

34. Ostrogorski, *Partis Politiques,* II: 69ff.

35. Albert Soboul, *Histoire de la Révolution Française* (Paris: Gallimard, 1962), II: 51ff.

36. Vilfredo Pareto, *Transformazioni della Democrazia* (Rocca San Casciano: Cappelli Editore, 1964), p. 53.

III

Dynamics of a Political Party

1. A MAJOR PREMISE

Most studies of political parties are limited to a major social process such as the growth of political elites, voting behavior, relationship between voting behavior and economic change, location of power within parties, and the relationship of the party to the distribution of power within the state. Other studies in this field are descriptive or historical, substantial monographs of major political movements. But the study of political processes is of such complexity that it requires a rigid limitation of the field of inquiry. In this essay we are concerned with the political party or movement as a dynamic social force, not as a consequence of social change but as a factor, an instrument by which social and political change is accomplished. A political party is an organized group, oriented toward political goals, that attempts by its actions to maintain the status quo or to change the existing social, economic, and political conditions by means of influencing attainment or the conquest of political power. Political power is the power of the state.

Thus, our approach and theoretical frame of reference need to be reduced to those elements related to the dynamic nature of the party, to its quality as an instrument of action and of change. Furthermore, sociology is a "generalizing discipline." This means that our frame of reference in a sociological approach has a "general quality" which permits application of our concepts to a substantial class of social processes.

Such an approach assists us in perceiving common, essential characteristics and relationships of those movements and at the same time permits us to perceive differences among the latter. In a certain sense, the very concept of a "frame of reference" is a paradoxical device. On the one hand it is a limiting device for it narrows and focuses the field of inquiry, and on the other hand it is a broadening device, a generalizing one, since by the process of selective reduction of variables it points to the essential relationships between facts or variables which have a wider application in similar situations or cases.

A study of the political party as a social force, a dynamic variable affecting social change or maintaining the status quo, suggests a major premise and a frame of reference. We begin with the major premise. In a sociological approach, the political party should be studied in its social, economic, political, and cultural context, that is, within the social environment it operates. For the political party attempts to conquer political power, to change the existing social, economic, and political relations: the social environment. Thus, the political party is studied in situ, in its continuous relationship within the situation, called also by theoreticians and practitioners, to mention Stalin as one of them, "objective conditions."[1] In fact, the political party is a part of the situation, part of those complex processes which we call "conditions." We separate the political party from the entire social fabric as a matter of method, since it is not possible to study the party otherwise, and afterwards, in another step, we relate the party as a separate variable again to the complex situation. An analogy is a rather risky logical device, but let us use it in this case. A heart is part of a functioning human body. In the study of a heart this organ is isolated; otherwise it is impossible to study its structure and functions. However, to understand how it functions the heart must be studied as a part of the human body. Separation, again, is only a matter of method.

The social, economic, political, and cultural environment, which we shall simply call *situation*, is a highly complex system of relations and processes. To this belong: (a) the basic economic pattern: the type of economy, the level of industrial and agricultural development, the general tendency, the trend of economic growth; (b) social-economic relations: the class structure; (c) distribution of economic and political power within the society; (d) social and political institutions; (e) value systems, especially ethnic and religious values; (f) historical traditions, historical antecedents that have shaped behavioral patterns in politics and institutions; and (g) organized political, economic, and religious forces: parties and organizations—briefly, social forces operating within the situation. Viewing the political party from the vantage point of the social environment (situation) the former appears as a consequence of the latter, while the latter, the situation, as an antecedent. We may suggest at this point only, without any further elaboration, that limitation of the "objective conditions" solely to economic relations explains only in part the emergence of this modern social force we have called the political party. Furthermore, the political party is not necessarily a mechanical consequence of economic-social relations. The party is also an independent variable, or an antecedent, in a certain sense at least, since it is an instrument, a factor of social change.

Initiation of social, political, and economic change may begin as a political and economic action of a party. A political party may change or maintain existing conditions by its activities. At this point we may suggest a general working hypothesis as a consequence of our major premise: The social environment (situation) influences and affects the political party; on the other hand, activities of the party affect the situation. This hypothesis is represented by a simple model (Model 1). The circle represents the situation, the triangle, the political party, the smaller inserted one, ideology. The arrows point to influence or causation. Model 1 suggests reciprocal causation or, in another approach, a mutual interdependence.

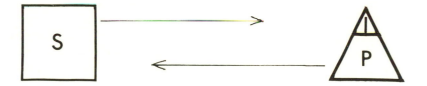

Model 1. Reciprocal Causation

2. A FRAME OF REFERENCE

Within a situation, what are then the major variables or components of a party? At this point, guided by the premise to narrow our study to the dynamic aspects of political parties, we shall reduce our frame of reference to three mutually interdependent components: (1) ideology (value structure), (2) organizational structure (apparatus), and (3) pattern of actions (strategy and tactics). Any political party must have at least these three components, as we shall see later. All three components are mutually interdependent; a change in one involves changes in the remaining two. Such changes, however, usually begin with changes in the goal structure, which is located in the ideological system.

3. IDEOLOGY

The party ideology consists at least of a general value structure and of immediate political goals. Such a limited ideology is usually called a "platform" or in Continental terms the "minimum program." Elaborate ideological systems contain an extensive philosophical and economic theory and an analytical method, in addition to a clear and sometimes detailed goal structure. We may use here as an example the Italian Socialist party of Proletarian Unity (during 1964-1965), a splinter group of the Italian Socialist party. This party followed a Marxist ideology and a democratic orientation and its theoreticians applied analytical methods based on historical materialism. Its writers used Marxist philosophy in addition to theories of democratic government rooted in European but especially in Italian traditions. The ideology, goal structure, and strategy of this party made it a distinct group. It was distinct from the Communists (regarded as the extreme Left) and from the Italian Socialists, which leaned more toward the other democratic parties, as well as different from the Social Democratic party, which was largely based on humanist philosophy and applied a humanist, personalist approach to social problems along with certain elements of Marxist theory.

Theory-oriented ideologies of European mass movements have a definite goal structure: immediate goals (minimum program), intermediate goals (reforms or changes suggested after achieving power during the tenure of a government), and distant goals (maximum program). The goal structure is usually anchored in a vision of a future society. The vision of the future society was called by Sorel, social myth,[2] by Manheim, utopia.[3] A vision, however, can also be realistic and workable.[4] Major American parties present in times of elections a "platform" that contains immediate and intermediate goals and a

general value orientation. At the annual conference of the British
Conservative party in 1934, Baldwin, the leader of the party, quoting
Disraeli, presented in a comprehensive way a "program." Disraeli,
said Baldwin, laid the principles of the Conservative party at the
Crystal Palace many years ago; they were "the maintenance of our
institutions and of our allegiance, the preservation of our Empire and
the improvement of the condition of our people."[5] In this comprehensive presentation, what Disraeli suggested was the status quo, as far as
basic institutions were concerned, and moderate social reforms. Here,
the ideology was presented as a clear program which in turn suggests a
sense of direction.

Where lies the strength and the appeal of an ideology? There is no one
simple theory that fits all cases. Pareto had for his time a valid assumption. For him, an ideology was a "derivative" of major "residues." Thus,
essential sources of social actions, according to Pareto, are interests and
sentiments; ideologies are only rationalizations of interests and sentiments. A social class "selects" those ideologies corresponding to its interest. Others select ideologies because of "sentiments."[6]

The materialistic school (to take as an example Plekhanov's interpretation of materialism), reduces the variables to one major "prime-mover":
the productive forces of the society, social relations in production. Interpretations of historical materialisms are many; differences in interpretation led to bitter ideological struggles. Therefore, it is better to quote
his text. Plekhanov argues that men do not make several histories but
"only one history, the history of their own social relations, which are
determined by the state of the productive forces in each particular period.
*What is known as ideologies is nothing but a multiform reflection in the
minds of men of this single and indivisible history."* He further states
that productive forces determine all social relations, and social relations
in turn—always anchored in the former—give rise to morality, to a set of
values. Economic relations, he continues, determine also indirectly all
the creativity of mind and imagination. Thus, socioeconomic relations
determine also the psychology of society, the prevailing beliefs, and
the concepts. But once the productive forces change, the changes in
economic structure will follow, as will changes in the "superstructure"
in beliefs and ideas. Plekhanov, however, concedes—he accepts here the
theory of the Italian philosopher Antonio Labriola—that survival or
concepts of the past social-economic periods play an important role in
development of ideologies.[7] Plekhanov's deductions are logical, but
logic does not always agree with hard facts. Essential as those changes

are, they do not explain all ideological trends and all sociological cases. Ideology is by no means in all cases solely a direct or indirect consequence of changes in the "economic base." On the other hand, underestimation of the socioeconomic situation leads, as Charles Beard has indicated, to major errors.

Ideology does reflect the socioeconomic situation and attitudes of its followers, but this is only part of the complex relationship. The choice of ideology may be a result of several factors. True, response to an appeal is strong in most of those cases when the appeal or an interpretation of an actual situation is directed to the economic interests of a social group. The process of even choice in such a case is, however, more complex. The psychological or value appeal of ideologies is of primary significance. For example, in Italy, after World War II, workers of the same factory, in the same wage bracket, were sometimes divided in their ideological choices; some were Social Democrats, others were Communists, and still others were Christian Democrats. Individuals in the same class position may respond differently to an ideological appeal when their personality or their values, which form the core of ideology, differ. Thus, every case requires a careful analysis of variables.

The central force in the development of ideologies of protest movements in Europe and America was, and is, social, economic, and political inequality. This inequality remains in obvious discord with our dominant value, the ideal norms of equality of the initial Christian interpretation of Judeo-Christian ethics. The dichotomy between ideal norms and real social conditions supplied argument and legitimacy to the fourteenth- as well as the seventeenth-century European religious protest movements. Political ideologies of social protest (as much as some political apostles may resent the fact) are a rationalistic continuation of the earliest religious protest movements that began with the first prophets.

But let us return to the complex problem of choice. The very existence of inequality may not always necessarily produce an ideology. The problem is how facts are perceived. The same economic facts may be perceived differently by two individuals embracing different value structures. Ideology influences the perception of social facts and their interpretation. Our ideology and values decide, under certain conditions, how facts are interpreted as well as the choice of facts perceived. The same fact of, say, a thunderstorm may be perceived and interpreted by a person of a primitive religious ideology as a miracle or as a warning of a deity; by a primitive hunter who has a magical outlook on the world it may be interpreted as evidence of the magical power of his medicine man; and by a scientist as a natural phenomenon. We may perceive and interpret misery as an eternal and unchanging part of a permanent system: the poor, or persons of a lower caste, are those who in their previous life cycle sinned and therefore were reborn into a lower caste. Within such an ideology, misery becomes part of religious evidence and a political economic appeal may have no, or little, meaning. A precondition of "class consciousness" is the concept of "class"—man cannot perceive his class position without first perceiving class. The concept is a result of a theory or of an ideology, unlike the medieval concepts of estates, which were juridical institutions. The term *proletarians* was not invented by proletarians. The appeal to class interests and class solidarity meets with a collective response once an ideology, or at least a new value structure, appears and modifies the previous values and attitudes and emphasizes the new social identity: a class identity instead of a religious or an ethnic one.

Shared, collective values as well as concepts combined with similar economic interests are indeed a fruitful soil for an appeal. To perceive fully such a common interest, a new outlook or a new emphasis is necessary; it guides and directs the perception. In a rationalistic outlook, serfdom or slavery are only stages of a historical development and are institutions opposed to basic moral principles of social justice. The Bible accepts the social institution of slavery and medieval theory condones serfdom. The dominant social, economic system (in a rationalistic approach) is no longer a part of an eternal religious and unchanging order; it is a transient and exploitative stage in human history. Once such an approach is assimilated in a digested, simplified way, once a person reinforces or discovers certain values and changes the thought pattern and begins to think in a different way, he begins to "see" the conditions differently; in other words, his perception, interpretation, and selection of facts are guided by new values. Now, since he knows that the social system can be changed and that his suffering can be removed, the ideological appeal becomes convincing and he responds to the appeal. The perception of social problems, of one's own class position, and the realization of the possibilities of change are a consequence of the development and popularization of social sciences and of the diffusion of an ideology as well as the result of real economic relations. Industrialization created new classes—above all, the working class. But the various types of proletarian and class ideologies were a result of the new philosophical and scientific trends, of rationalism, enlightenment, as much as of classic economy. When both trends met—

the intellectual and the socioeconomic—a new outlook, a new ideology, was created. Without the socioeconomic realities, the ideological appeal would not have elicited a response. An ideology appeals to a people when it corresponds to its various economic, psychological or ethical needs. Thus ideology is built on a set of fundamental values; we may call them core values. They guide the ideology and shape the educational, economic, and political institutions of a new society. In a conservative idea system, the set of values suggests rationalization of and support for traditional and rigid political institutions. Thus, fidelity to a dynasty in Russia, belief in sanctity of the emperor's person and his divine right to power formed the fulcrum of czarist institutions.

The core values are also represented in symbolic forms. Icononic symbols, which appear in pictorial form such as the tree or the bell of liberty, the flag, a poster of a worker with a red flag, verbal symbols, musical symbols expressed in national anthems, party songs such as the International—all of them are anchored in major values, core values which harbor the standards and goals man tries to achieve or norms of conduct. Once the values are destroyed, once the belief system disintegrated, the ideology breaks down. Once the basic norms and beliefs in monarchy were weakened and destroyed, new social institutions and structures appeared which were built on a different set of values.

History offers many examples of revolts of the exploited classes. Socioeconomic and political inequality was and is a source of spontaneous protest movements. These revolts were, however, shortlived unless reinforced by a comprehensive ideology. In medieval times religious and sectarian protest movements supplied such an ideological base and at the same time the continuity of a movement. Without an ideological underpinning and an adequate value structure, revolts ended nowhere. Social, economic, and political inequality existed in England long before the end of the eighteenth century. Seditions and unsuccessful protests erupted here and there. But effective political movements for social and political equality and universal suffrage appeared in times of the French Revolution under the influence of English philosophy, the American experience, the new rationalistic and scientific outlook, and French revolutionary ideology. This was the beginning of a powerful social movement that sometimes declined but was strong enough to reappear. Class division, oppression, and the misery of workers were part of the European urban landscape long before the French Revolution. And although the Industrial Revolution intensified the situation, a powerful social movement did not manifest itself until an ideology appeared offering a viewpoint and a critical interpretation of social-economic conditions and suggesting an answer as well.

The development of a scientific outlook and the growth of rationalism had its effect on political and social relations. A scientific outlook was not limited solely to natural sciences. Once scientific methods were applied to human society, once man rejected dogmas and began to explore the origin of social and political institutions, the origin of social inequality, of wealth and poverty, slavery and serfdom, the revolution began. The quest for a rational society, a society based on scientific and not solely traditional principles, was a necessary consequence of the scientific revolution and of a change in world outlook and values.

Thus, values are of significance. Their origin is often ancient and transmitted for generations through the processes of early socialization. An atheistic anarchist may advance ideas of a totally free society of equals not being conscious of the fact that his new values are a result of displacing into a rational philosophy his Christian ethics acquired in early childhood. He has internalized the basic values even though he disassociates himself from the institutional church and from the entire religious system. His values, however, are of a religious origin although he may not be conscious of it. Ethnic values are strong too and are a result of long and complex social processes.[8]

Traditional voting patterns (voting a Democratic ticket because one's father and grandfather were Democrats) and strong party or dynastic loyalties belong to a similar category.[9] Here ideology appeals to established values and loyalties. Socioeconomic conditions and class position alone do not explain the fact that sections of the *sotto proletariato*, the subproletariat of Naples, inhabitants of slums, voted a monarchist ticket after World War II, thus contributing to the election of a monarchist mayor, a shipowner, at that time the only monarchist mayor of a major Italian city.

The appeal of an ideology cannot be reduced solely to the concept of pragmatism, of economic interests or quest for power, powerful as such an appeal is, or to a single psychological determinant. Whatever may be said about political parties, especially parties of social protest, as much as they are an expression of economic interest and rationalization of a quest for power, they are also (at least some of them, or for parts of their membership) expressions of man's quest for moral answers, or for a rational well-working social and economic system, a quest to close the gap between ideal moral norms and reality. In order to achieve a system that is closer to ideal norms and to an ideal value structure, conditions must be changed; in order to change conditions, power is necessary—such is the line of reasoning.

Our century has already given ample evidence that ideologies also appeal to collective psychological needs although individuals are generally not conscious of the nature of the appeal. The quest for power and domination is a strong psychological drive quite common among men. Political parties supply avenues to satisfy the desire to rule and dominate and to overcome personal insecurities and complexes.[10] Some psychological needs at times can be psychopathological ones, or they may be a reflection of primitive hostilities and urges of aggression not fully controlled. An appeal to the mass extermination of a weaker nation may be effective in such cases. An ideology may also appeal to widely spread anxieties, personal insecurities, and the quest for a more sheltered place (for example, safe neighborhood or town). What we call the psychological variable or factor is by no means a single determinant. Every empirical case requires a careful analysis of factors, which we have reduced to three major variables: socioeconomic conditions, value structure, and psychological factors.[11]

The appeal to identity should not be overlooked. The great dynamic social movements of our century appealed either to class, or ethnic, or religious identity. Major ideological movements were class oriented (socialist, communist or related), nationalistic, or religious. Their ideologies sharply divided the society into in and out groups. The enemy was an "anticlass," "antination," or "antireligion." Eventually, the Nazi movement created out of the Jews an integral enemy, combining an anticlass, antireligion and antination in one single notion or symbol. Sharp ideological divisions were also corollaries of party centralism. Aggression or defense suggest a centralistic organization, which is better suited to a militant tactics and strategy. Ideology and party structure are interdependent. But in the last analysis, emphasis on a single identity—religion, nation (patriotism)—is an appeal to deep-seated core values and here we move again to the fulcrum of an idea system.

An ideology contains elements of both the psychological and the pragmatic-rational appeal of a party. The pragmatic appeal is concrete, frequently immediate: for example, the reduction of working hours, increase of salaries, lowering of custom barriers, civil rights, etc. The distant vision may be rational, even "commonsensical" but it also usually has an emotional, psychological appeal such as visions of a socialist state, eternal peace, and world federation. Presented in a reduced verbal form (i.e., Liberty, Fraternity, Equality) or in a visual form (iconic symbols), ideological concepts acquire the quality of symbols. Symbols contain a value, a psychological or emotional charge. However, there is no definite dividing line between a rational and an emotional appeal. As a consequence, rational goals and appeals can be reinforced by emotional appeal, while a psychological appeal can be reinforced by an additional pragmatic or quasirational persuasion.

The complex system of values and goals suggests a general direction toward which the party intends to move. As mentioned above, the objectives of political parties can be reduced to the major goals of either maintaining the status quo or changing the social-political environment. The goal is usually achieved by winning or capturing political power. The locus of political power is, of course, in the state and public institutions. We must always keep in mind, that the party is an organization oriented toward conquest of political power. Political power is always a major goal and at the same time a means to other objectives. Thus, to achieve or conquer power of the state is both an end and means of political parties. In the first case the ideology supplies a conscious or nonconscious rationalization. In both cases ideology offers the necessary legitimacy, the value support to justify political activities, especially the bid for power.

In addition to its function as a system of goals, values, and appeals, an ideology is a "collective representation" in Durkheim's sense, and it integrates a social group into a cohesive political party. This function of ideology has frequently been underestimated by deterministic and monistic theories and philosophy. The fact is that China in our time was united not through economic change or development but by a powerful ideology and through the political means of a centralistic party. The conquest of political power led to the control of the means of production. The change moved from the political to the economic level and not from the economic base to the political superstructure. The primary significance of political power and of ideology as the integrating force has been validated many times in history.

We may summarize the major function of an ideology as follows: Ideology rationalizes or states explicitly the socioeconomic interest of a social group or class; it contains value structure and goals and supplies a sense of direction for political action; it supplies rationalization of the quest for power; it is a powerful integrating force (here belongs appeal to identity); in appealing to economic and political interests and to noneconomic motivation such as psychological and moral needs, it harbors pragmatic, rational, and emotional appeals of the movements and, last but not least, ethical appeal. Generally, it is the ideology, the goals, that move the followers of a movement to action.

4. STRUCTURE (APPARATUS)

A well-coordinated pattern of group action is a condition for attaining a collective goal. Gaining political power requires an action of an organized group, which might be called the "apparatus." Without an organization, the goals set by an ideology cannot be reached. The organization—the structure of the group—and its ideology (goals) are essential elements of a political party.

Durkheim, in his studies of primitive religions, points out that religious ideas are always associated with an organized group. The latter is called the church. The group practices a religion which is a common social idea and value system. Durkheim's analysis suggests that the formation of a religious system always implies two essential components: an idea system and an organized group.[12] Independently and much later, Adolf Berle defined a political force in a similar, although operational manner. Berle's political force consists of two elements: ideology and "apparatus."[13] All social movements, that are dynamic, effect a change, and have a certain degree of permanency, require these two components, as well as a third one—a pattern of actions, a modus operandi.

The study of group structures and relations between groups is a subject matter par excellence for sociology. The structure of the party changes according to its function. In order to operate effectively, an underground party under a foreign occupation, with a tactical pattern of direct paramilitary action, must be organized differently from a conservative party in a free, representative political system oriented toward the maintenance of the status quo and toward the achievement of power through an appeal to a limited electorate. The experience of the last one hundred and fifty years suggests that the structure of the party, the way a party is organized, contributes substantially to its political effectiveness. Small, strongly disciplined parties, centrally controlled but still having a certain local flexibility, were very effective in conquering power in those countries where the mass of the population was politically indifferent or passive and democratic institutions either nonexistent or weak. In our times, small totalitarian parties of this type, supported by foreign governments and their armies, have conquered nations, paralyzed by fear or manipulated into submission. This, of course, is not unusual; history offers many examples of conquests of large and peaceful or passive and divided nations by small and well-organized groups.

5. TYPES OF POLITICAL PARTIES

In this section, we shall review briefly and classify selected "ideal types" of political parties. This classification focuses on internal structure, organizational pattern, and party discipline—not on ideology, values, or strategy.

A distinction must also be made among mass, vanguardist, cell, and cadre parties. I shall discuss all of these parties as ideal types. In reality the pattern is somewhat different and does not comply with the ideal-type structure.

All parties have some kind of control over their membership, but certain parties are geared more toward consensus, agreement, and persuasion, and others toward coercion and command structure. The selection of types and the classification of parties follow these basic patterns. However, the two significant types are the centralistic and the federalistic (see Chapter VII).

A Political Camp: Fulanismo

We shall start with a loosely organized movement which we shall call "a political camp." The Latin American countries perhaps fathered this type of sociopolitical movement. The three essential elements are a definite leadership or leader, loosely organized groups, and a vast mass of sympathizers. This type of movement usually has a definite goal and a definite target of action. Here belongs, for instance, the Mexican revolutionary movement in the time of Francisco Madero. Its target was clear—the overthrow of the dictatorship of Porfirio Díaz. Its goals

and ideology were definite: constitutional changes and democratic
principles were to be introduced into the Mexican republic. Later, the
revolutionary movement extended its ideological and practical socioeconomic goals. The early development of the revolutionary movement
in Cuba (now in power) could also be called a "political camp," although
there were already well-established groups at the University of Havana.
This type of a movement of a rather loose and informal structure is frequently focused around a prominent, perhaps charismatic leader.

The prominent Spanish writer and scholar at the University of Sala-
manca, Miguel de Unamuno, argued that some of the Spanish political
parties were formed around prominent and influential personalities,
and were rooted in personal loyalties rather than in definite and clear
political programs. He called this phenomenon *Fulanismo*. *Fulano* means
in Castilian (also in Portuguese), "Mr. Somebody." *Fulanismo*—I cannot
find an adequate English term—could be translated into French
Quelconquisme, a phenomenon of a political grouping around a personality (somebody).

This type of group also appeared in Portugal. In 1910, after the
proclamation of the Portuguese Republic, the three leading parties
were known by the name of their leaders: the followers of the Portuguese Republican party were called Alfonsistas (Professor Alfonso
Costa was the leader of the party). Partisans of the Evolutionary party
were known as Almeidistas (the name was derived from the leader
Antonio José Almeida) and supporters of the Unionist party were named
Camachistas, since the leader was Brito Camacho.[14]

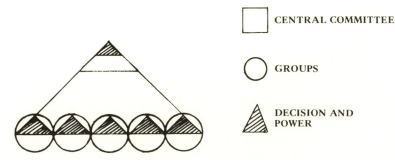

Model 2. The Federalistic Pattern

Federalistic Structure

The federalistic type of party organization is indicated in Model 2. For the sake of simplification, I shall call the central committee the supreme and, in certain types (see below), decision-making body of the party and omit distinctions among deliberating, legislative, and executive bodies. In a federalistic system, we distinguish the central committee and local groups. (I have marked the locus of power and decision with a triangle.) Power and decision are located in local groups and, in certain matters, in the central committee. But the central committee's power is relatively weak, and depends on the decisions and views of the local committees, whatever may be the internal manipulations and power structure of the latter. The locus of power and decision is indidated by the interplay of the triangles in Model 2. Although the federalistic pattern is a consensus-orientated structure, it is not necessarily free of coercive tendencies and devices.

Centralistic Pattern

In an "ideal type" of centralistic organization (Model 3), power is vested primarily in the central committee. The local groups have very little decision-making authority and limited or no power. In the Com-

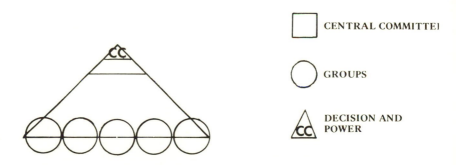

CENTRAL COMMITTEl

GROUPS

DECISION AND
POWER

Model 3. The Centralistic Pattern

munist party, for example, the supreme decision-making power lies with the central committee and not in the local party units. The organization

is a centralistic, command-oriented structure. (The origins and development of the centralistic party are discussed in Chapter II.)

Mass Party

In a mass party (Model 4) we can distinguish a central committee,
provincial and local committees, and the general membership of the
party. The party may be either centralistic or federalistic, having in this
case a vertical structure. The territory controlled by the party and the
organization which secures this type of geographical control will be
called horizontal.

CC   CENTRAL COMMITTEE

PC   PROVINCIAL COMMITTEES

LC   LOCAL COMMITTEES

M   MEMBERSHIP

Model 4. The Mass Party

The mass party appeals to a large audience or electorate. It is an
"open" party which accepts as new members all those who simply
declare that they approve the program or ideology. No elaborate methods
of screening or enrolling are practiced. The strategy of its leadership is
to win widest support. No rigorous discipline is imposed in democratic
mass parties, in countries which practice parliamentary democracy. But
a mass party may appear also in a highly disciplined form, controlled
by a cadre or by paramilitary units. It becomes then a mass party in
sense of membership, but in fact such an organization is a cadre party
(see below).

Vanguardist Party

The vanguardist party (Model 5) consists of a small, all-powerful central committee which makes decisions and a selected number of party members, called "activists," whose profession is politics and party activities. These members are selected carefully. Sympathizers have only a loose connection with the party. Their function is to give the activists and the central committee financial and political support. They have no direct influence on the central committee nor are they members of the political party.

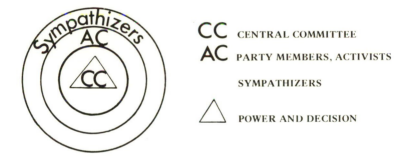

CC CENTRAL COMMITTEE

AC PARTY MEMBERS, ACTIVISTS

SYMPATHIZERS

△ POWER AND DECISION

Model 5. The Vanguardist Party

This type of party, which was formulated in its classical form in 1902 by Lenin in his book *What Has To Be Done*, is of early origin. Its beginnings can be traced to the end of the eighteenth century, to the Jacobins and to Babeuf, who led the "Conspiracy of the Equals," an attempted revolutionary coup at the end of the French Revolution. In fact, in Babeuf's writings we have indications of a vanguardist type of party. Later, in the middle of the nineteenth century, the French revolutionary Louis Blanqui outlined the pattern of vanguardist organization and planned the establishment of a "Parisian dictatorship." In 1875, the theory of a vanguardist organization of professional revolutionaries was advanced by the Russian revolutionary writer Peter Tkachev (see Chapter II, section 16).

Cell System

The "small units" pattern (Model 6) consists of two related patterns: the "cell" system and the "fives." In fact, the "fives" is only a variation of a cell pattern. Both types are forms of an underground organization; the difference lies in the level of secrecy. The "fives" pattern represents a tighter, more secret organization—a "deeper" underground.

Cells consist of five to ten or more members who act together, sometimes within another institution, party, or organization. The cell organizes political action and manipulates large organizations, while keeping secret the identity and operations of cell members. Cell members know each other and act together. They are also familiar with the "legal" (open) structure of their organization and its leadership and may partici-

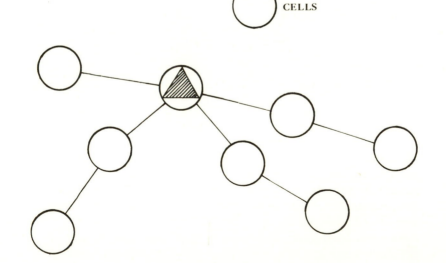

LEADERSHIP CELL
(COMMITTEE)

CELLS

Model 6. Small Units

pate in general meetings of the party. The cell system was and is also applied as an open (not secret) form of party organization. It was used, for instance, by certain Italian political parties.

The cell is frequently the underground structure of a legal party. Its leader, or liaison, may be known only by a pseudonym. The system permits wide penetration, indirect control, and manipulation of a vast network of a variety of organizations and enterprises, few of which realize that such operations are underway. In that way, a party controls a system of organizations much larger than its limited membership would normally permit.

The "fives" consist, at least in theory, of groups no larger than five. In an ideal type of the structure, no member knows more than five members of the entire political organization, and usually no fewer than two. The leader of the group knows four members of his five and one liaison member of the committee. The committee may also consist of five members; its "lines of communication" may, however, be different. A nonleader knows one member who brought him (or whom he has won) to the organization, and usually one other member, perhaps the leader. As a rule pseudonyms are used, and a simple inquiry about real names may be regarded as an attempt at treason. Special underground fighting squads (not the "regular" underground army) were probably organized in this way. In case of arrest or treason, the losses are limited, since none of the militants, with the exception of the top leadership, knows more than five, and them only by pseudonym. But theory is different from practical organization and action.

Secrecy and Origin of Cells

The cell system had its wide application in secret political organizations, in those vast networks of the underground movements which were fighting foreign conquest and domestic oppression. But such a pattern could also be chosen by those whose struggle, even sufferings, were intended or led to absolute power of a few in the name of some lofty ideas or prejudices.

This type of structure permits simultaneous application of a centralistic and federalistic principle. This may sound like a contradiction, but it is not in practice. An underground struggle calls for certain types and models of organization. Aggression and defense call for discipline, central control, and execution of major, largely strategic decisions. On the other hand, communication with the central committee is difficult in such a type of secret political activities. A dangerous situation calls for immediate decision and swift action. There is neither time nor possibility to ask for orders from a regional or central committee. The leader of this small unit assumes all responsibilities of leadership in such moments. In consequence, sections or cells must also have flexibility of freedom of decision and movement within the broader frames of strategic orders of the central committee. Risks are high, but a cell structure permits a high level of flexibility of action of a single cell because it limits the risks of losses and also of identification to a small unit of five (sometimes more). Secrecy of the rest of the organization remains intact. The network is unknown also to the members of the cell.

Man frequently advances flexible forms of organization which can cope with a variety of situations. In times of critical, massive change of his social situation, he is also forced to change the patterns of his association, being otherwise unable to cope with new conditions. This is, however, not always true. Sometimes attachment to institutions is stronger than the practical imperatives of daily struggle, even than survival. Patterns of organization change slowly; in addition, inventions in this field are rare. Is the cell system a spontaneous form of group response to political situations of massive pressure, such as oppression and terror, or is this one of those social inventions that developed in certain historical conditions and was later widely diffused?

It is difficult to discover the early beginnings of the "small units" model, especially the interconnected system of three or five. Historical evidence available seems to suggest that this type of underground secret party appeared in Europe sometime between 1850 and 1870, but initial types can be traced back as early as 1834. Two to four decades later, well-organized political movements—such as the anarchists, certain factions of socialists, and others—appeared that professed systematic ideologies. At this time secularization, or deritualization, of secret movements took place. This is just a hypothesis.

Now, we may ask a question: When and how has this rather unusual form of political organization developed? Where are its historical roots? This is a question of interest not only for a social historian or social scientist. This leads us, however, to the broader issues and history of secret organization, for the cell system was and still is primarily a technique of secret parties, although it was also used by legal, or manifest political organizations. First the distinction must be made between internal secrecy, external secrecy, and secret actions (or system of actions). When inner activities and relationships of an organization are "secret" but the existence of the organization and membership is not concealed, then the organization practices internal secrecy. When, however, the location, activities, sometimes even the existence and membership of the organization are concealed from society, from the nonmembers of the organization, then the organization has external secrecy. As a rule, external secrecy involves internal secrecy as well as secret operations. An organization which is manifest and not secret (for example, a government) may undertake secret actions or secret operations. In the latter case "secret" means known only to members or selected members of the same organization and concealed from others.

The secrecy of an organization may not necessarily involve any sinister or violent objectives or action. Internal secrecy was quite common in Oriental religious cults, which had their mysteries and secret rites. Jewish religion and Christianity were free of this secrecy. Today, a number of American associations and lodges dedicated to philanthropy and mutual aid practice internal secrecy, for example, the Masons and the Grange. These associations assimilated old, sometimes very elaborate rituals. Many other American orders practice internal secrecy connected with rituals, initiation, and status. Since American Protestantism has a very limited ritualism and liturgy, the lodges respond to some needs for ritual and symbolic behavior.

A political organization may combine external secrecy with violence. Such tactics of terror usually generate a "collective" fear, a fear that affects large sections of the population, exposed to sudden and often random attack. Death in such situations is always around the corner, and publicity given to a single assassination results in a collective identification with the victim. Who is next? Secrecy supplies elements of surprise and gives the actors the choice of time, place, and action. Actors may choose the time and place that are best for them and deadly for the victims.

A combination of secrecy, violence, and fear can give a party power and influence far beyond the limited number of its membership, and a sophisticated underground organization can manipulate fear in a highly effective way. The technique is a very familiar one to us, today in this twentieth century, but it also has an ancient history. It was practiced almost two thousand years ago by the Sicari in Jerusalem (see below).

Again, secret organizations, practicing both internal and external secrecy, are neither a new nineteenth- or even an eighteenth-century

phenomenon nor are they solely a European or Western one. Nor have
secrecy and systematic terror been used solely for democratic objectives
in fighting autocracy or in struggling against foreign rule and oppression.
Secret religious cults were and even are quite common the world over.
Secret criminal organizations such as the Mafia and the Camorra flourished in Italy for years.[15] Secret operations and organizations have been
used by right-wing extremists, fascists, and racists of various brands in
countries as distant and different as Roumania, Germany, and Croatia
during the interwar period. An underground, secret organization applying terror as tactics is employing a kind of social technique that can be
used for a variety of objectives: good and bad, democratic or authoritarian, or simply criminal, connected with organized banditry.

In the relatively early history, in the first century A.D., vast secret
organizations have been recorded, and they must have been in existence
prior to this time. Josephus Flavius, the Roman and Jewish historian
who wrote in Greek, tells us about the organization of Sicari, which
existed in the first century A.D. The Sicari practiced systematic, individual assassination. His general description suggests that they were not
simply "murderers," as he has called them, but organized members of
a religious or politico-religious sect. Terrorists of this sect assassinated
Jonathan, the high priest, in broad daylight. After his death, continues
Josephus, there were numerous daily murders. The panic created was
more alarming than calamity itself: "Everyone, as on a battlefield, hour-
ly expected death." The murders were committed in daylight, in the
heart of the city, especially during festivals. Sicari, dressed like others in
the crowd, mingled among the people, and after a murder they joined
the crowd and voiced their indignation. Thus it was impossible to distinguish them from the rest. The conspirators used short daggers; their
actions were swift.[16]

This is not an isolated historical case either. In Syria and Persia, the
Assassins, a secret order of the Ismaili sect of Islam, practiced systematic,
individual killing for two centuries. They enriched our vocabulary with
the word _assassin._ This again was a religious-political group. Their
ideology was theology; their organization a sect. A major objective of
the Assassins was to overthrow the existing religious and political
authority in order to impose their chosen leader (prophet). Their secret
activities and terror spread from the eleventh to the thirteenth century,[17]
and the Syrian branch of the organization came into contact with the
Crusaders.

In India a secret fraternity of assassins called the Thugs, worshippers of the goddess Kali, practiced their trade for more than three hundred years. They murdered and robbed travelers, after first winning their confidence. Between 1831 and 1837, more than three thousand Thugs were imprisoned by the British colonial authorities, and 412 were executed. In 1879, perhaps even later, they were still active in Punjab and Hindustan.[18] The sect may have originated as a religious underground against invaders of a different religion.

In medieval times, Europe had also its share of secret organizations.[19] Secret organizations were a social phenomenon throughout India, China, and Europe. The objectives, and the ethos of the organizations differed; so did most probably the personality types of members. But all of the secret organizations mentioned here—the Sicari, the Assassins, the Thugs, the Mafia, the Camorra (in Southern Italy), as much as the noble Masons and the idealistic and republican Carbonari—used a highly developed ritualism in their initiation, meetings, and behavior, and an elaborate symbolism of orders and ranks. The members were divided in a variety of ranks, and advancement from lower to higher grades was connected with rites and symbols. The Thugs even had their own peculiar vocabulary and signs.[20]

I have no intent to present the history of secret organizations here. I have used a handful of examples with the sole purpose of supporting by facts my contention that "secrecy," especially secret associations, appeared in the past history not only of Europe but also of Asia and elsewhere. Let us also mention the secrecy of magic, secret religious associations, secret "clubs" of men among nonliterate cultures (once called "primitive") in sub-Saharan Africa or among Plains Indians.

Thus, this type of social organization of selected and trusted membership is not limited solely to revolutionary parties. It is a quite general social phenomenon, and a patient student may sometimes discover that they were far more frequent in the past, are and were in general among many of the "primitive" cultures, and have declined with the advance of modern, democratic political society and with the progress of rationalism and scientific outlook.

Now, after this general discussion of the nature of secrecy, we shall return again to the beginnings and origins of secrecy in the modern, revolutionary parties and, in consequence, development of the cell system.

Early in the eighteenth century, secret and secular "ideological" organizations made their entrance in Europe. Freemasons were not an offshoot or a sect of a religious denomination. Nor were the lodges temporary conspiracies for seizure of power or change of a dynasty.

Those were associations bound by a philosophy of enlightenment, by
ideas of progress, elements of an elaborate idea-system. The Freemasons
with time became the nucleus of a movement for political progress.
Deistic, perhaps religious in outlook, but not a religious or sectarian
group, the Freemasons advanced a highly complex ritual, and the
hierarchy of secrecy, as well as status in the lodge, was combined with
rituals of initiations. Freemasons practiced internal and external secrecy.
The grand lodge appeared early in England (1717). In Italy, the first
Masonic lodge, with its secret rituals, was organized in 1733. The Italians
had their connection with England. It did not take too long for the
church to act; by 1738, Pope Clemens XII had excommunicated the
Freemasons.[21]

At the turning point of the French Revolution, in 1795, an elaborate
secret society of Pantheon, later called Conspiracy for Equality (Conspiration Pour l'Egalité), headed by Babeuf, was formed in Paris. We
have discussed in the preceding chapter more extensively its organization
and ideology, based primarily on the political philosophy of Rousseau.
This organization formed another branch root of the future secret
political party. The end of the Conspiracy for Equality was tragic,
but some of its leaders, among them Filippo Buonarotti, survived.
Buonarotti later wrote the history of this movement and published a
collection of documents pertaining to its activities. He was well familiar
with the structuring of this secret party. The space in his book given
to this topic seems to indicate that he understood its significance in
political struggle.

After 1815, another political secret organization appeared—
Carbonari. The Carbonari were dedicated to the struggle against autocracy which ruled the European nations at that time, and for political
rights and liberty. Carbonari were far more "political" than the Freemasons; their organizational form and initiation to secrecy followed,
however, the traditions of the latter. By 1821, France had its Charbonnière Française. The Charbonnières were patriotic and liberal, and
they were striving for a democratic republic. They were adversaries of
the Bourbons and of the monarchy, and this was their rallying program;
otherwise, their political views differed. Some of them were republicans,
others Bonapartists, and there were even some constitutional monarchists
among them. Filippo Buonarotti, at one time an active member of the
secret society of "Pantheonists" in 1795 (later called Conspiracy for
Equality [Conspiration Pour l'Egalité Dite de Babeuf]), now played a
leading role in the Charbonnière. He was, of course, well familiar with

the principles of secret organization. Buonarotti (and others of a similar life story) combined the traditions of the Pantheonists and Carbonari; moreover, he supplied the skills and experience.

Some political actors, innovating or revolutionary, span in their single life two or even three historical stages. But earlier political periods had the decisive influence on their personality. Thus, they continued to represent and advance ideas and strategies of those times into a new period, changing and adjusting the content or patterns to new, diverse conditions. Buonarotti formed a kind of spiritual bridge between the times of the French Revolution and the nineteenth-century struggle against European reaction. He was a political continuator of earlier secret political organizations.

Prior to the Revolution of 1848—as early as in 1834—a new pattern evolved, which already bore a striking similarity to the future "small units" or "cell parties." This new organization, called "Society of Families," was headed by Blanqui, Barbès, and Bernard. This was already a prototype of a future revolutionary cell party. Blanqui, at one time a Carbonario, was one of the "continuators," now a leader in the Society of Families and later a builder of revolutionary parties.

A cell at that time was larger (no more than twelve persons, however) and was called a "family." Families were organized in "sections," and each section received directions from a "chief of a section." The latter was subject to the decisions of a "commandant of quarters," who reported directly to "revolutionary agents" who formed the top committee and exercised supreme decision. A member knew only fellow members of his family. The Society of Families was antiroyalist, republican, and democratic.[22] The Families were subject to a secret hierarchical command. They had to obey orders issued by the leadership. The Society of Families already reflected a centralistic discipline pattern of a future underground political party. But the secret Society of Families was discovered by the police and its leaders were given very mild sentences.

Blanqui was permitted to live in Paris for a time, and probably during his confinement he invented a new type of secret organization very closely related to the future rational and efficient cell system. This son of a Girondist deputy in the Convention during the French Revolution, a radical democrat and republican, ardent socialist, believed in seizure of power by a secret well-organized group in those times of restoration of monarchies in Europe. The new organization was a more sophisticated continuation of the Society of Families and called "Society of Seasons."

This highly secret political society was divided into "weeks." The week formed the basic and the lowest unit. A week consisted of six persons and was headed by a leader called "Sunday." Four "weeks" formed a "month." Only "Sunday" knew the leaders of three other weeks. The four Sundays knew only one single "July," the leader of the "month." Thus a "month" comprised twenty-eight people, plus the twenty-ninth, the leader. Three "months" formed a "season," and they were under the order of "Spring." Only the leader of a "season" knew the leaders of three other seasons, and four seasons formed a "Year," which was headed by an agent of the revolution ("Agent de la révolution"). Paris had three "years" led by Auguste Blanqui, Armand Barbès, and Martin-Bernard. They formed a secret triumvirate, and they also had dictatorial powers. Their orders had to be obeyed and executed. In case of a victory, they would also be entrusted with this type of absolute power. The ideology of the Seasons was what is known as "Babouvism," an ideology of the Conspiracy for Equality (the Pantheonists), who professed a kind of radical egalitarian creed (the organization was already discussed in the previous chapter). The revolutionary leaders of the Seasons ordered their followers in the abortive uprising of May 12, 1839. The organizational pattern of the Seasons already had the basic features of the future cell party which became the general pattern of underground movements in Europe. Among its probable inventors we must mention, above all, the venerable descendant of Michelangelo, Filippo Buonarotti, the respected and radical democrat and republican who began his active political life in the days of the French Revolution. Blanqui met Buonarotti and was under the influence of this man whose political integrity was highly respected among the republicans.[23]

Thus, the lines of origin of the European secret political organization suggests the following historical sequence:

1. Freemasons (first grand lodge, 1717); England
2. Conspiracy of the Equals (1795); France
3. Carbonari (about 1797); Italy
4. Society of Families (1834); France
5. Society of Seasons

The Seasons seems to form a link to totally secular small units or cell party structure free from solemn rituals and trimmings.

And here, we may return to our subject of cell parties. It seems that between 1850 and 1870 a new type of secret organization began to

appear, mostly organized into cells, free from ritualism and extensive
symbolism, except for a solemn oath. The cells of five and three evolved
perhaps at this time. These were secular, deritualized, secret organizations; the emphasis was on tactics, ideology, and political efficiency. In
this sense, they were pragmatic, rational. They appeared as elitist or
vanguard movements (microparties), sometimes using the cell system to
structure their organizations.

The cell system was also applied by so-called legal or manifest (not
secret) movements in democratic states, and indeed sometimes it
increased substantially the influence of the party in times of election.
A party may establish small units (cells) in universities, department
stores, factories, and large establishments. In times of elections, the
cells distribute propaganda materials, organize local meetings, and
advance the party policy at trade union or shop meetings. In Italy,
some parties of the left identified with the working class had this type
of organization; however, by 1865 cells were rather in the decline, while
other forms of broader organization prevailed.

The other forms of secret organizations, called "circles" in Russia and
Poland, continued. Similarly, the ritualistic traditional type of secret
political organizations, which had their roots in earlier traditions, did not
entirely disappear and can be identified even prior to World War I, perhaps even later.[24]

Organizations based on the cell system appeared also almost a hundred
years later in the struggle against the German invasions during World War
II (as they did many times before, including the Revolution of 1905).
Few, if any, of the organizers, realized the historical antecedents. With
its experience in the Revolution of 1905 (against czarist Russia), the
PPS (Polish Socialist party) organized its underground network rather
rapidly in 1939 and 1940 in a way that was similar to that of 1905 and
sometimes on the same historical foundations (some of the top leaders
had belonged to the underground organization of 1905). During World
War II, sections of the underground were organized into small cells. At
the bottom, the movement was organized into cells of three or five.
Five leaders of the lowest five cells (*piatki*) formed the committee of five
which may be called a leadership committee or cell; thus only one member of the cell (*komitetowy*) knew his leadership committee of five
(*piatka komitetowa*). In every district, a district chief had contact with
the main committees of five, which controlled through this complex
chain the cells of the district. He also had a connection with the central
committee in Warsaw. The contact with the central committee was

maintained only by the district leader, and he knew only the pseudo-nyms of the members of the central committee.[25]

Interestingly enough, the structure and hierarchy of the underground PPS during World War II has a certain similarity to the structure of the Conspiracy of the Equals of 1795.[26] There is, of course, no evidence of any direct historical influence. Perhaps old insurrectionist traditions (the events of 1863 influencing the Revolution of 1905) or perhaps even simple logic suggested this model of organization. Nonetheless, the Poles had their share of tradition of secret organizations, which developed in Poland prior to the Insurrection of 1831. Cultural contacts with France were always active, and political connections since the French Revolution were of a traditional, even sentimental nature.

It may be of major interest that the Soviet Partisans during World War II were instructed to form, in addition to combat units, cell units of three, five, or ten. The group—reads the instruction—must be so organized "that partisans of one group do not know of any other units."[27] This sounds almost like an instruction for the Carbonari.

The Cadre Party

The cadre party (Model 7) is a command-oriented party. Cadres comprise carefully selected members of the party who are politically active and dedicated to the party (*activists*; in French, *militants*). Frequently they derive a number of privileges from party membership. This was true, for instance, with the Fascist and Nazi parties. In an ideal type of cadre party, we can distinguish the central committee, the cadres, and the mass membership, as in Model 7. The central committee is usually all-powerful. It controls the cadres and, through the cadres, the mass membership. Cadre parties were specially built and suited for dynamic political action.

Unlike the vanguardist model, the cadre party has an elaborate structure, a wide organizational network, and a substantial, frequently large membership. As a rule, once the party achieves power, the membership secures a privileged status. This was and is a manifest or legal party, unlike the secret cell model.

The cadre model however, has similarities with the vanguardist pattern. The top leadership has substantial, frequently dictatorial powers and even the cadre members have a special status vis-à-vis non-registered supporters (sympathizers.) In the past, the cadre party was quite often an elitist one and sometimes a continuation of an earlier vanguardist model. The cadre model may also control a system of cells. (All those models are presented here as ideal types. Overlapping features and similarities can be identified in the vanguardist, cell and cadre model and a combinations of all those models in a process of a development of a party appeared in the past.)

The Bolshevik party at the beginning and until World War I was a vanguardist one. During the Russian Revolution of 1917, it was transformed or evolved into a cadre model, always with vanguardist and elitist leadership on various levels of command. The vanguardist model was frequently used in the past for conquest of political power, while the cadre was for consolidation of the political conquest.

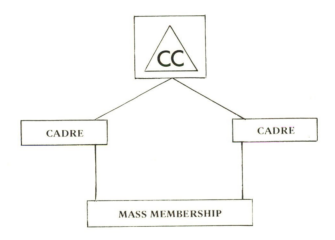

Model 7. The Cadre Party

Militarized Command Parties

We have finally arrived at a combination of a number of patterns, and this combination, containing elements of cadres and private armies, is especially suited for dynamic political action, political attack, and the seizure of political power. This type of party has a command structure.

We shall call such parties militarized command parties.

The structure of this pattern is diagrammed in Model 8. At the top we find the all-powerful central committee; below that are what we shall call intermediary committees—provincial or local committees connected with the party cadres. The party cadres and the central committee are closely related, on the one hand, to the mass movement and, on the other, to the cell organization. But this is not all. The central committee also controls, as we see in Model 8, private armies or political militias and partisan units.

Let us review for a moment the functioning of various parts of the party. The mass movements supply basic support, membership, and perhaps part of the finances. Usually the main source of the financial support of such a party, which is kept secret, comes from special interest groups, wealthy sympathizers or fellow-travelers, or foreign governments. The running of such an elaborate political enterprise is an expensive proposition.

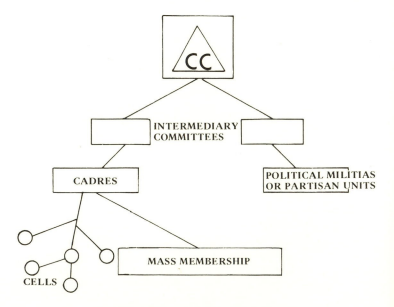

Model 8. Militarized Command Party

The masses of those parties are rather submissive. They are subject to the decision of the central committee and are directly controlled by the cadres, which obey the former. The central committee, the cadres, and the mass movement are "legal" and open. Contrariwise, the cells, the small units, are secret or underground. This supplies unusual strength and maneuverability to the party since it has both an open and an underground organization. Furthermore, the private armies or partisan units supply an element of physical force and terror to subdue opponents.

A complex militarized command party is a powerful political instrument of attack. It may force into submission a much larger but differently organized or passive opposition. It is multifunctional, since the various sections of the party perform different functions and operations. Still, operations are complementary and permit intensive action and simultaneous attacks. The horizontal and the vertical centralistic structure, combined with the cadre and cell systems and private armies, supplies a complex instrument that penetrates many aspects of life.

This complex political machinery, operated on the command principle, was developed and perfected between 1918 and World War II. It was first geared for conquest and later for the consolidation of power. In the latter stage, the party machinery was integrated with the powerful coercive machinery of the state. The political strength of the totalitarian state lies, among other factors, in this combination. A similar pattern was applied by the Nazi party. Emotional tension was built up by propaganda. Then ritualism and symbolism were used for collective psychological excitement, which in turn was channeled into hostilities and aggression. The integration of social structure and discipline with psychological intensity and manipulation supplied dynamism and force far superior to the sheer numbers of its membership.

Now, suppose that a political leadership applies this type of pattern of organization vis-à-vis a passive population or loosely organized political parties. Let us imagine a conflict in which a highly complex and combat-oriented political party faces a loosely organized, confused, and undisciplined mass of people. Of course, a militarized-command type of a party derives not solely from large numbers, but primarily from its structure.

A militarized party is also an instrument for the consolidation of power. Usually, after the capture or penetration of an area, a totalitarian regime breaks any form of organized political life, and sometimes even

organized religious or social life. In that way the population of the
area is immobilized and its organizations disrupted and delegalized,
while the command party, the conquering party, grows in power and
total control. Since this is the party having military units and control of
the government, the now disorganized population becomes helpless in
the face of the new and growing power system.

The basic policy of an authoritarian elite is directed toward pulveri-
zation of a society, destruction of all possible social bonds but those
of the monoparty and state. In consequence, the new elite tries to
establish the dominance of a single loyalty toward the party and ideology.
Children in the schools are taught that their first loyalty is to the party
and the leader and not to their parents. In that way the essential organized unit, the family, is weakened. Similarly, other forms of organized
life are disrupted and a virtual party monopoly is established over the
social organization.

Control of population movements may further increase the power
of the party. Any movement from one town to another, any purchase
of a bus or rail ticket, except by members of the ruling political party,
may require the permission of the police. In that way the conquering
party, even if it is not very strong in numbers, can move its militia,
its private army, very rapidly from one place to another by public
transportation.

What happens to consensus-oriented political parties when they are
threatened by the existence of a command-structured, aggressive, cadre
military organization? It is difficult to give a single answer. Herbert
Spencer and, later, George Simmel argued that conflict leads, as a rule,
to more centralistic forms of organization.

The fact that conflict strengthens the coherence of a group and
contributes to a change in structure, frequently leading to a centralistic
form, cannot be denied. The structure of conflict groups no doubt
bears many similarities. The organization of the aggressive party forces
the victims to reorganize into a more centralistic pattern. Experience
teaches us, however, that several alternative courses of action are open
to democratic parties threatened by centralistic command parties. In
interwar Germany and Austria, outside threat resulted in the development
of ancillary political militias of the democratic mass parties and their
allies. The German Social Democrats and trade unions responded by
their support for the *Reichbanner*, a voluntary republican militia, controlled by the democratic parties. The Austrian Social Democrats had
their own *Schutzbund*, a political militia. In a sense, the threat of

political violence did result in emergence of military structures attached to democratic parties. The latter had, however, also centralistic and bureaucratic tendencies.

A government of a democratic commonwealth, threatened by secret, centralistic parties which apply terror tactics, may use such powerful command structures as display of the army. Once democratic legitimacy is strong, a show of force free of any direct use of violence may suffice. A show of force may affect sections of the oscillating population, and invigorate democratic parties. This did actually happen in Canada, when in Quebec (1972), Prime Minister Trudeau displayed military alertness against weak and nonrepresentative, but violent and active secret organizations, directed against elective, provincial government. This was done, however, as the last resort, after several kidnappings. Of course, another possibility is a direct use of violence, but such action may already mean a beginning of civil war or result sooner or later in limitation or suspension of political rights and civil liberties.

In the situations mentioned, aggressive tactics of centralistic command parties were countered sometimes with, other times without, success by a "centralistic-command" response, either a consequence of structural changes of a party, formation of ancillary party organization, or by use of the army.

Seizure of power by European Fascists was usually accompanied by the use of violence, arrests of political opponents, and dissolution of the opposing democratic parties. Seizure of power by East European communist cadre parties was carried out in stages. The parties had a powerful outside support. Military pressure was also exercised by Soviet diplomacy. At a certain stage, other parties were gradually infiltrated and, in a decisive moment, forced into submission or dissolved. The leadership of opposing parties was imprisoned or forced into exile. Often a centrally organized party, supported by the pressures of the military and police apparatus, broke any legal resistance. There was no time to reorganize, or it was impossible to do so.

In these cases, the party structure was a major organizational device of discipline, strength, and dynamism. On the other hand, struggle against a centralistic and authoritarian government calls also for a centralistic command structure of parties advancing ideas of political, economic, and social democracy. Long before Lenin, the Russian revolutionaries realized the significance of party structure in a conflict situation. The Populists of the latter part of the nineteenth century discussed this problem. Eventually, after their unsuccessful attempt at mass revolt, the revolutionaries split, and the group that embarked on a terroristic action assumed a centralistic form of organization. When, in 1903, the Social-Democratic party split into the Bolsheviks and Mensheviks, the problem of party structure was again an issue.

New conflict strategies led to a complete merger of the political party with the military organization. What is called today a partisan war is a political conflict, waged by political armies or militarized parties. The "wars of liberation" and various kinds of revolutionary warfare are in fact conducted by such military groups of political quality. Blanqui's forgotten project of a totally militarized party comes again alive.

The Palestinian commandos form this type of a totally militarized party federation. The central committee of the Palestine Liberation Organization is an association of ten (or perhaps more) member-groups. They represent various ideological tendencies and supply a variety of orientations that may have a broad appeal for recruitment. Hostility against Israel and strategy of continuous or protracted armed conflict supplies the major strategic goal and psychological appeal. All member parties are in reality political militias. The party structure is a military one. The political leaders are at the same time military commanders. The "civilian" party, the party of free citizen "withers away" on the road toward a state of total power.

6. PATTERN OF ACTIONS
(STRATEGY AND TACTICS)

The party organization supplies an instrument of a coordinated group action. In a well working democratic system the pattern of action moves through formal, established channels. Similarly, the organizational structure of the party follows traditional, generally accepted patterns. Nevertheless the business of government, maintenance of power, or changing existing conditions require continuous activities, a modus operandi. Hence, the third essential component of any political movement is the pattern of action, sometimes elaborated into strategy and tactics. The party in a democracy may act in a number of ways. It may diffuse the ideology or solicit votes by means of mass communication, stressing certain facts and concealing other information.

To achieve goals or votes, political power or change, the party acts "rationally," even if the goals are not always rational. Actions are "rational" because such means are chosen by which goals can be attained under favorable conditions. "Rational" here means a proper evaluation of means. Since certain goals are distant and may require time or stronger support, the party leaders may divide the planned action into stages. Single movements within a given stage are tactical movements. The strategy suggests a general direction and distant goals, the tactics single political actions within the stage or entire plan.

The party acts and develops its general pattern of actions or strategy and tactics in a "political arena." A political arena may be defined as an ideal type of political market, a general situation within which political parties compete for power.[28] In a traditional democratic political arena the general strategy and tactics of the party are open. The goals are not masked, not concealed, but manifested and generally discussed.[29] A party may act through newspapers or local meetings. It acts in the parliament where its members, organized in a parliamentary club, form with other parties tactical alliances, support certain legislative moves or certain budgetary propositions as a matter of tactics to win support for other appropriations or reforms. But even in a democratic system tactical moves may conceal the real objectives. Thus, special publicity given to corruption or to the irregular private life of some public figure may serve electoral purposes in order to weaken the appeal of the competing party. This type of publicity is "tactical" in its nature and not necessarily a result of a special concern for honesty and efficiency in public life. In consequence, the way a case is "played up" is different when publicity is given only to an extent that is relevant and necessary in the public interest to safeguard ethics in public life, or if the purpose of publicity is to weaken or defeat a competitor to power.

An elaborate strategy and tactics are of special significance in a long-range program of conquering political power in an unconventional arena. Such is the case when a political arena is not one of a stable equilibrium of social forces or of a dynamic but orderly and rapid change but rather a rapidly changing and disintegrating situation that can be manipulated by the party. The party may also upset an orderly social change. A party through violent and terroristic action within such a social-political environment may affect a rapid transformation of a conventional political arena into an unconventional one of social disintegration and political confusion. This is done today by militarized centralistic parties through a combination of political and military strategy and guerilla tactics. In Asia and in Latin America, such strategy

and tactics have become a part of a general strategy of military and
political expansion and conquest.

Theories of party structure, strategy, and tactics are by no means
of a purely academic interest and have their historical significance.
Lenin, as we have mentioned, advanced the concept of a vanguardist
party structure; Mussolini and Hitler developed a military command
structure of mass parties; Stalin wrote down and presented a theory of
political strategy and tactics in his lectures at the University of
Svierdlovsk in 1926; Mao Tse-tung advanced further strategy and
tactics of direct action by combining political and military strategy
and war and revolutionary means. Mao Tse-tung's long-range strategy,
outlined in his essay *On Contradictions*, is based on Hegelian dialectics,
on a general proposition that change is determined by contradictions
and conflicts.[30]

7. INTERDEPENDENCE

The three components of our frame of reference—goals, organizational structure, and actions (ideology, apparatus, strategy, and tactics)—
appear in one form or another in every political party. The components,
however, are not separate, distinct blocs. Isolating components and
analyzing single variables is, again, a matter of convenience and perhaps
a necessary methodological device. The components, however, are
closely interrelated.

Change of the ideology, change of goal structure, affects strategy
and tactics. The change of ideology such as the acceptance of an
evolutionary instead of a revolutionary change affects of course general
strategy and also tactical movements. Changes in tactics affect organizational structure. Change from a parliamentary action to a direct
action, insurrection, affects the structure of the organization since
a centralistic organization in such a case is a more effective one.

Other institutions, not only political parties, can be classified
according to the types of the three major components mentioned
previously. The pattern of actions and structure of the organization
next to the human factor, such as leadership, determine group effectiveness. We understand by the latter the goal-achievement capacity of the
group within the limits of accepted and shared moral standards. The

standards vary. The moral standards of the Quakers are, of course, different from those of the Nazis. The Quakers are limited in their choice of actions by moral considerations while the Nazis had a much wider choice of alternatives since they were unrestricted by any moral consideration. Group effectiveness is by no means identical with moral strength, and goal achievement in politics is not tantamount to achievement of moral goals. Nonetheless, the efficiency of the party depends on the three major components adjusted properly to the "objective conditions," to the situation within which the party operates with an intention of changing or maintaining the existing situation.

8. REDUCTIONISM

Our frame of reference and the major premise do not and cannot embrace all variables. The fabric of a society is too complex with many variables interacting. Our observation of a political movement began with a (relatively) detached observation of the entire gestalt, a general political process. Such an observation offers a global picture, a general impression of a political development involving different personalities and the strength and the weaknesses of a party's strategy in a given situation. From this general observation we proceeded to a reduction of variables. We began with the identification of major, dynamic components that affect change, for any application of scientific method requires limiting the number of variables to those relevant ones for a working hypothesis of the subject matter. It is simply not possible to discuss or analyze an N number of variables at one time. Our minds do not work that way. However, we can list the major variables or the major problems, suggesting then an "inventory" of variables or problems. An inventory however is only a preliminary stage and largely descriptive in its nature. It is an attempt to identify major variables (or problems) and to indicate their relevance as a preliminary to any further exploration of mutual relationships or classification. A rigorous examination of social and political change or institutions requires narrowing the field of observation and a sharp reduction of relatively constant and variable components of the process. Reductionism as a research method is a conscious and logical process of eliminating less relevant variables in a given inquiry and focusing the inquiry on a limited number of relevant variables. The identification of relevant and less relevant variables is, of course, only an hypothesis. Reductionism as a method does not necessarily suggest that other variables are of lesser significance or without significance. The purpose of a reductive process is to identify the variables regarded as most relevant in a given approach and in a concrete inquiry. During an inquiry the relevance of other variables may appear and result in the reduction of previously selected variables and the identification of new ones. Our major premise of this discussion as well as the frame of reference are a result of such a reductive method.

9. AN OUTLINE FOR A STUDY OF
POLITICAL PARTIES AND
SOCIAL MOVEMENTS

Our frame of reference suggests a greatly reduced approach. A practical study of a social political movement may require the discussion of additional variables or components of political parties, relevant for students of the general political development of a country. The reduced frame of reference strengthens our focus of inquiry and narrows the field of research. We shall now proceed from our reduced approach to a more extensive and descriptive survey outline, a general outline for the study of social political movements. Such a descriptive survey includes a more extensive analyses of the size of the party and the number and kind of membership. In our reduced approach the problem of quantity is part of the structural-organizational analysis.

Political movements of significance are costly affairs. Even secret underground operations, which on the surface appear as movements without any specific economic support, require substantial financing, especially today in time of technical equipment and communication. The identification of the origins of financial resources of a political party, its general expenditures, and the distribution of expenses can indeed be very illuminating and assist in the identification of economic, political, and ideological interests. It may also shed light on the sympathizers of the party, members of different classes who, for ideological reasons, support the goals of the party.

The dynamic nature of a political movement depends, in addition to our three major components, on strong or charismatic leadership. The type of personality of a leader and the personality of the followers as well as the selection of leadership is an important area of psychological and sociological study.

Thus, a general survey of a political movement prepared for wider use suggests an overall, integrated approach. A departmental monism, a single discipline approach, may hinder full comprehension of this complex political process. An outline of a survey of a political party is given below as a general pattern for a suggested descriptive study. Today political parties represent a major social force of change not only in the Americas and Europe but also in the emerging nations of Asia and Africa. An analysis, even a balanced view, requires at least a general orientation of the forces at work in a political arena.

Tentative Outline
A Survey of a Political Movement

A. *Introduction*
  1. Origin of the movement
  2. Short history of the movement
  3. Identification of (a) economic interests, (b) ethnic or religious groups, (c) general political goals the party represents.
  4. The political arena: competing social and political parties

B. *Socioeconomic Environment (Situation) of the Party*
  1. Political conditions and institutions
  2. Social and economic conditions
  3. Class structure
  4. Major religious communities and institutions; significance of religious values; major ethnic and racial groups; ethnic values; patterns of intergroup relations.

C. *Ideology*
  1. A general description of the party's philosophy, and of the social and economic classes and interests the party can be identified with.
  2. The goal structure: "manifest" and "masked" goals, immediate, intermediate, and distant goals (minimum and maximum programs)
  3. Values and symbols emphasized

4. Image projected by the party ideology and activities:
   a. pragmatic-rational elements of the image (social, economic and political goals, demands, plans)
   b. ethical elements (norms emphasized)
   c. emotional elements
5. General appeal of the ideology: economic, political, psychological (a general summary of 1 through 3)
6. Flexibility and adjustment of the ideology to:
   a. changing socioeconomic conditions
   b. altered leadership
   c. differing needs

D. *Party Structure (Apparatus): Size, Ecology*
   1. Social class of members and voters
   2. Quantitative changes of membership and votes in time
   3. Territorial distribution of membership and voters (ecology)[31]
   4. Methods of recruiting party members
   5. Structure of the party (organization, apparatus)
   6. Decision-making: formal and informal power centers (who makes the decision and exercises power or influence)

E. *Pattern of Actions*
   1. General description of activities and planned operations
   2. Means and mass media used
   3. General pattern of strategy and tactics

F. *Leadership*
   1. General identification of party leadership and way leadership is exercised
   2. Class origin of party leaders
   3. Personality types
   4. Mobility of (changes in) leadership
   5. Method of selection and achieving position of leadership

G. *The Economic Base of the Movement*
   1. Estimates of party revenue and expenses
   2. Source of support
   3. How and by whom it is used

H. *Sociological Function of the Party*
   1. Function of the party in terms of social, economic, and political needs of its members and of social classes, as well as ethnic groups the party attempts to represent

2. Function of the party in terms of social-psychological needs of members and voters
3. Function of the party within the political, institutional structure (government, state)

I. *Evaluation*
   1. General evaluation of the strength and influence of the movement and of competing or opposing forces

A survey of political movements does not exclude the usefulness of the need for more extensive and specialized historical studies and monographs. A historical study of a political party has utility and significance of its own. In addition, a psychological and sociological approach profits greatly from historical material. Social events gain clarity in their historical perspective. The origins of a movement frequently explain future developments.

This outline for a general survey suggests a broad and general but also an integrated approach to the study of political movements. Of course, often not all of the necessary information is readily available. Moreover, not every section of the outline is relevant for every movement, and certain areas of information require a preliminary, theoretical frame of reference. This general survey suggests a descriptive and at the same time a broader approach than our focused, limited sociological analysis of the dynamic nature of political movements, of their

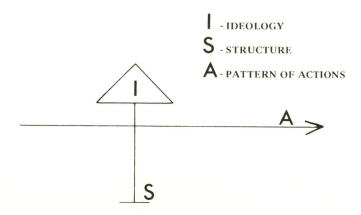

I - IDEOLOGY

S - STRUCTURE

A - PATTERN OF ACTIONS

Model 9. Model of a Political Party

nature as a social force effecting change. The latter approach narrows the inquiry to the major premise and to the frame of reference of the three major components which contribute to the dynamic nature of movements and which are essential in effecting social change in a social environment. Our frame of reference, demonstrated by Model 9, corresponds to a general hypothesis that the type of structure of the party, its ideology, its strategy and tactics contribute to its effectiveness in achieving power and influencing social change or maintaining the status quo.

NOTES

1. Stalin makes a distinction between the "objective" and "subjective" elements of political strategy and tactics. The objective element is the socioeconomic base within which the party operates; the subjective element is the party which changes existing conditions. Stalin's approach is pragmatic and based on historical experience. According to a dogmatic Marxist interpretation, the changes in the base (social relations in production) are decisive; the party is only a dependent variable. In Stalin's and Lenin's theory, the party affects or accelerates changes within the base. Since Stalin controlled absolute political power he could interpret Marxism as he wished. See Joseph W. Stalin, "On Strategy and Tactics," J. W. Stalin, *Works* (Moscow: Foreign Languages Publishing House, 1952-1955), translation by the Marx-Engels-Lenin Institute of the Central Committee of C.P.S.U. Also see Stalin's *Strategy and Tactics of the Proletarian Revolution* (New York: International Publishers, 1956), pp. 21ff.

2. The term "social myth" was introduced by Georges Sorel. In the introduction to his *Reflexions sur la violence* (Paris: Rivier, 1921), Sorel suggested this term for ideas and social visions which in reality are not achieved but act as a motivating force and incentive. He called his social myth a "happy finding," which indeed became a fruitful concept in social sciences.

3. Karl Manheim in *Ideology and Utopia* uses the term *utopia* to mean an idea system projected into the future which suggests and motivates action toward changing the status quo. *Ideology and Utopia* (New York: Harcourt, Brace, 1936), chap. 2.

4. Visions can also be classified according to their pragmatic potentialities, in terms of practical application and problem solving. According to the degree of "workability," visions in such an approach can be divided into utopias, social myths, and practical solutions. See Feliks Gross, *European Ideologies* (New York: Philosophical Library, 1948), chap. 1.

5. 1934 Conservative Party Annual Conference Report, folio 49, quoted by R. T. McKenzie, *British Political Parties* (New York: Praeger, 1964), pp. 144-145.

6. Pareto developed his frame of reference in *Trattato di Sociologia,* published in English as *Mind and Society* (New York: Harcourt, Brace, 1942) and later applied it in his discussion and analysis of political movements after World War I in *Transformazioni della Democrazia,* published first as articles in *Rivista di Milano* in 1920 (edition quoted is Cappelli Editore, Rocca San Casciano, 1964).

7. Karl Marx in his interpretation of historical materialism did not deny the significance of ideas, and Engels stressed the reciprocal causation of variables. Nor did Marx deny the significance of ideas and action in a dynamic process of social change (to mention only his theses on Feuerbach). However, he was not always consistent in the presentation of his theories, and his views changed over a period of time. During his life he reacted to current conditions, which no doubt influenced his views. The interpretation of Marx's theories, therefore, is a difficult problem. There are many interpretations, and some remind one of scholastic commentaries to holy scripture. A monistic position in this interpretation was presented by a talented Russian theoretician, George Plekhanov. In such an interpretation, changes in the economic base are the only determinant. See his *Essays in Historical Materialism* (New York: International Publishers, 1940), pp. 23-25, 48.

8. Early descriptions of ethnic institutions and values were influenced by individual and national prejudices. See, for example, Machiavelli's description of French national character, *De Natura Gallorum* (in *Tutte le Opere, Complete Works*, ed. Guido Mazzoni and Maria Casella [Florence: Barbera, 1929], pp. 730ff.) and his discussion of the origins of certain ethnic characteristics in his *Ritratto di Cose di Francia* (op. cit. p. 731). Nevertheless, parts of these early descriptions, including Machiavelli's, sometimes contain penetrating evidence of historical processes of transvaluation and change. Mesnard, in his historical-political studies, traced political values to early periods of development. Mesnard's work suggests mutual interdependence of value structure and political philosophy and institutions. For instance, he traces the development of liberty as one of the major Polish ethnic values back to the Renaissance. He shows a mutual interdependence of values, philosophy, and political institutions. Pierre Mesnard, *Il Pensiero Politico Rinascimentale* (Bari: Laterza, 1949), II: 31ff. The classic essays of De Tocqueville as well as those of the South American statesman, Sarmiento, written more than a century ago, give a surprisingly accurate picture of certain American values and institutions. These values can still be identified in present-day American communities.

9. American studies on voting behavior are extensive, and research has supplied ample evidence of the significance of traditional voting patterns of some sections in American elections, to mention only Paul Lazarsfeld, B. Berelson, and H. Gaudet, *The People's Choice* (New York: Columbia University Press, 1948). André Siegfried found a general tendency of an ecological and traditional distribution of votes in France. André Siegfried, *Tableau Politique de la France de l'Ouest sous la Troisième République* (Paris: Colin, 1913). For an introductory bibliography in this area, see Joseph S. Roucek, ed., *Contemporary Sociology* (New York: Philosophical Library, 1958), especially the essays by Joseph B. Ford, "Public Opinion and Propaganda," pp. 624ff., and Feliks Gross, "Political Sociology," pp. 201ff. For a survey of research and studies on voting behavior, see Rudolf Heberle, *Social Movements: An Introduction to Political Sociology* (New York: Appleton-Century-Crofts), 1951.

10. The individual psychology of Alfred Adler can be fruitfully applied to a study of an aggressive "political personality" driven toward the conquest and exercise of political power. See also: Harold D. Laswell, *Power and Personality* (New York: W. W. Norton, 1948). Erich Fromm interpreted the success of the Nazi movement in terms of collective anxieties and certain psychological dialectics, contradictions between two psychological needs—freedom and security. See Fromm's *Escape from Freedom* (New York: Rinehart, 1941).

11. A separate category, "values," is suggested here for methodological

reasons; their normative quality and function crosses the conventional border lines of disciplines. It may be argued, however, that values can be integrated with the general psychological category.

12. Emile Durkheim, *The Elementary Forms of Religious Life* (New York: Collier Books, 1961), p. 59.

13. Adolf A. Berle, Jr., *Natural Selection of Political Forces* (Lawrence: University of Kansas Press, 1950).

14. I owe the information on Fulanismo in Portugal and Spain to Professor Armando Mazques Guedes of Lisbon.

15. Albert Falcionelli, *Les Sociétés Secretes Italiennes: Les Carbonari, La Camorra, La Mafia* (Paris: Payot, 1936).

16. Josephus Flavius, *The Jewish War*, trans. H. St. J. Thakeray (New York: Putnam, 1927), Books 1-3, p. 423, Book 2, pp. 254-257.

17. Bernard Lewis, *The Assassins* (London: Weidenfeld & Nicholson, 1967), pp. 24ff., 47ff., 123ff.

18. Sir William Sleeman, *Thugs or Phansigars of India* (Philadelphia: Carey & Hart, 1839). See also *Encyclopedia Britannica* (*Thug*), vol. 21; John H. Lepper, *Famous Secret Societies* (London: Sampson, Low, 1932), pp. 296ff.

19. Thomas Keightley, *Secret Societies of the Middle Ages* (London: Charles Knight, 1848); see also, Lepper, *Famous Secret Societies*, p. 74, on French Compagnonage, a medieval association of craftsmen and workers abolished in 1789. Compagnonage survived the Revolution in spite of adversities.

20. See n. 21 below; also J. L. Sleeman, *Ramasseana, or the Vocabulary of the Peculiar Language Used by the Thugs* (1836), mentioned in *Encyclopedia Britannica*, vol. 21.

21. Angelo Ottolini, *La Carboneria* (Modena: Albrighi, 1938). For a well written and popular history of the Carbonara see: Indro Montanelli, *Italia Giacobina e Carbonara* (Milan: Rizzoli, 1972).

22. Lucien de la Hodde, *History of Secret Societies* (Philadelphia: Lippincott, 1856), chap. XXI.

23. Max Nomad, *Apostles of the Revolution* (Boston: Little, Brown & Co., 1939), pp. 14, 17-25; Auguste Blanqui, *Textes Choisis* (Paris: Editions Sociales, 1955), p. 105. See also his "Instruction for insurrection" ("Instruction pour une prise d'armes"), p. 214.

24. Between 1870 and 1880 in Poland after the defeat of the uprising of 1863 against Russia, secret political socialist organizations (later formed into a party called "Proletariat") were organized into secret circles. "Circles" were limited in number to ten to fifteen members. The members of each circle elected a treasurer and an organizer. The organizers of all or of a "section," or certain circles met in an "organizers' circle" and decided by a majority vote. At first, "Proletariat" was an organization of students, but later workers and even some army officers were attracted by its appeals. "Workers' Circles" were formed and met once a week. The delegates of workers' circles formed a "section" and met also once a week. This underground party probably had between fifteen hundred and two thousand members, a substantial membership when compared to similar Russian organizations, See Lucjan Blit, *The Origins of Polish Socialism: The History and Ideas of the First Polish Socialist Party, 1878-1886* (Cambridge: Cambridge University Press, 1971), pp. 32, 64, 83.

The "circle" organization has been, so it seems, the dominant pattern of the Russian Populists, a secret political organization, perhaps still in the years of 1875-1878 (prior to the development of terroristic tactics). Secret printing plants, however, had already at this time no more than four to five workers, organized in a tightly secret small unit (called later among the Poles "deep underground"). This high secrecy was achieved by social isolation, reduction of personal contacts with friends, even family. See Stepniak, *Underground Russia* (New York: John W. Lovell, n.d. [date in introduction 1882]), pp. 184ff.

The traditional forms of symbolic initiation and ritualism survived and continued, especially in the Balkan secret political organizations, until the twentieth century. But even in Poland, a patriotic socialist organization, ZET, during the last decade of the nineteenth century, kept a traditional ritualistic form.

L. Frances Millard, in *The Founding of Zet*, a highly informative study, describes the ritual: "The organization of Zet provides a sharp contrast to the socialist ideals it professed. Instead of equality there was hierarchy; instead of free discussion there was ritual and the absolute subordination of the individual member. The organization was based on a complex three-tiered system of the masonic type. 'Colleagues' made up the lower level; the more tried and experienced became 'comrades,' and at the apex came the most dedicated of all, the Zet 'brothers.' The lower levels did not know of the existence of those above. They communicated with the higher echelons by means of the 'older colleague' who was secretly a comrade, or through the 'older comrade' who was in reality a Zet brother. At the head of Zet stood a five-man Central Board, elected by a congress of brothers. One member of the board was openly elected and was known to all members at this level of the organization. Choice of the other four was by secret ballot; the successful candidates were secretly informed of their election by the 'open brother,' thus remaining unknown to all but each other throughout their term of office. Congresses were apparently held every academic year.

"This tight hierarchical structure was accomplished by an oath of secrecy and the use of secret signs and handshakes for each of the three tiers. The most obvious reason for this method of organization was the very real need to protect Zet as far as possible from discovery by the authorities; in an open system the arrest of one member would probably have led to complete disintegration. In conjunction with its conspiratorial trappings the organizational structure also served the attempt to foster complete discipline within Zet as well as the greater psychological involvement caused by the drama of conspiracy. This involvement was reinforced by the emphasis placed on the nobleness of the cause of independence. Members were committed to strive for the development of purity and strength of character, discipline, and subordination to the 'Polish idea.'" Manuscript copy of *Polish Revue*, courtesy of Mrs. Millard and Professor L. Krzyzanowski, the editor.

25. The information is based on this writer's interviews in Paris in April 1965 with Zygmunt Zaremba, for many years a member of the Polish Parliament (Sejm), a member of the central committee of the Polish Socialist party, and one of the leaders and chief architects of the Polish underground during the war; and with Dr. Michael Borwicz, who was commander of military underground units in the area of Miechov-Cracow during the war. Georg Simmel wrote in an abstract way on the general sociology of secrecy; see Kurt H. Wolff, trans. and ed., *Sociology of Georg Simmel*, (Glencoe: Free Press, 1950), pp. 330ff. Simmel is probably the first sociologist to pioneer in this important area of social organization, behavior, and values, but he had little, if any, personal experience or empirical data.

On underground cell parties see: Zygmunt Gross and Feliks Gross, *Socjologia Partii Politycznej* [Sociology of political parties] (Second, revised edition, Cracow: Czytelnik, 1946), p. 51ff. On secret organizations see also: Joseph S. Roucek, "Sociology of Secret Societies," *The American Journal of Economics and Sociology*, vol. XIX, Jan. 1960.

26. See "Organisation des agents principaux aux nombre de douze et des agents intermédiaires. Premières fonctions de chacun d'eux." (An instruction of an order of the secret leadership [directoire secret]), [Filippo] Buonarotti, *Conspiration pour l'Egalité dite de Babeuf* (1828; reprint ed., Paris: Editions Sociales, 1957), II.

27. John A. Armstrong, ed., *Soviet Partisans in World War II* (Madison: University of Wisconsin Press, 1964), pp. 655-656, document 2.

28. Harold Laswell and Abraham Kaplan have defined an "area of power" as a situation comprised by those who demand power or who are within the domain of power. Laswell, *Power and Personality*, p. 223.

29. Masked goals are those political objectives which are not revealed in party propaganda and at times not even in party programs. They are kept as secret decisions of the party leadership. Masked goals appear especially in totalitarian movements.

30. Mao Tse-tung, *On Contradictions* (New York: International Publishers, 1951). See also his *On Practice* (Peking, 1951).

31. Political ecology can be defined as a study of special distribution of political attitudes and behavior of voters and social groups or classes. André Siegfried, a French political geographer, was among the early students and pioneers in this field. He advanced a thesis on special distribution of political attitudes in France. According to his findings, the distribution of votes and party preferences in France followed the old historical divisions into *pays* and not the administrative divisions which were established after the French Revolution. André Siegfried, *Tableau Politique de la France de l'Ouest sous la Troisieme Republique* (Paris: Colin, 1913) and his *Tableau de Partis en France* (Paris: Giasset, 1930). For a general survey of this field see: Rudolf Heberle, *Social Movements*, pp. 218ff. "Political Ecology" in Gross, "Political Sociology," in Roucek, ed., *Contemporary Sociology*, pp. 206ff.

IV

The Underground Movements

1. THE PATTERNS OF THE UNDERGROUND

The term *underground movement* probably originated in Russia and Poland and most likely appeared in the late 1860s or early 1870s. The term was used for secret, political, organized groups which opposed and fought the Russian czarist regime. Originally, the type of organization associated with underground movements was used in struggles for political freedoms such as civil rights, freedom of press, speech, association, elective government, or freedom from foreign rule. It was also used by the early socialist movements in Russia and Poland.[1] As time went on, the term was used to refer to networks of any secret and militant political organizations, including those of the extreme right— for example, the Croat Ustasha, which introduced a reign of terror during World War II in Serb territories after gaining power. The concept of "an underground" gained appeal and glory during World War II, when struggle against German occupation called for heroism, skill, and organizational talents, and when risks were cruel: torture, death camps, executions.

Today in the United States, *underground* is used to refer to the publications of those who feel alienated from the politics of the "Establishment." Ironically, in spite of the name, the "underground" press of this type enjoys the most extensive freedom of press in the history of mankind. It is sold and displayed freely; it prospers, com-

bining politics with a sometimes vulgar sex. These weeklies and month-
lies have nothing in common with the underground papers of World
War II, published under German rule, when printers and distributors
daily risked their lives and freedom. The cause was clear and quite
different from the aims of those who adopted this name in the late 1960s
in the United States.

However, for our purposes, we are interested in the earlier meaning
of *underground*—a secret political organization with a wide network.
(The details of secret party structure and organization have been discussed in Chapter 3, "Dynamics of a Political Party.") The political
nature and orientation of an underground movement—in other words,
its political function—is related to the situation within which it operates, the goals the organization is attempting to achieve, and to the
political institutions it is trying to weaken or destroy. The goals of
a movement and the ways it responds to situations affect its recruitment. An underground movement in a given situation appeals to
certain classes and attracts certain personality types. The current
political, economic, and social situation is not the sole cause or variable
that originates such a movement. Historical traditions, ethnic and
political values, even existing or traditional types of organization are
contributing causal factors. And in reverse, traditions of underground
struggle affect the ethnic values and political culture of a nation. All
these variables interact.

The underground movements of our century had and have an
ideology, goals, definite forms of organization, and tactics. The risks
and dangers frequently attract different personality types than those in an
orderly democratic process. The underground party does not resemble
legal parties in a pluralistic, democratic system. Moreover, there are differences between underground patterns of various nations, and between
underground movements of various orientations. Underground movements in the past served a variety of objectives. In this essay, we shall
limit the data and theme primarily to the traditions and experiences of
underground movements in Poland.

Some nations, like Poland, have century-long traditions of underground movements, traditions originated and reinforced by struggle
against foreign and oppressive rule. Nations that have enjoyed freedom
from foreign rule and long periods of democracy seldom have any
extensive national experience in underground struggle. A nation without such traditions, or with only weak historical reminiscences, may
devise an underground structure, however, once overrun by a foreign

invader. But the building of a network from beginnings can take time and sacrifice. This was the case of France when the German troops over-ran the country during World War II; it took time before the Maquis and the whole network of the underground organization emerged. In contrast, when Polish territory was overrun by the Germans, the underground movement mushroomed almost overnight. Poland had had an insurrectionist tradition for nearly a century and a half, and knowledge of the insurrection of 1863 and the revolution of 1905 was not solely from books; it was a part of a living tradition. For example, Tomasz Arciszewski, who was one of the top leaders of the Polish underground during World War II and who was elected prime minister of the government in exile by the underground Polish Council of National Unity, had been a leader of the Polish anticzarist under-ground half a century earlier. His colleagues were men who knew the techniques of underground warfare and had the necessary desire for and devotion to the cause of freedom to wage it. There was a definite, historically established and accepted pattern of underground struggle. When the Germans came, the pattern was rapidly adjusted to the new conditions.

While the Poles followed a one hundred and fifty year old pattern of insurrectionist resistance, the Yugoslavs carried on a tradition of underground partisan warfare that was shaped by centuries of struggle against the Turks. When their country was overrun by the Germans, the Yugoslavs formed detachments of Chetniks under the supreme leadership of General Draja Mikhailovich. The Chetniks withdrew into inaccessible mountain hideouts and from there launched their attacks. When Communist partisans under Tito appeared on the scene much later, they also adopted the Chetnik methods.

Even geography had its significance in the formation of patterns of resistance. Underground strongholds were hidden in the forests of Poland, the mountains of Czechoslovakia, and the Eastern Carpathian slopes and the Prypet marshes of the Ukraine. The Poles built an elaborate underground state. The Yugoslavs established their high political authority in the mountains. The Czechs followed a traditional pattern of slow, passive resistance and sabotage, so well and satirically described by Jaroslav Hasek in *The Good Soldier: Schweik* (Garden City, 1930). Some Poles in their underground parlance called the pattern "Czechization of resistance," meaning that, if the struggle is hopeless, the adversary strong, and there is no hope of outside support, then passive resistance may be the wiser, subtler, and more effective course.

The Belgians also organized their World War II resistance movement early since the tradition of anti-German resistance developed during World War I was still alive. The vicinity of the British coast also played a significant role in their underground strategy.

In Russia underground movements had flourished for a hundred years in a struggle against a native, despotic, traditionally established rule. Since the time of the Decembrists, through the Populist tradition of the sixties and seventies and down to the turn of the century, the movement and its underground tactics were developed by, and for a long time limited to, revolutionary elites. In the last quarter of the nineteenth century the underground had no popular support, but at the turn of the twentieth century it began to win followers from the liberal middle classes and the workers and, finally, on the eve of the revolution, from the peasantry.

Each country produced its own kind of underground and its own techniques of resistance, in which national traditions and values played a powerful role. The variety of patterns resulted from a diversity of historical experiences and other factors.

2. IMPACT ON SOCIETY AND CULTURE

Space does not permit a detailed discussion of all these national variations. We offer here a description of the Polish resistance and compare it at some points with others.

Insurrection against foreign occupation and rule has been a part of Polish history since the eighteenth century. It developed in the area that was under Russian rule until 1918 and furnished a romantic image to the rest of the country. As a consequence, "insurrectionism" evolved into a cultural complex reflected in value attitudes, personality, history, politics, and also in specific skills and techniques, perpetuated by tradition.

Those who participated in insurrections were respected and often revered. Their social status was high. Some of the 1863 insurrectionists still survived after World War I and saw a free Polish republic. The very title of *powstaniec* (insurrectionist) was honored. The insurrectionists' courage and devotion to the cause of freedom, the years of Siberian exile, were part of conversation and evening stories, were taught in the schools, and became topics for term papers and master dissertations. Then came those of the younger generation, who struggled in the Polish socialist underground at the turn of the century against the czarist rule. They played a prominent role in the interwar politics of Poland. The semidictator Joseph Pilsudski was at one time one of their leaders. This period, including the revolution of 1905, produced a political myth, a legend that at one time supplied an element of strength to Pilsudski's ideological appeal. Once Poland was free, the tradition of these underground struggles against Russian rule went into history books and popular sentiment. Every year, representatives of the social-democratic labor movement (PPS—the Polish Socialist party) paid homage at the Citadel of Warsaw, at the place below the gallows where Polish socialists perished. Flowers and wreaths marked their graves and flags were lowered.

The leaders and militants of a not so distant past now moved into history books. Hero worship became a part of political lore and tradition. *Hero* in Polish was not easily or frequently used; heroes were not among the living. An act might be heroic (*bohaterski*) but still the actor must not be called a hero (*bohater*). This would sound pretentious and even embarrassing.

Historical journals of the 1930s devoted to the modern history of Poland published scholarly articles on the underground and the earlier periods of resistance. The insurrectionist ideology and the underground struggle even influenced belles-lettres and the arts. One of the leading Polish novelists, Stefan Zeromski, devoted his talent not only to the romanticism but also to the moral dilemmas of the underground. His *Dream about Sword and Bread* depicted the concept of heroism of an underground Polish fighter at the beginning of this century. In *Roza* (The Rose), he dramatized the great issues of the underground, appealing to the youth of the time from the stage of national theaters. Stanislas Brzozowski in his novel *Flames* fascinated the reader with the underground and its philosophical issues, while Andrzej Strug in *Underground Men* gave moving and true sketches of the life and character of men of the PPS at the turn of the century (Strug was one of them). All three writers are "greats" of Polish literature and their works are considered classics. Artur Grottger, one of the Polish national painters, devoted his talent to the painting of the insurrection of 1863, the resistance struggle, underground action, and Siberian exile. A passerby in one of the main squares of Warsaw might have been impressed by a simple monument, marked P.O.W., which commemorated the military underground or-

ganization of 1917 against the Central Powers. Streets were named for
the heroes of the revolution of 1905—Okrzeja, Montwill Mirecki, and
others.

Memorials of the underground and of the resistance were every-
where—in novels, theaters, history, paintings, and monuments; in
folklore, stories, and songs. Some of the songs, like "Varsovienne"
and "Forward Warsaw to Struggle," were sung in many countries.
Annual celebrations of many kinds formed a symbolic and ritualistic
mechanism through which the values and tradition were reinforced
and the experiences renewed. People lived them over and over again
through these celebrations, and heroes rose again from the ashes.

National traditions were a part of family traditions too. In the home
of one Polish architect, once a member of the Polish socialist resistance,
one could see on the diningroom wall a framed page from a newspaper
of 1831 with an account of the death of his grandfather in an insurrectionist battle. On the same wall was another relic—a framed piece of
blood-stained linen and the story of the heroic sacrifice of his uncle
in the insurrection of 1863. And finally there was a picture of the late
architect himself, surrounded by Russian gendarmes armed with swords,
on his way to Siberia—just before he escaped to Austria. Here was the
story of three generations. His widow, her children, and their friends
told fascinating stories about the insurrectionists. She was a *dromader*,
a witty, charming, and courageous lady who carried underground publications across the border to the Russian area. Such a home atmosphere
in the 1930s was fairly typical of some of the Polish intelligentsia,
whose roots were in this old, insurrectionary tradition. Among workers
of social-democratic views, the underground traditions and stories were
a part of their social history. After all, in the areas under Russian rule,
the socialist movement was active underground for many years, and it
existed legally for twenty years, from 1918 to 1939. All four presidents
of the interwar era (Narutowicz, Wojciechowski, Pilsudski, Moscicki)
were either sympathizers or leaders of the pre-1914 Polish Socialist party.

There were of course strong opponents of this tradition. There were
trends in Poland that tried to steer public sentiment, especially that of
young people, away from these values and ideas. At the end of the last
century, the "positivists" advocated constructive work for the economic
advance of the country. The insurrections, they argued, were never
successful; they had only weakened the nation. They further argued
that in every uprising the dedicated and the patriotic, but above all
the young generation of participants, had perished. There were times

when the positivists were influential among certain social classes, and
their "voice of reason" was effective. Later the National Democratic
party, a rightist movement, violently opposed the insurrectionist strategy.
In the long run, however, the tradition and ideology of insurrectionism
shaped the values, traditions, and personalities of the Poles.

The underground struggle developed specific political skills. In 1863
an underground state was organized complete with a national government, army, police, and courts; even national loans were floated. The
national government was, however, apprehended by Russians, and its
leaders were executed. Undoubtedly the experience of 1863 influenced
the model for the underground state formed in defiance of the Nazi
occupation in 1940. During World War II, the fate of the underground
national government of 1863 was cited in the underground press to
justify the formation of a government-in-exile in London and an underground council in the occupied country.

Historians, theoreticians, and tacticians of insurrections evolved a
political and sociological theory. In the early 1900s Joseph Pilsudski
was a prominent leader of the Polish underground and of the Polish
Socialist party. He was editor of the underground paper *Robotnik*
(The worker), the central organ of the party. Joseph Pilsudski wrote
books and articles on theory and praxis of the underground struggle.
In 1912, encouraged by a democratic-socialist leader, Daszynski, he
published a remarkable book entitled *Bibuła*. Literally, the word means
"India paper" (comparable to onionskin), on which underground newspapers and pamphlets were printed for easy distribution by smuggling
or by mail. Thus, the word came to mean any underground publication.
Pilsudski's book is a combination of personal reminiscences and a
manual for underground editors. It describes the skills essential to the
editor of the underground press—that most independent and intransigent
press of the world, free from censorship and advertising—and answers
the critical problems that confront him: how to operate secretly, where
to find paper supplies and printers, how to store the publication, and
how to distribute and circulate it.

In a lecture given in 1912 on the mobilization of the Insurrection of
1863 (part of a series of lectures, which later were published), Pilsudski
analyzes his subject with a practical goal in view—the future. The key
to insurrectionist mobilization, he argues, is the transformation of a
small revolutionary vanguard into an insurrectionist mass army. In his
Military History of the Insurrection of 1863 (1912), he discusses another
aspect of this branch of political science—the problem of civil and mili-

tary organization in an uprising.

A number of pamphlets and articles on the techniques of underground struggle appeared at this time. Among them was a handy booklet on how to behave while in prison. It discussed the rights of a prisoner and supplied an alphabet for communicating with other political prisoners by knocking on the walls or iron pipes. There was even a training school for revolutionaries in Cracow, the outer base of those who fought against czarist Russia.

When the Germans overran Poland, all of these traditions and skills were put to a test. They were strong. The values which had been continuously reinforced were challenged by a new situation; the response was positive and underground organizations began to grow. Old skills and techniques were put into operation, then tested against new experiences and revised and adjusted accordingly.

3. SOCIAL STRATIFICATION AND THE UNDERGROUND

A national underground movement represents a collective response to a political situation and in consequence it is rooted in a social structure and in certain social classes. For example, the Populists in Russia were students and intellectuals; the Polish socialist movement was supported by intellectuals but to a far greater extent by the workers. In contrast to these, the Polish anti-Nazi underground was a national mass movement, similar to that in France. It cut through all social classes, with strong organizations among industrial workers, peasantry, and intelligentsia.

A strong underground movement, a mass movement, should have an appeal to large sections of the population. The Polish insurrections of the eighteenth- and nineteenth-centuries failed because the democratic appeals of the leaders did not win mass support. Even Kosciuszko, who had the experience of the American Revolution, was unsuccessful, despite his serious effort to win the peasantry. Secret societies and juntas may operate without what is called in everyday parlance mass support, but an underground mass movement usually attempts to appeal

to the urgent needs and to the hopes of the people. Its leaders and
theoreticians attempt to convince them of a better tomorrow—a release
from the semifeudal conditions or liberation from foreign rule or an
oppressive dictatorship.

4. VALUES AND ATTITUDES OF THE UNDERGROUND: "IDEALISM" AND "FUNDAMENTALISM"

An underground movement is related to existing social, economic,
and political conditions and should be considered in this context. Oppressive authoritarian or foreign rule may stimulate an underground
and democratic response; sometimes this is the only active, political
alternative. An underground political structure can also be used,
however, by movements directed against democratic institutions. For
the present, we shall narrow our discussion to the former and postpone
the latter to section 9 of this essay ("Some Comparisons and Comments").
   The philosophical meaning of values may be only vaguely realized
by a group of insurrectionists. The goals are simple: liberation from
foreign rule or from an oppressive government. Next to these basic values
of freedom and justice, the generally accepted value for the Poles was and is
niepodleglose. Because of the negative prefix (*nie*), it is difficult to translate this value symbol exactly. The closest translation in English is
"independence," in the sense of nondependence on, or nonsubjection
to, foreign rule. The emphasis on the negative prefix is rather unique.
The Polish national anthem is built around it, as are many other
patriotic songs. "Poland is not lost" (*Jeszcze Polska nie zgineła*)
is the national anthem, while another popular patriotic song begins
"We shall not surrender the soil of our fathers" (*"Nie damy ziemi skad
nasz ród"*). The songs are not of aggression but of defense against conquest
and submission, songs born of defeat, not victory. They reflect the past
and its values. In the insurrections and underground, the symbol of
independence was historically connected with concepts of political
democracy and equality so that all three were joined in a sort of association of ideas.

These three symbols, "Equality, Liberty and Independence," were
printed on proclamations by the insurrectionists of 1794 and appeared
on the seals of the national government in 1863. Furthermore, they
gave a new name to the social-democratic underground during the Nazi
occupation when the PPS changed its initials to WRN ("*Wolnosc,
Rownosc, Niepodlegloso*"—Liberty, Equality, Independence). These
were also the values of the revolution of 1905. Commemorating the
insurrection of 1863, an underground paper in February 1942 con-
cluded: "The insurrectionists fell in the battlefields and at the gallows.
They left to us a glorious page of Polish history, a heritage of national
underground and of courageous armed struggle. This page has an in-
destructible symbol, the seal of the National Government with its
slogan: 'Equality, Liberty, Independence.'"[2]

The dominant issues of a political movement are usually formulated
in the form of short slogans. This can be observed, for instance, in the
symbols of the French Revolution, as well as in the slogans of the Polish
resistance. In a predominantly Catholic France and Poland the use of a
symbolic trinity moved on well-established emotional and intellectual
"tracks." The Trinity was assimilated, diffused or projected (probably
unconsciously) from a religious belief system into political ideology.
Three symbols associated in such a religious-traditional way are intense
in their message.

Perhaps a major value or concept, strong in Polish political, especially
insurrectionist, tradition is idealism (*ideovost*): dedication to a cause
because of a moral commitment, an ethical imperative. A man who is
ideovy or faithful to his principles does not expect any reward in terms
of glory, power, or profit, and is willing to carry his principles to a
point of self-sacrifice, even for a cause which is lost from the beginning.
This is of course an ideal type, not necessarily and not frequently real.
A man dedicated to such principles is *ideoviets*, and can be trusted. An
ideoviets is not identical with an idealist; he is a man of action as well
as of principles. His idealism is tested by willingness to sacrifice of his
time, career, life chances, and liberty.

Self-sacrifice in such a context was a norm of conduct, and respective behavior was expected from the leadership, at least in crisis situations or in national disasters, even if such an act was of no practical
avail and was from the very beginning hopeless. (In this respect the
Poles and the Serbs had similar traditions where ethnic values had some
affinity. They celebrated days of national defeats as days of victory.

The Serbian defeat at Kossovo in 1389 and the Warsaw uprising in 1944 were instances of heroic resistance without victory; suffering and self-sacrifice are revered.) A Polish political leader should prove his devotion by self-sacrifice. Years in the penitentiary for a political offense, for the struggle for independence is an honorable distinction, a testimony to self-sacrifice, to noncorruption. A labor candidate with a commuted death sentence had a good chance while elections were really free. In short, men who have sacrificed themselves are men whose devotion can be trusted because they have put the public interest above their welfare.

The social-democratic mayor of the city of Radom in the late thirties used to walk like a soccer player with his hands moving and his legs and feet turned toward the inside, leaning forward a bit. I once asked him whether he had ever played soccer, but his answer was negative. His way of walking had been acquired during the long years in czarist *katorga*, when he was sentenced for his underground activities against the czars, the worst type of hard labor. He had been in chains, his legs in irons, and in this way did he acquire this particular gait.

Self-sacrifice and suffering do not always lead to glory. The underground soldier is an unknown soldier. Such was the social reality of the underground struggle in Poland and it was reflected in novels. One of the masters of Polish prose, Stefan Zeromski, used this theme in his *Dream about Sword and Bread*, mentioned above:

> When a Japanese officer, sentenced by an alien courtmartial to be shot for serving his country, was asked before the execution what he wished to do with the money found on him, and whether it was his will that the money be sent to his children, he said: "I donate the money to the International Red Cross. I have no need to be concerned about the fate of my children for after my death the Mikado will care for them."

> The abject world recoiled in its heart on having heard this simple answer, and since the Japanese cause was won—the greater was its admiration.

> Beyond you, oh Polish soldier—when you are hanging lonely from the hook of the gallows, when you are falling into a bloody ditch of the condemned with a heart pierced by bullets of the Tsar's soldiers—when you are dying a slow death in the Siberian steppe— waves no banner of a distant might. *Beyond* you there is nothing.

Behind you there is only a grave dug to the size of your corpse.
Before you armies stand. No one's love will nourish your children
when you die.

Your compatriots will renounce you, your neighbors will forget
you for in their hearts a feeling does not last long, and a thought—
as it was discovered long, long ago—does not last an hour. Therefore
the gutter receives your children. A privy—as it already happened—
will be their shelter, and a cut throat, as soon as they grow older,
will be their tutor. The near world and the distant world will not
listen entranced to the rhapsody of your death, for your cause
is not won.

Your heroism, therefore, is greater than the Japanese.

Against you, behind the files of the mercenaries, stands everything.
Aversion, fear, hate, the landlord's screams, the manufacturers'
sounding alarm, the cowards' secret intrigues and the deep (dark)
ignorance of misery. . . .

It is your lot to be dying for sacred ideals, to be dying without the
last solace of a brave man, without glory. But you did not go for the
sake of glory! You have sent yourself to wrest the world—against
the will of the world—from under the scepter of darkness. Your task
it is to annihilate man's oppression of man.

From under the suffering of flesh to unearth the human spirit and
to implant love and the right to happiness among people. You have
therefore challenged the might and the authority of the world. So
next to your martyr's cross, for even greater glory, they will place
the crosses of thieves.

For only Polish poetry will not abandon you, will not insult you,
oh soldier! She alone will not fear your dreams and your deeds.
Even if your cause were lost—she will remain faithful to you. She
will see and retain in her memory your days and nights, your suffering, effort, labor and death. She will place your head, battered by
mercenary rifle-butts, on a cushion of the most enchanting poems,
which she will for you alone take out after years from the splendor
of an age-old tongue. She will cover your naked body—that has no
golden belt and red *kontusz*[3] when the people of Lodz again and
again unearth it from the mass grave to give it a coffin of pinewood—
the only thing that the people can give—with a mantle of dignity

woven from the most enchanting hues of art. . . . She will place in
your torpid, lifeless hands, which are powerless in death alone, your
golden dream, the dream of so many generations of youth, the
dream of the knight's sword.[4]

Andrzej Strug's hero in *Underground Men* sacrifices his life to the
goals of revolution. His death still serves a purpose. A battle at his
funeral invigorates the movement:

Everything went off as it should. There were wreaths, there were
wide red ribbons and about a thousand people. They sang the *Red
Banner* over the grave. There was a funeral oration and the crowd
was listening—only the oration could not be finished. The Cossacks
charged into the cemetery and trampled the graves with their
horses. . . . And there was quite a fight, and several score arrested—
and great emotion.

A thing like that strengthens the people and sends gusts of wind
through the musty air of conspiratorial cellars. You were useful
even after death. You died in somebody else's bed—for the coffin
they dressed you in someone else's *surdut*[5] and in someone else's
hand-me-down shoes. . . .

Look—what did we ever have of our own? For years we didn't have
a place we could call our own. A minute that was ours? Personal
affairs?

One never particularly thought of such things—yet we were always
down—but always. . . .

It was a dog's life. . . . *(From The Obituary)*.

After World War II a change could be noticed in attitudes toward
self-sacrifice. A strong criticism arose against the policy of squandering
human life without a visible chance of victory. Political movements in
exile, on the whole, were opposed to the suicidal policy of self-sacrifice
in a futile struggle. The value had been modified by experience.
   In Russian cultural values, the concept of suffering and self-sacrifice
emanated partly from orthodox religious ideology. Penitence and self-
inflicted bodily suffering could also be found in sectarian movements.[6]
The Populists were removed from religious traditions but shared the
attitude toward self-sacrifice that penetrated Russian cultural values.

Selfless dedication to ethical-political principles was associated with their humanism. Their ethics however were in frequent and dialectical conflict with their tactics of terror. This also appears in Russian revolutionary literature.

Self-sacrifice may reflect a Machiavellian revolutionary creed. An extreme interpretation of this norm has been expressed by Bakunin, the anarchist, in *The Catechism of the Revolutionist* (written sometime in 1866). This document was attributed for a long time to Sergei Nechayev, whose story became a theme of Dostoyevsky's *The Possessed.* However, Max Nomad gives convincing evidence that Bakunin was the author. No doubt Nechayev carried the document to Russia; he shared the views. Most of the Populists rejected the Machiavellian philosophy credo of *The Catechism.* Although it was a creed of a minority, it does reflect where the concept of self-sacrifice can lead to. *The Catechism of the Revolutionist* begins: "The revolutionist is a doomed man. He has no personal interests, no affairs, sentiments, attachments, property, not even a name of his own. Everything in him is absorbed by one exclusive interest, one thought, one passion—the revolution."[7] The very title of Bakunin's principles, *Catechism*, indicates a religious influence in terminology.

During the first half of the last century among the Polish and Russian émigrés in Paris, a movement called "Messianism" grew. Towianski and Mickiewicz, the Polish poet, were its leaders. Poland was called "Christewicz" of nations. Through Poland's sacrifice (partition and foreign rule), salvation would be achieved. The Messianistic movement was a mystical one, religious as well as political.

In a well-working democratic, parliamentary system, compromise is respected and necessary. It is an important political technique. Lord Morley, in his classic book *On Compromise,* quotes Burke: "All government, indeed every prudent act, is founded on compromise, and barter." One could hardly find a Polish political writer who would expound a similar theory. While the British have stressed compromise in politics, the Poles, Russians, and Yugoslavs have stressed the principle, or "fundamentalism."

In the national politics of Poland and Russia, compromise had a bad reputation; it was considered almost on a par with opportunism. Statesmen who understood its significance had difficulty in using compromise techniques; when they did use them, they took pains to disguise them. A high value was placed on fundamentalism and on those who did not yield to compromise. Politics without or with little compromise is difficult, of course, and may even be impossible. The strong emphasis on principles, however, permitted the Poles to maintain their values and their political ideals under tribulations. Such were norms as reflected in Polish literature and noticeable in discussions and even behavior. Reytan, a member of the Polish Diet who in the eighteenth century rejected any compromise with the enemy over partition of Poland, was a national symbol.

World War II and subsequent foreign occupations and influence, a catastrophic defeat for Poland, also had a noticeable effect on Polish attitudes. The attitudes began to change toward an acceptance of an imperative of a compromise. But attitudes and norms of this type are subject to change; a crisis situation or a sudden change of political situation may again affect them. Those who were born or were in their early childhood during World War II voice their doubts about wisdom of the past history, although the heroic past is respected and deeply felt. So often this past is also a part—indeed a tragic part—of family history. In conversations, discussions, articles, views are expressed about political realism, the end of romanticism in politics, the imperatives of modern times. Those attitudes, under present conditions, cannot be measured by rigorous, quantitative techniques or opinion polls. Such views appear again and again, however.

Other attitudes also grow under a prolonged occupation or underground struggle. These have their serious, and frequently negative, implications. Let us imagine a child who was ten years old in 1939 in Warsaw when the city was occupied by the Germans. The Soviet occupation and a communist rule followed. When the boy reached the age of twenty-four, he would have grown up in the traditions of the underground struggle. Killing enemies was a virtue; forging papers was a necessity, often a condition, of survival (as was true under Nazi rule); lying to the conquerors became natural, necessary behavior. But once the conquerors have gone and a free government has emerged, the attitudes and behavior do not change at once. A negative attitude of distrust toward the very symbol of government may survive. The resistance developed high skills of destructive opposition; constructive opposition is an entirely different kind of political action. Some of those trained in underground techniques may, once in power, use these same ruthless methods to dispose of the opposition.

The underground democratic leadership could not control all the groups that operated illegally. In my conversations with underground leaders and members of underground forces, I heard again and again one comment: "This was a jungle." Native Polish right-wing extremists had their underground, too. They killed a number of Polish democratic leaders and persons of Jewish faith. The extremist right-wing underground was small, however ruthless and merciless. Various bands assumed a role of "independent" underground groups. Some of the bands engaged in banditry and took full advantage of the confusion. In towns and on the highways, the German Nazi conquerors ruled by terror and cruelty. This was "the gray jungle." In the forest and in the towns on the periphery of the underground grew another human jungle—the "grey" one.

As time went on, some of the boundaries between political and nonpolitical action began to blur. A holdup of a public institution and "confiscation" of their money had full legitimacy in an occupied and terrorized country. But . . . some of the Poles collaborated with the German enterprises; they made money and grew rich while others starved. Their expropriation seemed also legitimate. Such expropriation—in terms of technique—was an armed burglary. Even if not frequent, it took place. There were bands controlled by no one but their chieftains. Their deeds were on a borderline of banditry. Ethnic hostility was strong, religious hatred manipulated. And those sentiments also led to actions and destruction.

In the Vilna region especially, isolated groups of the guerrillas killed some Jews who survived the German holocaust. But even here, at least some cases had this strange aspect, frequent in Polish experience, of active and humane solidarity on one hand and hatred on the other.

In one case, a Polish squire (*Szlachta Zagononowa* corresponds to small gentry or a squire) who owned less than a hundred acres hid a number of Jewish families. At times of acute danger, the families were kept in cellars (*ziemianki*) dug in the fields and covered with earth. A number of such families were hidden by his tenant farmers. Mr. K., a Catholic, who organized this rescue operation himself, as well as his Catholic tenant farmers, risked their life. The place was visited several times by Lithuanian storm troopers, dreaded by the Poles even more than the Germans for their ruthlessness and cruelty. They were unable to find the refugees. After the German retreat, the Jewish families "surfaced" to life.

A detachment of guerrillas operating in this area invaded Mr. K.'s farm and killed two families, including a Polish-Catholic woman, a tenant farmer who was hiding the families. However, Mr. K. was warned by a member of this detachment, who was his kin, that his refugees were in danger, and he succeeded in hiding a number of them. (This writer interviewed Mr. K., who lives in western Poland now, and two of the survivors, now in the United States.)

With the corroding march of time, the external influences had some effect on the guerrillas. The extreme rightist elements tried to find their way into the ranks, and they represented the old inveterate prejudices and hatreds. However, the Socialists and the Peasant party had their own military organizations, integrated with the guerrillas. The Communist People's army was relatively weak and subordinated to the Soviet orders.

The underground had a tragic aftermath: it had a profound impact on moral standards. It had produced men and women of unusually strong moral principles, unyielding and noble—but it also had broken the morals of those who had lost hope and principles or who made an "adjustment" to the grey jungle.

Waclaw Zagorski, a captain of the underground Polish guerrillas under German occupation, touched on this dilemma: "We all tried a taste of the underground, and in this jungle we all believed at one time that the day will come when no one will be persecuted, followed, and trapped like an animal, no one will kill anybody, no one will need a disguise or false passports, or look for shelter in a strange home.

"Our underground paths have crossed and led to various places. Some in this struggle have forgotten their real goal; for them it was only important who kills whom, who instigates the oppression of man against man; their goal was only their own freedom. From the underground they went into the depths of this jungle where only the might of the stronger prevails, where a Chekist joins forces with a Nazi SS stormtrooper."[8]

Zagorski's dilemma is more profound. The underground of World War II was a school for selfless and heroic men, but it was also an experience in brutal struggle. It uprooted thousands who could never return to normal life. It trained people in the use of violence and also taught them the ultimate in sacrifice—life laid down for a cause.

The law of selection is at work in a "political jungle." Among the courageous and the selfless, casualties are heavy, while collaborationists and opportunists often may survive.

5. PERSONALITY TYPES

The response to seizure or conquest of power is not the same in all social classes or among all citizens. Some resist; others yield and collaborate. The attitude toward the conqueror or usurper may coincide with social stratification. Frequently, however, the attitudes are not necessarily distributed according to class structure. The personality factor has a significant share in attitude formation. Some individuals have strong values, others have weaker or different ones, and still others put different emphasis on different norms. The interaction between social environment and personality is reflected in the attitude toward the usurpers.

The European experience permits us to single out eight personality types that developed under oppressive foreign rule or native dictatorship.

The Resister. The resister is an active opponent of the regime. He forms and joins the underground and organizes an active struggle.

The Wallenrod. This term originated with a popular ballad by the Polish national poet Adam Mickiewicz. The hero of the ballad, Konrad Wallenrod (Valenrod), was a Lithuanian trying to avenge the suffering of his people inflicted by the Teutonic order. Konrad joins the order, becomes its grandmaster, and leads it in war against the Lithuanians, but purposely leads it to defeat, not victory. His treason was a moral act, for the Teutonic order had shown no mercy to his people. Konrad Wallenrod captured the imagination of the Poles, who coined a term in his name: "Wallenrodysm" (pronounced "Valenrodism"). A man who "wallenrodes" collaborates with the enemy, but for the purpose of destroying him. Strangely enough, the history of Poland does not offer too many Wallenrods, although so much has been spoken about them. There was no one in a historical sense to be compared with the story of the grandmaster of the Teutonic order. However, there were probably some minor ones in the resistance, for example, resisters who owned cafes and restaurants and catered to higher German officials, showing them friendship and outward allegiance, and in that way obtaining information for the underground. In the so-called blue police, which was collaborationist, officers were planted by the resistance.

In resistance lore, tales are still circulated about Wallenrods who were killed by mistake by the very resistance they had served. Only the top leaders knew their real identity and assignment. Despite its romantic implication, the role of a Wallenrod did not agree with the nineteenth and mid-twentieth century Polish cultural pattern. In a Polish adage a man "fights with an open visor."

The Sympathizer (*sympatyk*). The sympathizers do not join the underground; however, they support the movement, morally as well as materially, as the need arises. The term was generally used by the Poles during the revolution of 1905, and A. Strug in his novel, *Underground Men*, tells the story of a *sympatyk*, a friendly but not organized or "disciplined" supporter.

The Positivist. The positivist is not an adherent of a foreign or authoritarian rule, but recognizes that the conquerors or usurpers are more powerful than his countrymen and that open rebellion cannot succeed. Therefore he suggests some sort of modus vivendi that could create the best possible conditions for the conquered.

In the history of Poland, positivism has had its tradition, although one that has been challenged. Before the insurrection of 1863 Wielopolski suggested such a solution for the Poles within the Russian empire, but the youth and the Insurrectionist party rejected his policies, especially when the oppressive measures of the Russian government followed. After the collapse of the insurrection, the positivist movement gained and has been known since by that name. The term is used here in a far broader sense than its original meaning had. Polish positivism after 1863 was a definite, well-developed philosophy. The Polish Conservative party in the Austro-Hungarian empire followed a similar line. Under German rule the positivist concept was completely rejected. Now among the intellectuals in the Soviet bloc, positivism has been revived as a policy of cultural survival and economic development under the Communist rule.

True Believer. The true believer is one who shares the ideology and loyally supports the ideologies and interests of the conqueror. After the German occupation of Poland, among the true believers were the *Volksdeutsche*, members of the German minority who embraced Nazism. In Norway, under leadership, a party was formed affiliated with the German National Socialists. Some of the true believers honestly support the party policy for ideological reasons; the rest are positivists or opportunists.

The Opportunist. The opportunist joins the conquerors or the

new elite out of self-interest—for money or status. The lower stratum
is the *lumpen* opportunist, the criminal or amoral elements. Under the
German rule in Poland, this group was not insignificant. Various types of
opportunists appeared, and the new experience soon affected the everyday
language of the city and urban and criminal folklore. New marginal or
criminal occupations were identified in a language of the street, which
made clear-cut, sometimes striking, distinctions. These "professional"
types carried appellations difficult to translate into English. Here belong
the *szmalcovnik,* men or women who made considerable money denoun-
cing Jews. It was difficult for the Germans to distinguish Jews from non-
Jews, but the Poles were accustomed to the variant accents in Polish of
certain Jewish groups who used Yiddish, and the *"szmalcovnik"* readily
helped to track down victims. When the Germans fled Poland on the eve
of the Russian invasion, another group, the *szabrovnik,* was making
money by stealing the contents of abandoned apartments.

   The Ambivalent.   When a conquest succeeds, most people are
bewildered by the new situation. They want only to adjust to it and
survive. In order to survive, anyone must more or less obey the laws and
orders of the victors. The more courageous ones offer as little cooperation as possible. Others who fear for their lives and those of their
families are overly eager in their willingness to obey. Some hate the
regime and sympathize with the resistance, but being fearful for their
survival, they collaborate. They try to resolve this inner conflict. It is
a conflict of conscience. The conquerors represent the "negative" pole
on the value scale, the resisters the "positive" one. But the hiatus is
wide, and the polarity of norms cannot be reconciled, shifted to the
middle. It is also a practical problem. To resist means to risk life or
liberty now; to collaborate may mean to risk it in the future, once the
resisters win. And in Eastern Europe and the Balkans, a peasant remem-
bers that three powerful emperors have lost their empires in his own
lifetime. Out of this conflict grows the feeling of ambivalence, of not
being able to join one side or the other. The ambivalent, finding himself
in one situation, "attaches" himself to the appropriate group, and a
short time later, when in a different group, he becomes either pro- or
anti-Communist, pro- or anti-Fascist, whatever the situation calls for.
He shifts his position, even changing his basic attitudes, from day to
day and within the same day. In his office in the morning, say in
Hungary, he is pro-Rakosi, loudly praising his merits and policies. In
the evening he meets his old friends; they are "anti," so now he is
anti-Rakosi too, and voices his opposition.[9]

   The Survivor.   A survivor wants to live and thus avoids dangers and problems. He does not sympathize with the conqueror or those who have captured power and imposed their rule. He "keeps out of trouble" and tries to survive. A survivor is often a man who dislikes the regime, who even has a moral aversion to its policies but feels helpless, and sees any effort of opposition as futile. After all, he is too weak to change the world. He may have a family, or a person dear to him, and he tries to protect them from danger. Of course, conditions may turn one into an opportunist and another into a resister. In principle, however, a survivor has a major goal: to live and escape persecutions, and at the same time to do his best to remain honest. This is not an easy task, and not a new dilemma.

A gifted Italian playwright, Vittorio Alfieri, wrote in 1777 a brilliant study called *About Tyranny* (Della tirannide). The second book of this volume is dedicated to three major themes, each of them with a special chapter: (1) How to vegetate under a tyranny ("In quando modo si possa vegetare sulla tirannide"); (2) How to live under tyranny; (3) How to die under tyranny. One can vegetate, he suggests, in a servile, timorous way, which one could not call life—in respect (honor) for the human species. It is a vegetation. But, if one wants to survive, keep at a distance from the tyrant, from his satellites and the honors he may offer, from his corruption, distant even from the walls of his palaces, from his gardens and territories. Choose this distance from those who rule, retire into solitude and think. You may think in your loneliness, exchange your views with some trusted friends, and eventually even write. Almost two centuries later, Pasternak has chosen this type of life.

Tyranny in every place and at all times—writes Alfieri—is always a tyranny. He compares his contemporary European tyrannies to Asiatic ones. His definitions are still interesting. Alfieri wrote in times of the Inquisition, and when he writes about the priests, one may consider the Inquisition in Europe at his time. "I say"—writes Alfieri—"that fear, militia, and religion [hierarchy,] are three pillars of tyrannies, European or Asiastic." Democracies also have their militias, he argues further, but this is an entirely different type of an armed force, since it is under elective, democratic control and cannot be compared with the heads (*capi*) of the armed forces of a tyrant. The officers and government of a republic are controlled and constrained by laws and by parliaments. His *sacerdoti* priests are, of course, those of higher hierarchy in times of religious persecutions. Change *despot* to *supreme leader* or to *Führer* or *Duce*, his *priests* to *party ideologists,* and *aristocracy* to *party elite,* and a modern authoritarian establishment seems to appear. Election of a tyrant does not make him mellow or less despotic, argues Karl A. Wittfogel (in his *Oriental Despotism,* Yale University Press 1950).

The nature of absolute rule, the patterns of political behavior of the subjects of the tyrant was well known to Aristotle as well as to Montesquieu. The continuity of absolute power, the repetition of political patterns, is rather striking.

During the first years of Communist rule, the Czechs developed their own taxology. As the story was told in the streets of Prague, the Communists are divided into three types: rock, wood, and water Communists. The rock Communists are firm like a rock. The wood Communists hide in the woods and come out when they see who is winning. The water Communists jump into the political waters, and they know how to swim.

The same person, who in a democratic state under the rule of the law is a law-abiding, peaceful, even a respected citizen, under totalitarian rule may become an accomplice to cruelty, oppression, brutality, all in order to survive. The ambivalent remains, however, continuously in a dilemma between survival and treason, collaboration or resistance.

After liberation, the story of a resistance shapes the cultural pattern and attitude of a nation. Usually the leaders of the resistance take or come to power; the virtues of the resistance are now emphasized, exaggerated, glorified, and become a part of the new national myth. While the occupation lasts, however, there is some kind of moral stratification according to values and attitudes. If the occupation is mild, the positivist attitude spreads; if it is repressive, as that of the German totalitarians, the resistance movement gains in strength, but at the same time the drive to survive forces people into ambivalence and opportunism. A long and cruel occupation eventually divides the people into a small group of resisters and a large group of opportunists and multivalents.

6. LOYALTIES

Ambivalence appears in problems of loyalties. Men of the resistance remain loyal to the authority which they recognize: an underground committee and usually an exiled group. Their compatriots must, if they are to survive, make some show of loyalty to the new rulers. A strong underground movement affects the loyalties of weaker personalities, especially the ambivalents, which otherwise may shift in favor of the usurpers.

During the German occupation in Poland, the underground movement exercised an effective social control through a special organization: civil resistance.

The civil resistance was divided into passive and active phases. Passive resistance took such forms as slowdowns in factories and sabotage of railroads. One of the functions of active civil resistance was maintenance of loyalties toward the Polish republic and exercise of social control over the pattern of political behavior. Through the underground press and radio (via London, listened to in Poland), the chief of civil resistance set the rules of political behavior toward the Germans. According to Stefan Korbonski, former chief of civil resistance, special rules were issued for diverse social classes or occupational groups—farmers, workers, physicians, lawyers, clergy, and many others. For instance, physicians were to provide special certificates to Poles that would release them from forced labor; factory managers must make every effort to raise the salaries of workers; the public was urged to boycott certain places of entertainment; and the "Ten Commandments of Civil Struggle" were published in *Bieuletyn Informacyjny*, an official publication of the Polish underground.[10]

Special underground courts were instituted to try the cases of those who had broken the rules of civil resistance or those who were guilty of collaboration with the enemy. Three kinds of penalties were administered: admonition, infamy, and the death sentence. The death sentence was executed by special underground platoons. The invocation of national infamy, an old Polish institution, and milder admonitions were published in the underground press and called for a boycott.

7. TYPES OF UNDERGROUND ORGANIZATIONS

Theory and practice have contributed to the development of various types of underground organizations. Our classification of types follows, in very general lines, historical experience. Here are the major types, which appeared in the past. This typology is not a perfect logical exercise. No sharp, distinct lines can be drawn between the types, and sometimes they do overlap. Broadly three types of underground organizations may be distinguished: junta; secret society; underground mass movement.

A *junta* is a secret military conspiracy. Its members control strategic elements, such as an army or police. The time span of the underground life of a junta is relatively short, as its goal may be an immediate seizure of power. The German military anti-Hitler plot on 20 July 1944 had this character.

A *secret society* is a limited underground movement, without a broad and strong support of, or contact with, a nation or a social class. Examples are the Populist movement in Russia in its initial stage, the Decembrists, and the Carbonari in Italy. Their contact with the peasantry or workers was weak and their emphasis was often on the development of a revolutionary elite.

The *underground mass movement* has usually a broad social base, wide support of organized members and sympathizers, and effective contacts with a social class or with the nation to which it appeals or at least certain segments of a nation. The underground organizations in France, Yugoslavia, and Poland during World War II, with their wide ramifications, may serve here as an example.

The junta is typical of a coup d'état or revolutions "from above." Without question, a small organization having at its command regiments of soldiers who obey orders is well suited for such actions. This type of an organization can act swiftly and efficiently.

In contrast to the junta the underground mass movement aims at revolution from "below"—a revolution in which the multitudes are moved to action. In the last stage of the latter, the underground movement merges with and usually leads an open revolution with mass participation. Such were the cases of the revolution of 1905 in Russia and in Poland, and the Warsaw Uprising of 1944.

The secret society may move both ways. The Russian Decembrists formed a combination of a secret society and a junta. Secret societies of officers and intellectuals had access to as well as command of structured, disciplined sections of the army. A revolution based on this type of an organization and respective tactics was called by the early nineteenth-century historians and theorists, to mention the Italian writer Vincenzo Cuoco, a "military revolution." Their tactic was a "revolution from above," directed against the central government, designed to capture political power at the top. This type of revolution, which was planned by the Decembrists for 1825, was also typical during this period in Latin countries, especially Italy, Spain, South America. Two generations later, from late 1860 to 1905, a secret society of Russian Populists evolved into a Social Revolutionary party, which in a later stage (1917) rode on the waves of a revolution from below and turned into a powerful mass party. It is difficult to indicate precisely the moment a secret society has been transformed into an underground mass movement. In general terms, the type of organization is indicative of, and determined by, the type and conditions of struggle: the junta indicates a revolution from above, an underground mass movement, a revolution from below. All three types of movements may have a party structure which is again adjusted to its goals, tactics, and conditions of struggle. (The structures of such parties is discussed in Chapter III.)

8. LEADERSHIP

Leadership in the underground demands specific abilities, skills, and—in times of crisis—dedication and strong convictions. Here belongs the ability to make decisions and respond immediately to a situation. A president of a republic may be hesitant, his decision may sometimes be procrastinative, and he will still survive. The national leader of an underground movement and his organization usually have fewer alternatives (options) open to them, or situations are pressing and call more often for immediate decision. The means of communication are different from those in open political life. In a democracy a gifted orator may sway the voters by means of radio or television. A statesman may win the public through his writings, or by presenting his views and ideas in a parliament or in public meetings. But an underground leader is known only to a few. He does not make speeches and appeals, and does not sign articles with his true name. His ability lies in organization, secrecy, underground strategy, judgment, and decision.

Organization of secrecy is a skill. The leader at the top of the underground hierarchy knows more about the whole organization than members of the individual cells. Only the few members of the central committee know most of the details. Members of the cells, even leaders of sections, receive only orders and information that are necessary and limited to their narrow assignments. They share the ideology and are dedicated to final goals. They do not ask questions. As a rule, in the Polish resistance all members used pseudonyms, as was the general practice in the socialist underground at the end of the nineteenth century.

The underground movement is under constant pressure, it is continuously spied upon. Leadership calls for "knowledge of the people," understanding of personality and character, evaluation of their trustworthiness. The leader who admits a man into higher secrets of the organizations takes on a heavy responsibility, for one traitor, one weakling, may bring death to many. An underground leader is, in this respect, a personnel manager in a large secret enterprise engaged in dangerous and risky activities. The intense nature of outside pressure and of hostilities integrates the group, forces a close cooperation, and favors dedicated friendship. These conditions may also affect the leadership, since the informal relations call for high degree of personal trust.

Under conditions of a ruthless conquest and unyielding resistance, the leaders of an underground are not elected in political conventions. The leadership is a vanguardist one selected from a few trusted people. Thus the organization is in a sense an elitist one—centralistic with strong discipline. Democratic controls cannot operate under conditions of continuous danger and high secrecy. Sooner or later the leadership becomes a group of professional revolutionaries.

A competent military leader of underground forces possesses specific qualifications such as an understanding of social forces and social problems. Success of his struggle depends largely on popular response. The underground army is not a regular army, discipline cannot be enforced the way it is in a conscripted or professional army. All men are volunteers, they can desert almost whenever they desire. The morale and ideological commitment of the underground army is therefore of primary significance. On the other hand, the success of underground operations depends on the support of the population.

A nationwide underground movement, directed against a foreign and conquering power, as the Polish movement was, also has a vast and specialized network of organizations with its corresponding civilian-political and military leadership. The personality of underground leaders varies, of course. A brief profile of a national military underground leader may serve here as an illustration. General Monter, field commander of the Warsaw uprising, can be considered representative of an underground military leader of a national movement. He was a professional officer of the Polish army, with higher military and civilian academic education. While in the regular army, he had strong democratic leanings. His underground assignment, however, gave him experience that helped in the development of specific qualities. He does not remind one of a prewar European army officer with strong caste feelings. In civilian clothing, he was free from the stiff military behavior pattern one is accustomed to finding among continental army officers. His ideal of the army was a citizen army. Monter understood the primary significance of ideology in the formation of an underground army. Without an ideology that appeals to underground soldiers, an underground army is hardly possible. Only a democratic ideology, he explains—in conversations with this writer—could appeal during the uprising to the large mass of the people and to an underground army led against a totalitarian conqueror. On the other hand, the program of the underground also had to appeal to the general population, especially to the working class and the peasantry. Monter's emphasis was on popular support through proper ideological appeal with clear candid answers to major social problems, oriented toward more political, social, and economic equality and just, proper distribution of national income. "I did not choose the moment of the Warsaw uprising, nor was it chosen by national leadership," he continued. "Two factors had to be evaluated: the strategic situation and the mood of the population, the psychological factor. The Russians were approaching and Germans now faced a regular army just at the city limits. The Soviet army was on the other bank of the river. On the other hand the psychological pressure from below was strong. We felt this. If the leadership would not order an uprising and lead the revolution, a spontaneous popular struggle would have begun, without any central leadership. There was little choice."[11]

9. SOME COMPARISONS AND COMMENTS

An underground movement should be analyzed or studied in a "context situation," in its relation to and interaction with the social, economic, and political situation at a given historical period. This is of course an elementary, also an essential step and approach. But the simple statement that an underground movement is solely a consequence of social, economic and political conditions is only part valid; it is a kind of a part-truth which may be misguiding, even false.

Man responds in a variety of ways to the same situation, a number of alternatives (options) are usually open, and the relevant problem is why A responds differently from B, why many Germans responded to similar situations, such as crisis, unemployment, differently from the majority of British, why some sections of the Frenchmen responded differently to the German occupation than others. Differences in perception of situation are usually explained by class position of the subject, or on the other hand by his values which are rooted in religious ethos, sometimes displaced from the latter into politics. These theories, useful as they are, supply only a part of the answer.

Related but different experiences may assist in posing the question. Sometimes, one single idea-symbol in a specific situation has a powerful appeal which blurs class and party lines, and even religious differences within one creed. Israel is an unusual experiment. In twenty years a stable and prosperous democratic republic, with pragmatic socialist institutions, has been built in a desert by immigrants who arrived after brutal persecutions and settled in an entirely new and different geographical environment. The appeal of a homeland—a historical, powerful social myth, a "single vision"—cannot be overlooked here as a powerful stimulus. After suffering in concentration camps one could expect a kind of collective psychological breakdown rather than an outburst of national energy.

Georges Sorel recognized early the power of a "social myth" in his *Reflexions sur la violence* [Reflections on violence]. It was also this social myth that motivated Israeli resistance, organized into an underground. The underground network the Israelis built so effectively did not come from nowhere. It was built by Polish and Russian Jews, and it followed traditions, experience, and skills which appeared in those countries three quarters of a century earlier, and at times were practiced in political struggle against foreign invasion and native political oppression. Again the underground "technique" had an old tradition.

The social and political plight of the European Jews was in this case a *necessary* but not a sufficient causal variable. Only in association with the psychological appeal of a historical, social myth and with traditions and skills, and last but not least, massive economic aid, the causal combination became *sufficient*. The combination of all, at least in this specific case, resulted in an effective underground political activity.

The historical underground movements of Eastern Europe and World War II are different from terroristic activities in the United States, in Quebec, Canada, and in Belfast, Northern Ireland. The question here is, where is the cause, the stimulus? In the first case, the two groups must be treated separately: the black militants and ethnic extremists on one hand, and student radicals on the other. We speak, of course, about the late sixties.

The terroristic activities of student "microparties" cannot be easily explained by economic deprivations of the participants or by oppressive political, social, and economic conditions. The terrorists are not poverty-stricken proletarians, nor do they represent trends within the working class, although they may identify with its symbols. They are students, largely from the middle-upper class, or in the second case, members of marginal classes of an ethnic or racial minority. They are not laborers, textile workers, miners, mechanics, or teamsters. Terroristic activities in the United States have not originated among impoverished families of Appalachia, among unemployed coal miners, but among well-fed students living comfortably. Some of the young, semi-underground activists among American blacks also do not belong to those really deprived. The American "submerged"—part legal, part secret radical groups of the 1960s—began their activities during a booming, if later declining economy—thus far in human history, a period of an unprecedented wage scale.

There is no political oppression. The "underground" operates in a nation whose people enjoy wide political freedoms and respect for personal views. Cries of and accusations about "repression" do not change the hard fact that America today is one of the major examples (next to Great Britain, Holland, Canada, Australia, and a few other nations) of a nation enjoying a rule based on advanced political and religious toleration, perhaps one of the most advanced in the history of mankind.

True, these "microparties" are not the classical underground organizations. The paradox is that the American microparties advocating violence did operate largely (not entirely) as legal movements. Violence was advocated openly, even on televised interviews of some of the leaders. It is a strange American phenomenon: the extremist microparties were legal but also submerged, their violent counterparts operating secretly in a kind of "underground." From time to time caches of weapons were discovered and confiscated. The groups were small, but

their right to violent activities was defended by some who "follow the
trend" or have a totalitarian and elitist bent and by a wide public
opinion dedicated to a candid expression of political views in a variety
of ways, even if one personally rejects violence.

The following is part of a news release of 2 January, 1970 from the
U. S. Department of Justice about some of the academic activities of
what was called radical student movements:

> Typifying some of the other activities of the various factions . . . was
> the dynamiting of four high powered transmission towers in January,
> 1969, in and around Denver, Colorado.

> The new heights [were] reached during the year 1968-1969, in
> connection with campus disruption. There were demonstrations on
> over 225 college campuses with 61 incidents of arson and bombing.
> Over 4000 individuals were arrested, nearly 2000 building seizures
> or sit-ins occurred, and known damage to campus facilities soared
> over $3,000,000. At least one death and over 125 injuries were
> reported. Continuing the trend, the current school year has seen
> approximately 215 demonstrations thus far, including 24 sit-ins or
> building seizures. Additionally, 52 demonstrations have been held
> against the ROTC program and damage thus far attributed to the
> demonstrations has amounted to well over $1,000,000. There have
> been 16 incidents of arson on campuses, two bombings, over 350
> arrests, and 33 police officers have been injured.

> It was neither by accident nor coincidence that the demonstrations
> held in Washington and San Francisco in November 1969, had
> accompanying anti-U. S. demonstrations in other countries throughout
> the world on the same day.

Indeed, in medieval times student violence was not unknown, but it
was never directed against the university, against buildings or libraries.
Even scholarly and personal manuscripts of the faculty were not spared
as was the case in New York, at the Columbia University campus.

The Vietnam war and the struggle for elementary rights of a racial
minority are a major causal variable. This seems to be a valid argument.
The problem of and the issues raised by the militant and violent microparties of racial and ethnic minorities were different, however. They had
a narrow social base and directed their appeal to the socially deprived
living in slums of the large metropolitan areas. Here, the socioeconomic

position of sympathizers of the militants may explain, in part, support for the latter.

There is a specific class element here, but perhaps not a distinctly social and economic one, and certainly not a very simple one. Here is a problem of generations. The students serve in the army and with other young men fight the war. This war—for a number of reasons—was an unpopular one with substantial sections of American college students. Many believed the war was wrong and chose to actively oppose it. In other historical situations, American students have protested war. It does provide a stimulus and reason for a protest. However, a variety of ways of protest were open; why was a tactic of violence and semisecret microparties chosen?

A quasisecret, underground organization has a variety of appeals. Extreme sacrifice appeals to the heroic sentiment. Ideological appeal cannot be reduced to the rational or the irrational, both explained by rigorous methods and disciplines. The tedium of life and routine of everyday activities strikes a contrast with heroism during great moments of mankind, moments that were made known to future militants and their admirers by college textbooks, movies, and novels. The past affects the future by its images, by heroic panoramas, and happy outbursts of victory.

Heroic appeal is often solely an intensification or an expression of a powerful ethical motivation more than often underestimated or simply disregarded in a rigorous empirical approach. The dialectics of *real* and *ideal* is a powerful moving force. Our ethics suggest devotion, mutual aid, equality, social justice. This is ethics of a Judeo-Christian tradition, which also motivates agnostics. Young people acquire these values in childhood, and although they may leave the formal church or lose the faith of their ancestors, they still carry their ethics, which motivate them strongly. The hiatus between ideal goals—an ideal image of society—and daily reality acts as a powerful incentive in our civilization rooted in Judeo-Christian ethical traditions. Other great religions may accept misery and suffering as normal conditions of man. We do not. Our outlook is optimistic—society can be changed, all can enjoy and share products of our hands and minds; hunger and war are not a historical necessity. But a comfortable life becomes a sin and produces guilt when other people suffer misery and hunger. The religious motivation is here again alive and projected into political perceptions and calls for heroism, sacrifice, and martyrdom. These sensitive young who enjoyed the wealth and comfort of their parents, wealth arrived at by meritless inheritance or what they see as ruthless business, may be affected even more than others.

There is also an additional "political" class element: political power. A new class of educated people has appeared in America. This class is larger than in previous generations; it embraces a subclass of students and faculty members of more than seven and a half million. A numerically small and marginal fraction of this class, but still visible and conspicuous at times, acting as "style-setters," made a bid for power in the late 1960s. The followers rationalized their will with a negative ideology, which they advocated with a fiery dedication, a kind of a political piety. Tactics suggested this choice of part legal, part secret microparties and of violence. These small groups had been unable in a working democracy to win majorities and impose their will. They were heard better and hoped to impose their will by means of semisecret microparties, which had a tactical advantage: elements of surprise, and aggressive action, which influences the weak and also leaves an impression of a powerful mass movement. The slogans and symbols of those movements were democratic and egalitarian. Their leadership and political objectives were, in spite of symbolism, primarily elitist. They saw themselves as a group of future leaders.

The new "underground" activitists frequently professed "proletarian" ideologies. They spoke and wrote about liberating workers and identified their programs with the fate of labor. However, American labor did not identify with them. The black and white radical groups claimed representation of an abstract, nonexistent international working class, while they were opposed by real workingmen, whom they derogatively called "hardhats." The socioeconomic situation of the American working class has had little, if any, connection with the emergence of the American terroristic underground movement of the 1960s. In fact, it is difficult to find in the past any groups so strongly alienated from the workingmen as these more recent underground extremists.

The appearance of these groups cannot be explained by a single major cause. True, the war in Asia and civil rights issues concerning the relative deprivation of certain sections of the population provided a social situation which was conducive to various types of strong protest action. But the specific type of political behavior and tactics—to suggest a hypothesis—was a result of a combination of factors, and among them the socioeconomic situation was not necessarily the "sufficient" one, with the exception of specific cases within the black militant movement.

And this would also call for a lengthy analysis of a rather complex causality.

This general discussion suggests a need for a multifactor analysis, and a pluralistic not a monistic, single causal model.

In the Canadian province of Quebec, in 1970 members of a terroristic underground movement, Front de Libération Québecois (FLQ) kidnapped and murdered Pierre Laporte, a member of a provincial government, and later abducted a British diplomat. The government was forced to declare a state of emergency in an attempt to protect public order, and even life and freedom of prospective victims. In a historical perspective of two centuries, Quebec is a conquered province—the French lost, the British won. The economic position of Quebec, especially that of the French population, does not equal the highest living standards in Canada. But such conditions have existed for many years, perhaps for two centuries. Why then did the underground movement of the extremist French-Canadians appear in 1970? Why did a terroristic struggle begin at that time? A number of democratic methods are open to the struggle for improving political, social, and economic status. In this case, as in the others, the class position of the actors and social and economic conditions are not sufficient by themselves to explain an underground organization in Quebec, even if its program claims so. Moreover, the Quebec "front" took full advantage of democratic institutions and political freedoms Canadians enjoy in their country. The ethnic tension, however, was a factor, as well as nationalistic tendencies combined with a radical ideological appeal. In this specific case, we may identify ethnic tension and ethnic identification as one of the causal variables, but again, it is not a sufficient one. Ethnic problems, as was mentioned, did exist before and did not move the French-Canadians to underground struggle.

The case of the underground Irish Republican Army (IRA) in Belfast in 1969-1971 bears some similarity with Quebec. The underground, the so-called Irish Republican Army, operates in a democratic country where citizens enjoy extensive political rights. The Irish are Catholics, the English largely Protestants; hence ethnic tension is intensified by a religious one. Moreover, socioeconomic conditions and class divisions coincide to a degree with ethnic and religious divisions.

Thus, the ethnic and religious conflict was intensified by class conflict.

The Irish workers in Dublin earn probably as much as or perhaps less than their kin in Belfast. Dubliners, at least, do not conceal that many

of them are better off in London than in Dublin.[12] The ethnic and
religious differences are almost absent in Dublin, but not those of class.
However, differences in the Irish capital were not conducive to open
conflict or violence similar to what has been happening in Belfast. In
consequence, the causes of the emergence of a secret Irish army in the
Ulster area cannot be reduced to the single one of socioeconomic
conditions in the area. True, it is a major, contributing, perhaps even
necessary cause, but in this case, so it seems, not the only or a sufficient
one. Again, here, as in other cases, underground and violent activities
are a consequence of a combination of causal factors in specific,
historical, traditional contexts.

General habits of thinking and modes of thought are anchored in what
we may call a "monocausal model," a single causal chain consisting of an
antecedent and a sequent, popularly called a cause and an effect. The
"why-because" habit of thinking is a basic pattern, and whenever we try
to understand a problem we usually think that way. Thus, a general
category of "socioeconomic conditions and class" is an easy and
habitual model for explaining anything that happens, to disrupt social
order. In such an approach, it is given as general, single (but not always
entirely valid) cause of all possible effects. True, it is a "background
category," important but not sufficient for discovering the nature and
the causes of all social ills, or all social phenomena.

We may move perhaps a step further in our search. Eighty years
ago, Lombroso and Laschi wrote an almost entirely forgotten book on
revolutions.[13] Most of the findings are dated today and some of the
theories are untenable. But incidents cited and some of the data are
still of interest. Lombroso and Laschi suggest that propagation of
revolutions can be fostered and facilitated by changes in communica-
tions: steamship and telegraph (in their time) supplied materials to
newspapers rather rapidly when compared with the eighteenth century.
They also point to the fact that once a revolution took place in a
Spanish-speaking nation, the trend seemed to move to other hispanic
republics in Latin America. Thus, modern communication may have
contributed to the diffusion of Spanish-Portuguese revolutionary actions,
they argue.

What we call today an underground movement is a broad network of
secret organizations. This involves the structuring of group and specific
behavioral patterns in a certain way. Institutional and behavioral patterns have diffused frequently in the history of man, and the institutional
and behavioral patterns of underground movements, as any other, may
also have a tendency toward diffusion.

In our time, by 1970, underground organizations with elitist tendencies—most of them practicing tactical violence—have appeared in the United States, Canada, South America, Europe, and Asia. They have appeared also in democratic countries and their action is frequently directed against democratic institutions. There is more to it. This is a tactical pattern of political aggression, and the tactics and timing of various actions may suggest a coordinated movement. Some of the "activists" are trained outside their own territories; Cuba is a good example. The way such movements are financed and supported may suggest the nature of this coordination.

But—an argument follows—patterns may diffuse by themselves provided that certain social, economic, and political conditions exist. The answer is not simple. A behavioral pattern may "propagate" in a variety of conditions.

The "submerged" microparties of today's America (which enjoy the freedoms offered by an advanced democracy) are entirely different from and can hardly be compared with the underground in France during the Nazi occupation. A handful of rather comfortably living boys and girls reading an "underground" paper in New York or San Francisco or a few young editors publishing an "underground paper" in Greenwich Village, with their telephones, business offices, distribution, and salaries, protected by laws and a metropolitan police force, enjoying freedom of press is, again, a different political phenomenon from the Russian underground world of the last quarter of the nineteenth century. They have, of course, appeared under entirely different conditions. Under the czarist rule, there was no freedom of press or freedom of political association and assembly. In Russia, an entire underground way of life came into existence. It was called *podpolshchina,* in Polish *podziemie.* It seems to me that only in these two languages a term has been coined—and a good one—to represent underground cultural and political life.[14] Various underground parties, literary activities that could not pass censorship, and intellectual trends belonged to this underground world. This was not a matter of one or two microparties or underground secret societies; the Russian and Polish undergrounds developed into secret intellectual and cultural movements. A like phenomenon is appearing again in Russia today, especially as a literary underground movement. Books are copied by hand and diffused. This time, however, there is no organized movement, only a spontaneous, unstructured, intellectual exchange and discussion—at least according to the scarce news one receives.

10. EIGHT INFERENCES

A wider comparative approach to underground behavior and organizations leads us to a few tentative conclusions:

1. Underground movements have appeared under a variety of socioeconomic and political conditions and in nations with different political practices and institutions.

2. The type of organization and behavior varies under different conditions; movements differ in their ideology, appeal and recruitment because of different conditions.

3. In the twentieth century, socioeconomic imbalance seldom has resulted in the kind of underground networks that appear during foreign occupation or extreme political oppression. In our times, especially, socioeconomic problems have not been a sufficient cause for the emergence of an underground movement, although it is a necessary or contributing one. In the 1960s and 1970s, the underground network in the United States was mainly the result of political and ethnic tensions and intensive war protest, and its primary appeal was either political or ethnic-racial.

4. The underground pattern may diffuse by communication from one place to another or by imitation. It may also spread as a result of an organized, coordinated tactical pattern of political aggression.

5. An underground organization usually has some kind of an "external base" abroad (associated group or party) from which it derives at least part of its support. Underground movements usually have an internal and external base of operations. By the "internal base" we mean the organization within the area of secret activities, opposition, or struggle; by the "external," a kind of "supply base" from which support in the form of money and equipment, as well as moral and political support, comes.

6. Historically, political underground movements were directed against foreign conquerors or authoritarian or autocratic regimes, and their struggle included demands of political rights and basic freedoms. During the twentieth century, the techniques and tactics of these historical underground movements have been used against democratic institutions and governments by only partially submerged groups within society. Thus far, however, in democratic countries having relatively stable governments, where social policies are progressive and living standards high, the underground organizations have been limited to small secret socie-

ties (which we have called secret "microparties"). Thanks to political freedom, they have tactical advantages not available to those movements which oppose or opposed authoritarian or autocratic governments. Potentially, they can exist and survive better than the latter. In certain cases their membership and ideology may be indicative of the appearance of authoritarian tendencies, of attempts to impose the rule of a small and ruthless political minority over large majorities. The use of the tactics of violence by such organizations may considerably affect the stability of democratic nations and lead to drastic measures, which in turn may limit political liberties.

7. In democratic countries, underground movements thus far have appeared primarily in times of a serious political crisis—such as an unpopular war opposed by large sections of society—and during intense ethnic or ideological tensions.

8. Underground patterns have developed in a variety of ways, for they originate under specific historical conditions. Foreign conquest may force a nation or groups within that nation into resistance. Once the underground struggle becomes one of the few remaining alternatives of political action and liberation, it may sometimes continue for generations (e.g., Bulgaria, Serbia, Poland, Armenia). Similarly, an underground struggle against an autocratic rule may continue for several generations (Russia). Skills and patterns acquired in such struggle may leave their imprint permanently on traditions, values, institutions, and political behavior. When such a struggle is limited to a relatively short historical period (e.g., Denmark and Holland during World War II), then basic political patterns and values probably remain unaffected.

In the United States, dynamic social policy which would answer the urgent problems of the deprived, marginal classes could weaken support for, and the rationale of, some of the microparties dedicated to violent action. Such a policy is, after all, an imperative for other moral and political reasons. But a pattern has been established, a way of life has been tried by some of the young, a political and social style has been introduced.

11. POSTSCRIPTUM, MARCH 1972

The time distance gives us today a better perspective of the American unrest. The postwar civil rights protest movement of long duration grew in emotional intensity in the late 1960s. This intensity of sentiments could be sensed rather than measured. At a certain point, the highly sensitive issue of a long and unpopular war in Vietnam, perhaps a general, rising feeling against war and international violence, supplied a new impetus. It was the war issue which at a critical moment triggered a torrent of massive protest movements on campuses and affected directly the attitudes toward the government.

Small, well-disciplined groups with their tactics of violence played a visible and conspicuous role in this historical drama. In case of a massive and prolonged violent street action, there was a chance that those groups could take over the leadership of a leaderless mass and further their own political aims.

A hope of an end of hostilities with withdrawal of American troops from Vietnam, even if slow, had its effects. The civil rights movement gave its positive results. The change was visible. In banks, department stores, factories, even in construction, blacks were and are employed in a higher proportion than ever before. Black mayors were elected. Also, the economic slump had its consequences on employment outlooks of the new generations. The violence subsided; so did the intensity of protest movements. On the campuses, the influence of marginal, radical groups began to decline rapidly. New problems appeared. And the new entering freshmen classes were also different. The American "underground" by March 1972 was in a process of dissolution.

NOTES

1. *Underground* in its literal meaning (subsoil) appeared early in the Russian language; the dictionary of the Russian Imperial Academy of Sciences lists it in a 1793 entry. A political metaphor meaning a secret movement based on the idea of "underground—*podpolnii*—seems to be closely associated with the Populist movement (Narodniki) and appeared probably between 1860 and 1870. *Underground* in the political sense of an illegal, secret movement is listed in the third edition of V. L. Dal's *Dictionary of the Russian Language (Talkovyi Slovar Zhivogo Velikorusskago Yazyka)*, published from 1903 to 1911. The term *podpolschina* is given, which meant an underground society—not only an organized association, but an underground way of life, an underground community. Since the term was included in a dictionary, it must have been in use for a long time and generally accepted. In Polish, at the beginning of the twentieth century, the term was already in general use and appeared in novels (Strug).

2. *Pola Walki, Cele i Drogi Podziemnego Ruchu Robotniczego w. Polsce, 1939-*

1942 [From the battlefield, the goals and ways of the labor underground in Poland, 1939-1942] (London: Nowa Polska, 1943), p. 50. This publication is an anthology of articles published by the underground press during the Nazi occupation.
3. A *kontusz* is an old Polish dress worn by the gentry.
4. Translated by Stanley F. Zukowski.
5. A *surdut* is a type of coat.
6. Jean Decarreaux in an interesting article—"Sainte Russie," *La Vie Spirituelle* 140 (July 1954):38-60—analyzes the concepts and personalities of Russian saints, and finds self-sacrifice and suffering as one of their strong attributes. They work more for a collective resurrection than for individual salvation; the sanctity of these saints, writes Decarreaux, was original. One trait is *podvig*—a term difficult to translate, close to the English "performance," the German *Heldentat*—choice of heroic acts, choice of a life requiring suffering, exposition to cold and physical pain. The other one is *strastoterpetz* or *passioniste*: "le chrétien qui accepte sans résistance, comme un sacrifice volontaire, une mort violente à l'imitation de l'Agneau divin. . . . Sauf au dernier moment il peut n'avoir eu dans sa vie aucune disposition particulière à la sainteté. . . . Il a simplement accepté, quand elle se presentait, et parfois en regrettant la vie, une mort douloureuse dans le Christ."
7. Max Nomad, *Apostles of Revolution* (Boston: Little, Brown, 1939), p. 228. Nomad gives the full English translation of Nechayev's *Catechism*. According to Nomad the *Catechism* was written by Bakunin. His opinion is based on *Reminiscences*, memoirs of Michael Sazhin, an old and trusted follower of Bakunin; see p. 227.
8. Waclaw Zagorski, *Na Skrzyzowaniu Podziemnych Dróg*, "At the Crossing of Underground Roads," *Robotnik Polski* (London), (July 1947).
9. Alfred McClung Lee developed psychological and sociological concepts in this area of ambivalent behavior which are seminal in the analysis of personality, especially in crisis situations. See his "A Sociological Discussion of Consistency and Inconsistency in Intergroup Relations," *Journal of Social Issues* 5, no. 3 (1949): 12-18, and his "Attitudinal Multivalence in Relation to Culture and Personality," *American Journal of Sociology* 60 (1954-1955): 294-299. For a comprehensive and penetrating presentation of theory of multivalence, see his *Multivalent Man* (New York: Braziller, 1966).
10. The organization and working of the civil resistance was described by Stefan Korbonski in *w. Imieniu Rzeczypospolitej* [In the name of the republic] (Paris, 1954).
11. These comments are not an exact quote; they are the essence of conversations recorded from memory. Janusz Zawodny writes about problems of a platoon leader during the Warsaw uprising (1944) in his reminiscences, "Raport Dowódcy Plutonu A. K. powstania warszawskiego" [Report of a platoon commander of the Home army], *Zeszyty Historyczne* 176 (1969):176-190.
12. International comparison of living standards by means of statistical indexes as well as comparison of "real" (purchasing power) wages may be misleading. The price of wine is more important for a French worker than the price of beer, while an Irish worker may care little about wine, but beer is a part of his weekly expense. Wages are, however, generally higher in the United Kingdom than in Ireland, and the migratory flow of workers moves from Ireland to England. Comparison of wages gives a fair approximation. According to the United Nations *Statistical Yearbook* (1970), monthly wages in manufacturing in Ireland for 1967 were 85.1£ for men (M) and 48.2£ for women (F). At the same time, the lowest minimum wages in the United Kingdom were 66.6£ and highest mini-

mum wages 116.0£ per month. UK statistics did not differentiate between the sexes on this table. *Statistical Yearbook 1970* (New York: Statistical Office of the United Nations, 1971), Table 175, pp. 554, 556. The International Labour Office in Geneva notes weekly wages in manufacturing. According to the ILO wages for manufacturing in Ireland for 1969 (M+F) in shillings were 309.3. This time the data for United Kingdom were reported separately for men and women: again weekly wages for M in shillings: 510.10, F:242.5. *1970 Yearbook of Labor Statistics* (Geneva: International Labour Office Geneva, n.d.), Table 19, pp. 565, 567.

13. C. Lombroso and R. Laschi, *Il Delitto Politico e Le Revoluzioni* (Torino: Fratelli Bocca, 1890), p. 47.

14. See n. 1 above.

V

Political Assassination

How does it happen, that certain changes from liberty to servitude and from servitude to liberty occur without bloodshed [while] others are full of blood? It depends on this: whether the state which is subject to change was born in violence or no; because when it was born in violence, accordingly it was also born in injury of many. In consequence, it is unavoidable, that when the state weakens and declines, those who suffered want to vindicate; and this desire of vengeance breeds blood and death of men.

Machiavelli, *Discorsi Sopra La Prima Deca di Tito Livio*, Bk. 3, chapter VII

1. LEGITIMACY AND VIOLENCE

The humanizing effects of democracy and our civilization have had an impact on our perception of history. It seems it is almost forgotten that the use of violence and assassination in order to achieve political power or to remove an adversary or change a dynasty was a general historical phenomenon for centuries in societies organized into the complex political form of a state. Next to assassination as a means to gain wealth and property, assassination to gain political power seems to be tragically frequent in past history.[2]

Western civilization, in a slow, historical process, has humanized political institutions. Humanization means here limiting or abolishing violence, cruelty, and killing in the business of internal government. It seems that a decrease in political murder and assassination as a means of transferring power or changing dynasties developed slowly, influenced in medieval times by the Western church and philosophy.

The major concept which contributed to the decline of political assassination in the transmission and succession of royal power during this period was the concept of legitimacy rooted in the duality of Church and state. It was the ecclesiastic hierarchy that validated the hereditary legitimacy of the dynasties and maintained in that way a control over the orderly transfer of power. Of course, political murder was still abundant in medieval times. The Church itself indulged in mass terror toward dissidents. There were ups and downs in this long process. Henri Pirenne, the Belgian historian, writes about the great intensification of "unspeakable violence and treachery" and calls the tenth and fifteenth centuries "epochs of political assassination."[2] Nonetheless, a foundation was laid toward the concept of power based on legal and philosophical (or theological) premises as the only "legitimate" power. The paramount legitimacy of elective and representative power, already established in antiquity, whether in Greece or Rome, continued in medieval cities and corporations. Advanced and formulated in England, diffused from there to distant corners of the world, representative and democratic legitimacy has greatly contributed to the humanization of politics, especially to crisis stages of transmission and succession. The complex legal and philosophical concept of legitimacy of power became fundamental in Occidental politics. Few ideas in our civilization can be found which contributed more to political and cultural continuity in Europe and America than this one. Only late, and in the few states where well-established concepts of democratic legitimacy—based on general will or majority rule—were associated with political freedom and relative equality, or absence of excessive exploitation, did a nonviolent power transfer and nonviolent political struggle become fully accepted— "institutionalized." It became a shared value, a political custom or way of life.

2. SULTANISM: ASSASSINATION AND TRANSMISSION OF POWER

In imperial Rome political assassination was frequent. In the time of Emperor Constantin, it became a method later called *sultanism*— a continuous murder of competitors or all possible pretenders to power until no one but the ruler survived. The Swiss historian, Jacob Burkhardt (in *The Age of Constantin the Great*), coined the term. Sultanism reappeared in totalitarian states. Hitler's elimination of Roehm, General Schleicher, and so many others in the infamous bloodbath of 1934, and Stalin's purges, were assassinations of possible competitors. In the fourth century A.D., Licinius, a competitor of the future emperor, Constantin, did away with "families of Galerius Severus, Maximus Daia, including their innocent children." Even the widow and daughter of Emperor Diocletian were assassinated, and Constantin later arranged for the assassination of Licinius. After the death of Constantin, his brothers, first Constantius, next Dalmatius, were murdered, relates Burkhardt.[3] It was the same Constantin the Great whose merits for the establishment of the Christian Church as a ruling religion of the Roman Empire are well known. This was, however, a period of transition and the disintegration of old value systems and legitimacy. At such times power was based on the personal loyalty of one's bodyguards rather than on legitimacy.

Byzantium inherited this political pattern. Sultanism continued in a variety of shocking cruelties, almost until the fall of the empire. Between 477 and 1374 as many as twenty-nine Emperors of Byzantium were murdered, poisoned, blinded, mutilated. This procedure reappears in the Third Rome—Moscovy and Russia. Ivan the Dread assassinated his own son. Peter the Great plotted the murder of his son Alexis, who died from torture before the "official" execution. Catherine the Great conspired and was instrumental in the assassination of her own husband, Czar Peter III, who was murdered in prison. Diplomats reported this political murder without emotion, as a kind of normal procedure, writes the historian Albert Sorel. After the death of Catherine, Czar Paul, more liberal than his predecessors, was assassinated, and his son, the glamorous Czar Alexander, was directly involved in this conspiracy.[4] Nor is Western history free of royal assassins. But the sequence and consistency in

Russian history is perhaps characteristic. The continuity can be traced back to the late Roman Empire.

While principles of legitimacy grew slowly in Western Europe, by no means free from political murder, in highly civilized Muslim Spain in the eighth century, political assassination was frequently practiced. "Of a total of twenty [governors, appointed from Damascus or North Africa] only three survived as long as five years: those who did not fall in battle were murdered by their rivals."[5] In the Ottoman Empire political assassination as a process of consolidation and transfer of power was part of the general use of violence in politics and absolute rule and, as we shall see, may have contributed to a "political style" or political cultural pattern in which assassination and individual terror became one of few avenues of struggle against autocratic rule. When Sultan Murad III (1574-1595) left twenty sons (out of forty-seven children who survived), his successor Mohammed III (1595-1603) ordered the murder of his nineteen brothers in order to eliminate competitors.[6] This pattern of eliminating competing dynasties by assassination, although in a far milder form in terms of means and number of victims, continued in the Balkans, especially in Serbia, even after liberation from Ottoman rule, from 1817 until 1903. Once a political pattern is established and "internalized" in the political behavior of individuals, or "institutionalized" in groups, it has a tendency to continue and becomes difficult to extricate. Turkey is no exception; indeed, it tends to be representative of the pattern. In Persia the succession of the two major dynasties was "seldom undisputed and decided without bloodshed."[7] Sultanism has been a major political device in Persia.

In Italy during the Renaissance, political assassination became an art. It reappeared when the old, medieval legitimacy based on dynastic heredity with succession validated and legitimized by ecclesiastic authority was considerably weakened, and when the old, elective or aristocratic power in parts of Italy was eroded by violent conquest and treason.

These brief historical notes could be extended into a voluminous survey to support the proposition that eliminating violence and assassination in internal transmission and succession of political power is a consequence of a long historical development, perhaps of paramount cultural significance, and that nonviolent succession and transmission of political power is not necessarily universally typical in a history stained with blood and violence.

3. POLITICAL ASSASSINATION AMONG NATIONS: COMPARATIVE DATA AND MAJOR TYPES

The patterns and incidence of political assassination of chief executives and high-level political persons vary among nations and political cultures. Historical experience, ethnic and religious values, distribution and patterns of political power, as well as social stratification and socioeconomic conditions, are among the major contributing variables. To blame solely the economic situation for political terror is a gross oversimplification and frequently a fallacy. In fact, in times of intense class tensions and class violence in the past, individual terror as tactics was seldom, if ever, practiced. This was primarily a political tactic. One single variable—legitimacy—seems to be of singular interest. Although by no means a sufficient variable of itself, it is perhaps an indicator of things which happen; I mean here a legitimacy that supplies continuity of institutions and facilitates and enhances social change in modern times. When the legitimacy of power—the value structure supplying the legal and philosophical basis of the exercise of power—is weak, unstable, or disintegrating, a tendency toward a high-level political assassination seems to increase.

Political assassination persisted and reappeared in the Balkans and in the parts of the Middle East which were also under Ottoman rule for a long time, where political assassination and government by violence was widely practiced. Once successful the violent succession of a ruler was legitimized ex post facto. Iraquis and Syrians today practice violence and individual assassination in succession of power, which was frequent among the Arabs of the eighth or ninth centuries, but there is no necessary historical connection.

Professor Karl M. Schmitt of Texas University, in his report submitted to the task force of the United States National Commission on Causes and Prevention of Violence (1968), estimates that over thirty chief executives or rulers or former rulers were murdered in South America in one hundred and sixty-two years since the assassination of Dessalines in Haiti. Bolivia, with about ten victims, tops the list. However, Guatemala and Colombia, two nations of intense political violence, had a very low incidence of assassination of chief executives. Otherwise, according to the estimates of Schmitt, in Guatemala only in the last two or three years the number of victims of political violence runs as high as three thousand deaths, and Colombia political violence continued for twenty years (1940-1960) at a cost of two hundred and fifty thousand people killed. In Argentina, Brazil, Chile, and Cuba, although there were no assassinations of their chiefs of state, there were several attempts. None of these nations has enjoyed political stability; none has been free of violence.[8]

The low level of assassination of chief executives or leading personalities in stable democracies is rather striking. Professor Murray Havens in his report submitted to the Commission cited above lists two such attempts in the entire history of Australia: the first one in 1868 directed against Alfred Duke of Edinburgh (by an Irishman), and another one in 1966 against the leader of the Labour Party, Caldwell. Since 1792, there have been only two assassination attempts of this kind in Sweden, the second being in 1909 and directed against a foreign and oppressive ruler, the visiting czar of Russia.[9]

In both nations the legitimacy of power is strong, and generally accepted and recognized by the people. Few question the legal and philosophical basis of power, the underlying values of democracy and of constitutional monarchy. The political institutions are here firm and at the same time elastic; they absorb without significant shocks political and social changes. Sweden is ethnically homogeneous. Both nations have high standards of living, a relative prosperity of the working classes, and an extensive system of social services.

Strong legitimacy of institutions is not, however, the sole variable in the relative safety of chief executives. Ethnic values and behavioral patterns, frequently included in definitions of the vague concept of "national character," do influence political behavior in internal politics. We should not overlook such simple physical data as frequency of contact and exposure in public meetings of the chief executives. The latter is very high in the United States.

We realize here, however, the shortcomings of comparative statistics in defining the act. Different countries may have different legal definitions and norms. The figures are used here for orientation and should be considered as tentative.

We may proceed, with this reservation, to the attempts of assassination against officeholders in the United States. According to the research prepared for the Commission on Causes and Prevention of Violence by Professor Rita James Simon, since 1789, the entire history of the United States records eighty-one assassination attempts, both successful and unsuccessful, all against officeholders. Nine of these, of which five were successful, were directed against presidents or candidates (high-level assassinations). In most cases, they were a result of "individual passion and derangement." "Cross national quantitative analyses," according to the report of Task Force I, "show that the incidence of assassination correlates strongly with intense levels of general political violence and political instability." We learn also from the Commission's Task Force I report that the higher the office the higher the probability of an attempt of assassination. However, of the approximately 1,100 men elected to the United States Senate in its entire history, two were assassinated; of the 8,350 congressmen, three were assassinated, and there were seven unsuccessful attempts, five, however, in one single attempt in 1954. It is also a higher probability that an attempt will be directed against an elected public officer rather than an appointed one, even if the latter is a powerful and prominent one, for example, secretary of state or justice of the Supreme Court. The legitimacy of power, the democratic principle and ideology, despite the present violent experience, seems to be widely shared and has contributed to a basic political continuity already observed more than a hundred years ago by Alexis de Tocqueville. Political assassination in most cases in democratic countries has been an individual act, a result of psychological obsession or derangement, frequently in times of political crisis or rapid political change. Professor Rita James Simon concludes that "the level of assassination correlates strongly with the level of political violence."[10]

Not only does assassination vary in time and space in a quantitative sense, it varies also in its quality and nature, scope and objectives, motivation and tactics. Roughly we may distinguish:

1. Political assassination as an isolated act, frequently carried out by a deranged person. The assassins of American presidents, perhaps with the exception of the Puerto Rican nationalists who attacked President Truman, "evidenced serious mental illness," according to a careful study of the Task Force of the National Commission on Causes and Prevention of Violence.

2. Sultanism, assassination of competitors to power. Related to the latter are assassinations in order to secure power for a new elite, to remove the one who controls political power.

3. Individual terror, systematic and tactical assassination directed against the representatives of the ruling groups or government with an objective to weaken the government, the political system, destroy the existing legitimacy, affect ideological, political, and social change. Individual terror is generally a tactic for achieving power; mass terror has been applied in the past and present to consolidate and maintain power.

4. TACTICAL TERROR

Political assassination can be a systematic activity, a part, even a major one, of political tactics advanced by an organized political group for achieving an ideological goal. Tactical terror has been historically recorded as early as ancient Palestine and the medieval Near East (see Chapter II, section 5.) In modern times it appeared in the nineteenth century as a consequence of opposition to domestic autocracy and oppression or foreign rule.

After the French Revolution, what is called "the reaction" in central and western Europe closed the avenues of peaceful development of representative and democratic institutions. Monarchies and autocracies representing the interests of the ruling classes lacked the will and initiative to resolve the burning social problems of the new industrial society. Here the traditions of the French Revolution suggested effective types of a popular revolution with a wide appeal and mass support. In Russia, however, which lacked a tradition of a successful popular dissent from below, and where the peasantry were either passive or loyal to the czar or only sporadically rebellious without broader political goals of basic change, where the government was autocratic in the Oriental sense rather than in terms of European monarch, individual assassination appeared as a political tactic. It spread to the Balkans, again as a tactic in response to foreign oppression and massacres.

During the second half of the nineteenth century, a theory of individual terror developed among revolutionary Russians in their struggle against autocracy. Unlike political assassination as an isolated act, individual terror—in terms of nineteenth-century revolutionaries and later in terms of some resistance groups during World War II—is a systematic, tactical course of action with political objectives. Individual terror attacked directly, above all, key decision makers or administrators or acted in lieu of punishment against persons responsible for cruelties and oppression. One of its functions was retribution and deterrence. The leaders of the organization expected that assassination of an oppressive administrator would deter his successors from inhuman, oppressive acts.

Such was the goal of the assassination of high Gestapo officers in Poland during World War II. In Russia, however, the major function of individual terror was to weaken the government and the autocratic institutions of the czarist empire.

It was in this terroristic revolutionary group in autocratic Russia that democratic ideas flourished. There were several factions of course, some of them minor, whose objective was establishing a dictatorship as the means or as a transitory stage toward a society free of any coercion. Here rationalism worked in harmony with perfect ideals and logical contradictions, impressive and convincing for novices. Theories were also advanced (by Morozov and Tkachev) that terror should continue under constitutional rule, since even under such rule, a tyrant might appear; they indicated contemporaries—Bismarck or Napoleon III. Individual terror by its power of intimidation and elimination of future tyrants would keep the future, perfect world free from autocracy. These advocates of regicides were, however, in a minority and formed an insignificant faction or separate party. The main party, the core of the "People's Will," had democratic traditions and clear democratic objectives. In 1878, the "People's Will" stated clearly and sharply in an "Urgent Note" its differences with the group which "indulges in Jacobinistic tendencies and methods of a centralistic organization."[11] The Russian revolutionary movement of those times was not economic; it was primarily political, as Thomas Masaryk put it: "It was an aristocratic struggle for freedom waged against Tsarist absolutism."[12]

5. INDIVIDUAL AND MASS TERROR

There are times in history when violence is one of the few roads left open for those who fight for the rights of man against the bestiality of others. Man was and is forced sometimes to use violence in his struggle for freedom and emancipation.

The experience of a hundred years teaches that a clear distinction must be made between 1) struggle and violence against domestic autocracy, 2) foreign conquerors who exterminate nations or reduce the populace to near slavery, and 3) individual violence waged against republics and democratic institutions, as the Fascists, Nazis, and their satellites did.

Violence generates violence, and blood calls for more blood. Individual terror, even in the name of the highest ideals, may create in the end political habits which move into the pattterns of stable political life, and continue even when conditions change.

Before World War I, individual terror in the Balkans and in Russia was to a large extent a tool of those who were "out," those who opposed autocratic institutions. After World War I, systematic individual assassination was used by the extreme right against democracy. Political techniques are similar to tools. Some—not all—are "neutral" per se; they can be used for a variety of contradictory objectives. The objectives are decisive in a political and, above all, a moral sense, since ideology and objectives control the choice of means. Mass terror can be and is a political tactic of the "ins," of those in the saddle, in an effort to consolidate power and, frequently, to eliminate groups of innocent people defined as a class, a race, or a nation. Thus, the objectives of mass terror are broader than solely rule by fear.

6. SOCIOLOGICAL ANALYSIS:
THREE VARIABLES

Political assassination and violence are not abstract occurrences. This type of individual violence is sociologically meaningless or necessarily misinterpreted by an outside observer unless it is viewed in its three major contexts: 1) personality, 2) group, and 3) situation.

Most European and Russian political assassinations have been organized and planned by an ideological or political group, or when the terrorist was a lonely actor he counted on support, at least moral support, of certain ethnic or ideological groups or politically oriented social classes. The goals, values, ideology, and tactics of a terroristic party suggested the purpose of the act, the function the act should play.

Thus, the act first must be analyzed within the context of the ideology, objectives, and tactics of a party. We may call it the group context.

The party, again, does not act in isolation; it responds to a situation. The act of individual violence is an act of response to the social and political situation, therefore the social act should be studied in this context. We may call it situation context.

The assassination of a Turkish Pasha by a Dashnak (Armenian) revolutionary as an isolated juridical issue is a crime. The same assassination in a context of a situation of persecution and extermination of Armenians is an act of self-defense and counter-terror: it is a political act. In the context of the ideology of the Dashnaks and in their perception, killing such an enemy is a revolutionary act of a democratic and socialist Armenian party. In these terms the act has its ideological legitimacy.

The relationship of the three variables given above is essential. In an oppressive situation, such as under the German rule of World War II, an otherwise humane person may resort to violence and organize a terroristic group. On the other hand, in a humane democracy, individuals obsessed by a drive for power, combined with ethnic or racial hostilities, some of them deviant, may embark on terroristic action against democratic institutions. Various situations appeal in this sense to different personality types. But the situation is closely related to the act. Model 10 is presented here to illustrate the three interdependent variables.

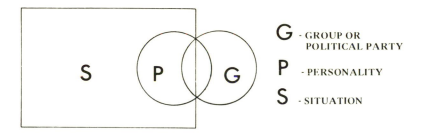

Model 10. The Context Situation: Three Interrelated
Variables of a Political Assassination

Three variables have to be considered in an act of tactical political assassination: 1) The group or political party, which supports the actor; 2) the personality of the actor; 3) the social-political situation to which the party and the actor respond. All three variables are closely interrelated and not isolated factors. Therefore, the act should also be analyzed within a triple context of these variables.

It is beyond the scope of this short essay to discuss mass political assassination—that is, mass terror—which has been used in the past to consolidate and maintain power. An elaborate enterprise of mass terror paralyzes a society by manipulating fear. It destroys for a time the will to resist and at the same time, for a long period, the chances of individual terror. Stalin's and Hitler's rule, as well as the earlier example of the Inquisition, seem at least to suggest some historical evidence, that mass terror does not necessarily result in a violent, individual response. Even conspiracies against Hitler were isolated and weak.

7. IN SEARCH FOR CAUSATION: TENTATIVE CONCLUSIONS

Now is the time to answer the crucial questions: What are the causes of political assassination? When and why does political assassination strike? In search for answers to our problems we frequently try to discover one single "root" cause that will explain an entire issue. This tendency for a single causal model dominates our everyday thinking. A single, firm argument is a most convincing answer of course. Consequently, at first glance a convincing answer to our query should also be one that offers a single major cause as a determinant in all acts of assassination. But a close inquiry suggests that there is no single cause, that political assassination under various conditions may result from a variety of causal variables, and that a simple monocausal answer, convincing as it may be, cannot be easily validated by the variety of data.

Our general discussion suggests, however, several tentative conclusions.

I. First of all, violence appears in a variety of forms and it is a result of a variety of conditions. There is no one type of violence.

II. Political assassination is one of the types of political violence.

Violence and assassination has appeared frequently in the past and present struggles for power, especially during struggles for succession. Among some nations, political assassination during long historical periods was frequent. Among others, individual assassination was seldom used or not practiced at all, or its use decreased or practically disappeared.

III. Diverse factors can cause political assassination. Consequently, there are several types of political assassination and each of these types usually corresponds to different causal syndromes. Past experience suggests four major patterns: 1) "isolated" (*A* and *B*); 2) traditional; 3) crisis; 4) tactical.

1. *Isolated assassination.* Even in a stable political system with a strong and accepted legitimacy, isolated cases of assassination do occur. We may distinguish two types of isolated assassination: *A*, with limited or no outside support, and *B*, a single occurrence supported by interest or political groups.

A. Sometimes, this may be a desperate act of protest of an emotional, intensely motivated person. More frequently, however, this is an isolated and single-handed act of a deviant or a disturbed individual, helped by some, perhaps, but seldom if ever by a network of a party. True, this type of act may spread as a consequence of an incipient crisis situation, or when a situation is so perceived by the prospective assassin. Still, the assassin is rather an isolated individual, and his act is not connected with a general tactical pattern of a party.

B. Isolated acts of political assassination may also be carried out by paid assassins, or by ideologically committed persons, loyal to a government, a dynasty, or a ruler. Others may act in the belief that the assassination must be carried out in the national interest. The act is not tactical, however; it is not continuous. It is a single, isolated act. In such case of an isolated pattern, the actor is hired and paid, or recruited for ideological reasons by an interest or political group, or even by a government.

2. *Traditional assassination pattern (sultanism).* Among certain nations and during certain historical periods, power was frequently transmitted by means of assassination of competitors to power. In ancient Rome, in Arab countries of the early medieval periods, in the Ottoman Empire, assassination of competitors to power was widely practiced and was later called "sultanism." Such practice diffused the pattern of individual violence and assassination into political struggles and led to armed defensive tactics of prospective victims. Thus political customs and traditions as well as oppressive forms of government contributed to a relatively wide and frequent use of political assassination. Even after the decline of the Ottoman Empire, the patterns of political behavior continued in the Balkan countries, where such practice was more intense, at least in certain historical periods, than in the countries of northern and western Europe (especially in the Scandinavian countries, and in England, the Netherlands, Belgium, Switzerland, and France, to mention the typical cases). We shall call this type of political assassination "traditional," since it is rooted in historical, traditional patterns and attitudes toward individual assassination in politics.

3. *"Crisis" assassination pattern.* Increase of political assassination in democratic societies has been noticed in times of weakening or breakdown of political legitimacies and political polarization over major issues (such as war). Such processes correspond usually to strong social-political divisions. Institutions once generally accepted, rules once generally approved, are now rejected by sections of a nation. Once

shared values lose their former appeal. Or, in reverse, the government's policies are questioned and challenged by a vocal part of society, precisely from the viewpoint of basic values. Actions of the government are regarded by a substantial minority as violations of the basic value system. This weakening or breakdown of values occurs usually in times of intensification of political and ethnic tensions, antagonisms, and violence. Such assassinations are related to a political crisis situation, in a sense are a symptom of it. For want of a better term, we may call this pattern "crisis assassination." Political assassinations of the 1960s in the United States were of this nature.

4. *Tactical assassination.* In the past, usually in times of extreme political oppression or of oppressive foreign rule, individual assassination was practiced as a political tactic against members of government or foreign authorities. Assassination in such case was systematic (tactical) and oriented toward a definite political goal: weakening or destruction of the government in power. Tactical terror has also appeared in areas of traditional assassination, being used (e.g., Bulgaria, Armenia-Serbia) as a defensive tactic against persecutions.

Tactical assassination may be and is carried out against democratic governments or representatives of democratic institutions, especially by totalitarian, secret microparties advocating violent social change. Such tactics may contribute to a process of delegitimization of a government by accelerating the process of weakening or disintegrating legitimacy. Tactical terror may in consequence also appear as a variation of traditional or crisis pattern.

This is a tentative classification, and there are no sharp divisions between these four patterns; they frequently overlap.

IV. The sociological nature of political assassination appears when the act or attempt is considered in relation to the three major variables: the social and political situation and process; the actor and his personality; the political party or groups he represents and which support him.

NOTES

1. This chapter is concerned primarily with individual, "high level" assassination, i.e., the assassination of chiefs of state, kings, presidents, chief executives, members of government, leading political personalities.

2. Arbitrary assassination, murder, rape, and violence against peasants and burghers, entire villages and cities, was a way of administration of political power,

a matter of routine for some of the ruling families like the Ezzelinis who have made history with their ruthless cruelty in times of Renaissance: see Antonio Perria, *I Feroci Ezzelini* (Milan: Sugar, 1971). "There was an undercurrent of violence in all levels of society," writes the English historian Hale about fifteenth- and sixteenth-century Europe. J. R. Hale, *Renaissance in Europe 1480-1520* (London: Collins, 1971), p. 27; see also the entire section 3 of Chapter I, pp. 25ff, and Henri Pirenne, *A History of Europe* (New York: Doubleday, 1958), II:227 ff. Jacob Burkhardt, *The Civilization of Renaissance in Europe* (New York: Harper, 1958), I. 22ff.

The cruelty of those times sometimes seems incomprehensible to most people. However, what followed in the twentieth century in Germany makes the Renaissance a violent interlude but not an exceptional one. After all, Adolph Hitler was worshipped by the masses and respected by foreign governments and ambassadors. He has shown the immense capacity a man has for cruelty, aggression, and violence and the variety of means man has invented for total submission of entire nations. No quantitative research or data can further illuminate this historical image. Since it reappears again and again in human history it can only prompt the sane and humane to attempt to understand it and learn to prevent it in the future.

3. Jacob Burkhardt, *The Age of Constantine* (Garden City: Doubleday, 1956), pp. 266, 271, 277.

4. Albert Sorel, *Europe Under the Ancient Regime* (New York: Harper & Row, 1964), pp. 39ff.

5. Harold Livermore, *A History of Spain* (New York: Grove Press, 1960), 1960), p. 67.

6. L. S. Stavrianos, *The Balkans Since 1453* (New York: Rinehart, 1958), p. 159.

7. William S. Haas, *Iran* (New York: Columbia University Press, 1946), pp. 95ff.

8. Karl M. Schmitt, "Assassination in Latin America," in James F. Kirkham, Sheldon G. Levy, and William J. Crotty, eds., *Assassination and Political Violence, A Report to the National Commission on Causes and Prevention of Violence* (Washington, D.C.: U.S. Government Printing Office, 1969), pp. 537-544.

9. Murray C. Havens, "Assassination in Australia," in *ibid.,* pp. 571-576, and Klas Lithner, "Assassination in Sweden," in *ibid.,* pp. 579-580.

10. For detailed information, see Chapter I, "Deadly Attack Upon Public Office in the United States," Chapter II, "Assassination Attempts Directed at the Office of the President of the United States," and Chapter III, "Cross-National Comparative Study of Assassination," in *ibid.,* pp. 9ff, pp. 49ff, pp. 113ff.

I have quoted a study by Professor Rita James Simon with the assistance of Mrs. Sandra Philips; "Political Violence as Directed at Public Office Holders," *Report of Task Force I* of the National Commission on Causes and Prevention of Violence, a document which was available in a mimeographed form when I wrote this essay. It has been published since, however, in *Assassination and Political Violence,* as quoted above.

11. "The Urgent Note," *Obschchina,* no. 8-9 (October 1878), signed by Vera Zazulich, Stepniak (Kravchinski) and others; reprinted also in Vladimir Burtsev, *Za Sto Lyet (1800-1896)* (London: Russian Free Press Foundation, 1897).

12. Thomas G. Masaryk, *The Spirit of Russia* (London: Allen and Unwin, 1919), II: p. 107.

VI

Dress, Rituals, Symbols, and Myth-Making:

Symbolic Manipulation

1. ON SYMBOLISM OF DRESS

There are phenomena and problems that we are aware of and which we come up against in our own experience, but find difficult to grasp, to arrest the whirl of change and momentarily to fix them in time and place. Our everyday, prosaic clothing belongs to this category. Clothing not only protects us from the cold and rain; it is also a symbol, an important element in the system of symbols that man uses while he builds complicated and powerful social organizations.

The weight and material of our clothing in various climatic conditions is perhaps less important than our diet, but nevertheless it is of biological significance. Just the same, scholarly interest in this aspect has been relatively small. Stefansson, an intelligent enthusiast of the Antarctic, has been one of the few people interested in the function of clothing. He demonstrated that the clothing of Eskimos is more intelligently conceived for and adjusted to the biological needs of a polar environment than our own contemporary city clothing to the demands of the climate and urban environment in which we live. The biological suitability of clothing should be measured by its usefulness with respect to the environment, that is, whether it protects man and makes movement and work possible.

A resident of New York, writes Stefansson, returns home from work in January in clothing weighing perhaps fifteen pounds. This clothing

would not keep him reasonably warm for a period of fifteen minutes
if he sat still at a temperature of fifteen degrees below Fahrenheit. An
Eskimo from northern Alaska in the clothing he wears in January, which
weighs ten pounds, would suffer less from the cold after fifty minutes
of immobility at a temperature of fifty degrees below.[1]

However Stefansson ignores an important problem: man is a symbolic
creature and man's clothing frequently serves a symbolic function. The
bishop's attire is primarily a symbol of his religion, his function, and his
ecclesiastic power; what is more, it is a system of symbols adjusted to
the symbolic church environment and to the esthetic styles of an
earlier period.

The cap and gown of a professor or a university student is a symbol
of learning and status rather than clothing in the biological sense. A
bearded and long-haired youth parading through Washington Square in
New York City might wear a heavy golden chain around his neck, like
Lorenzo de Medici, a cowboy hat, and jeans that have been spotted
white by bleach. His is a very recherché outfit and our young—perhaps
rich—fellow has probably spent a great deal of time in order to achieve
this dirty and pauperlike fashion. The way he dresses is only a part of a
peculiar symbolic system (the hippie subculture), which negates conformity, and of a whole environment (e.g., Greenwich Village and the
East Village in New York City, Haight-Asbury in San Francisco) to which
this symbolic system primarily belongs. Our hippie, convinced of his non-
conformity, is a conformist—very much so—in relation to his symbolic
environment. Symbolically, his clothing is just as conformist as a monk's
habit in the Middle Ages.

Thus, clothing fulfills many functions. Besides purely biological
functions, it also fulfills sociological and psychological functions (as a
symbol or element in a symbolic system). It is also an expression of
esthetic evaluations which in turn may also perform a biological function:
that of sexual attraction.

The social functions of wearing apparel are also connected with the
symbolism of power. The symbolism of dress has throughout history
reinforced and expressed the differences between classes and estates.
The fact of political or religious domination of one person over another
has been reflected in this symbolism. Even the act of socially "liquidat-
ing" a person or military degradation at one time required a symbolic
act expressed in dress.

Thus the act of degradation and moral death during the Inquisition
was connected with a change in the symbolism of dress. The penitent's

garb, a sackcloth or some kind of degrading attire, were symbols of the
victims of persecution. They gave the street mob the right to mock the
unfortunates and also provided the faithful with a sense of security and
superiority, for they could identify with the symbols of those in power
and of the church. Concentration camps during World War II also practiced a symbolism of degrading people. In these situations, clothing
served an antibiological function, for it was usually inadequate for protection, and it served as a symbolic foretaste of death. So, then, man's
degradation, as well as his elevation, call for a symbolism of dress,
sometimes a complicated symbolic system that has been preserved to
this day in the coronation ceremony in England or the assumption of
ecclesiastical office.

Man produces material symbols by which he measures social relations. Dress is one of these symbolic products. The miter, the crown,
the party emblem, the military uniform, diplomatic attire—all these
"artifacts" (to use an anthropological expression)—play a symbolic
role in ruling and domination. In certain historical periods, they have
been the expression of established social relations. In this sense, they
are "functional" for those who utilize them.

But this is not all. Dress also has a psychological function. We feel
more positive or happier when we wear certain, selected materials and
styles. Even Stalin and Mao Tse-tung created their own fashions; Mao
probably "feels well" in a military uniform; Stalin perhaps "felt well"
in high boots, the symbol of power and the common man.

Sometimes, colors and styles reflect compulsive urges, far deeper
needs. The homosexuals who inhabit the West Side of New York
are easily recognizable on Broadway by their attire and gait. They have
produced a style of their own, preference for colors and hairdo, and
also stores which cater to their taste.

Man chooses his clothing not only for its quality or value, but also
because of style and taste. *Style* is "social," "collective," imitated or
followed by majorities. It is imposed by the collectivity. *Taste* reflects
the individual, the choice he makes within a range the collective style
offers and within his economic condition. The interplay of individual
taste and collective style is expressed even in traditional or national
(regional) costumes in Europe and Latin America. Some wear their
hats at a dashing angle, pin a feather to them, while others are more
unassuming. The national costume is an expression of the community,
of collectivity, the way it is worn is an expression of individual taste.

In industrialized and democratic countries, where the working class is not poor and can exercise a wide choice when buying clothing, there is a style range in every price category. And here the buyer makes a selection which not only reflects the biological utility of the clothing, but also the personality and taste of the buyer.

The symbolism of dress also influences man's behavior. An individual belongs to many groups and plays a number of different social roles during his life. The same man may be a member of a religious community as well as of a veterans' organization and sports club. In his veteran's garb he behaves differently than when in his athletic outfit. He also plays different social roles. The same university student acts differently in formal evening wear than when he's on campus in his worn blue jeans and shirt. Before the war, a worker on May Day, wearing his best suit to the celebrations, acted differently from the way he did in his work clothes during a raucous meeting at the union hall. Generally, on May First, the parades of men in Sunday clothes were orderly, calm, and peaceful. Man finds it hard to risk his Sunday suit or parade uniform.

In a plurality of its functions, dress is sometimes a self-contradictory phenomenon. The esthetic choice of clothing may be contrary to its biological utility. The attractiveness and sexual appeal of dress may also be contradictory with its climatic usefulness. We look for the "lack of logic" in dress when its symbolism obscures or negates its biological utility. The uniform of a prewar cavalryman, buttoned to the neck, may seem very "manly"—the high boots contributing to both "manliness" and importance—but during the heat of the summer and from the point of view of freedom of movement, this uniform was biologically not very logical. Likewise, a low-cut evening gown in the winter, attractive though it may be in other ways, is contradictory to one of its biological functions: protection against the cold. Thus, symbolism and social functions of attire are relevant and seminal. Otherwise, dress would always be as biologically logical as that of Stefansson's Eskimos.

I have no intention of dealing systematically with this complicated problem in this short essay. Let me just suggest a few remarks and observations. I beg the reader to bear with my digressions and the marginal thoughts that occur to me on this theme. This subject leads us later to broader problems: the social significance of certain types of decoration and architecture, as well as the manipulation of masses during our historical period. Let me add that what I write are only hypotheses, tentative observations of a hurried passerby.

2. CHANGE AND DIFFERENCE: JAPAN, ROME, AND CONTEMPORARY FASHION

A quarter of a century ago I was impressed by the street dress in Yokohama, Kobe, and Tokyo. The Japanese kimono was then in common use. Men, women and children were dressed in beautiful, colorful clothes, in that climate more suitable for rest than for work. Even longshoremen wore Japanese attire: sandals, special stockings called *taby*, (in which the big toe was separated, like in a mitten), gloves—in its way a fitting outfit practical for work. The kimono affected the way people moved, making women unusually graceful. The shape of the high wooden sandals stressed movement. This combination of clothing and movement created a peculiar rhythm, a colorful flow to the street activity.

At that time I examined a collection of old Japanese prints, etchings, and lithographs at the Tokyo Museum and delved into their history. It struck me that Japanese dress had changed very slowly and very little. It was difficult for me to discern changes, probably more apparent to specialists or even to any Japanese used to the traditional form of dress. I thought then, gazing at the ancient likeness of a Japanese woman, that if any passerby in Yokohama put on a two hundred or even a three hundred year old kimono, he would not stand out on a Japanese street; he would probably calmly stroll down Dragon Street or sip tea at the Motomashi tea house without arousing any interest. His dress would differ little from other people's. The monk's garb in our civilization has also changed very little—the habit of St. Francis would cause no curiosity on an Assisi street today. At the time I am speaking of (almost thirty years ago), traditional Japanese dress, extremely ancient in style, was in popular use in Yokohama.

Twenty years later, I had an opportunity to see a large collection of Chinese paintings in the Metropolitan Museum in New York. My impressions—this time in a different field—were strikingly similar indeed. May I quote here from my notebook a few hurriedly written lines of a dilettante: "Chinese Exhibit. September 23, 1961. What strikes me, I cannot see any changes of style. For hundreds of years the style seems to be static, unchanged, the same. Perhaps the topics have changed, the subjects but no striking differences in style, to compare those of Gothic and Impressionism. Only in one of the paintings, *Mountain and the*

Clouds, I noticed an effort to change the style, otherwise the same style, the same modes and ways of perception. If history is change, then style is the very essence of history. And the Chinese style, for many centuries, was an expression of a static society." Perhaps . . . but let us return now to Japan, Yokohama and the kimono.

Let us compare the kimono with our civilian clothes, not with ecclesiastic garb. In my young years in Cracow, the old capital of Poland, there once appeared a man with some aristocratic connections who claimed the right to the crown of this ancient nation. He walked the streets in a blue azure gown, a replica of a twelve-century princely outfit. According to him, the Anjous used to dress this way. Once in a while he appeared on horseback. He was quite distinctive, and passersby were not quite sure whether it was a hoax or something more serious. In 1958, a visitor appeared in Rome—a very handsome, white-haired gentleman, with a hairdo and beard reminiscent of the Three Musketeers. And indeed he claimed to be a straight descendant of d'Artagnan, as he sipped coffee at a sidewalk cafe. He attracted curiosity, even in this town of red-gowned Jesuit students riding ladies' bikes.

An Englishman in a Norman outfit, parading through Oxford Circle in London, sporting a casque and sword, would look very different from the other people on the street, although—as it sometimes happens in England—it is possible that not much attention would be paid to him. After all, he has the right to his eccentricity! Or if a student, in a costume from the time of the American Revolution, wearing a tri-cornered hat, appeared at the public library in New York—I think he would be noticed, although most probably no one would make any remarks. After all, New York is still New York.

Differences in our Western garb are substantial in this historical sense—in comparison with fashion from one or two hundred years ago—not to speak of one thousand. Change in the Japanese national costume, as can be seen from paintings and illustrations, has been very slight and slow. It was the same in ancient Greece and Rome, where for centuries differences were barely discernible. Later, in the times of the emperors, they appeared—perhaps under the influence of the East and Eastern institutions. Religious dress is symbolic, as I have already noted, for example, the monk's garb is—or rather used to be—more or less the same. Is not the present change in nuns' habits also a manifestation of other, much more profound, changes in the Catholic Church? And similarly, was not the lack of change in clothes a reflection of an unchanging or barely changing social structure? Today we are used to rapid changes in clothes, fashions, and styles.

The style of women's clothes changes periodically, as does the "dress" or model of cars. Might not the change in clothes be a symbolic manifestation of other changes, changes in esthetic judgments, in customs, and also of increasingly rapid social change? I am only posing these questions; I do not attempt to answer them in this essay.

There was a striking difference between the Greeks' style of dress and that of their neighbors to the east, whom the Greeks called barbarians. Style is a general set pattern accepted by the society or group. It was probably the Greeks who originated the concept of style. But style itself is usually created spontaneously, by the voluntary conformance of a group to new patterns, to changes introduced by so-called innovators.

Wandering through the Metropolitan Museum in New York, I have noted the differences in decoration and attire between two civilizations—the great civilizations of the ancient East and of ancient Greece and Rome. One is struck by the unusual simplicity, I would even say modesty of ancient Greek and early Roman dress. In the southern hall of Greek and Roman antiquity at the Museum there are sculptures whose beauty lies mainly in their style, shape, and simplicity. The gods and philosophers are either naked or very simply dressed. The lack of adornment on their hands or necks is striking. There is a little more jewelry in statues and paintings of women, but not much. In the northern hall of the Museum can be found rich collections from Egypt, Assyria, and Chaldea. Their gods are strange—with animal heads or wings. What is arresting in these civilizations is the richness of ornamentation, the marvelous pieces in gold and precious jewels that adorned the body.

But let us return to dress. The simplicity of Greek dress was noted by Thucydides, the illustrious historian of Hellas as long as twenty-five hundred years ago. In describing the costly clothing of rich and aged Athenians, their linen tunics and golden hair-clasps, Thucydides writes: "The Athenians abandoned this ornate clothing only recently, adopting the more modern dress of the Lacemaemonians." This was an unassuming way of dressing. In Sparta, the rich tried to adopt the life-style and simplicity of the common man. They also introduced the fashion of competing in athletic exercises without clothing, naked save for a coating of oil unlike the barbarians. "To this day—writes Thucydides—among certain barbarians, especially in Asia, where prizes are awarded for wrestling, the athletes wear belts. At one time the Greeks did this as well, drawing these belts across their waists." But even the ornate dress of the Athenians that Thucydides describes was simple. Later the even simpler and less ornate Spartan dress became popular in Greece.[2]

For a long time republican Rome remained under the influence of Greece. But the Roman Empire was the synthesis of Greek and Asian influence: Republican institutions and the paramount concept of citizenship were of Greek and Roman origin; the technique of ruling over large conquered territories appeared quite early in Asia and Egypt. The latter called for a different legitimacy of power, a divine legitimacy; the Asian rulers were gods, just as the later caesars were. But at the same time the Roman Empire kept Greek and Roman republican laws and order for its citizens and cities.

Together with Eastern political legitimacy and institutions came also Eastern customs, style, and dress. This influence is apparent in the rich Byzantine dress of Caesar Justinian and Theodora pictured in the Ravenna mosaics. How many jewels and precious stones adorn the clothing of the rulers! Also from the East—before Christianity was adopted—came the religious cult of political power: the deification of the emperor, and splendor in custom and dress. Republican power was secular, based on elections, on citizens' choice, but the emperor was considered a member of God's family, and the dead emperor-god, forged into a statue, became the object of a cult.

The German sociologist Simmel writes that individualism increased during the early Renaissance, which was apparent in clothing. Everyone who could afford to, dressed originally, developed his own fashion, so that general fashion trends were difficult to establish.[3]

And here again man's quest for individualistic manifestation on the one hand and his social tendencies on the other (the dialectics of opposites: the individual and the collectivity) were expressed in this symbolism of dress. Man is part of a group and acts as a member of society, but at the same time is a "person," an independently acting individual. In his double role he finds himself in constant inner as well as social conflict: as an individual, a personality, with his drive toward independence and freedom of action, and at the same time as a member of a society, in his "collective" identification as part of a group, the individual searches for style and conforms to fashions that the collective society imposes on him. Thus, ladies change the length of their dresses in accordance with orders issued in Paris. Men suddenly grow beards and sideburns. They "discover" these changes by means of the press, films, or the street. The individual as part of the whole adjusts to fashion, while as a person he manifests his individuality, stresses his personal taste by details or color. This conflict between the pressures of collectivity and the propensities of individuality is also apparent among the working class of the industrialized and prosperous West. This conflict is reflected in the colorful though modestly priced leisure weekend clothes, free of the symbolism of work, the factory, or office. The patterned or brightly colored shirts and pants, fantastic caps—all the rather attractive splashes of color on Coney Island or Brighton Beach in Brooklyn reflect a revolt against the conformity of Monday, although at the same time they become a new conformity—of Sunday. There is no escape from society and its symbols.

3. DRESS AND SOCIAL CLASS

The development of estates and later class stratification was accompanied by symbolic differences in attire. The dress of the rich and ˈ powerful was an expression of their taste, good or bad; it protected them from the elements, adorned them, enhanced their beauty or sexual charms. It also emphasized class or estate differences. These differences were marked by color, cut, or special symbols, so that color, trimmings, jewelry, or weapons distinguished the owner of the symbol. In other words, the symbol emphasized higher or lower social position, differentiated the ruler from the serf. The symbolism of dress—the uniform, miter, crown—affected social behavior and even the way of speaking. The master spoke in one way, and the servant in another.

The color of clothing sometimes had a double meaning: a ritual one and a political one. In the latter, the color of clothing or symbol denoted the ruling group or political elite. The differentiation of social-political and ritual functions by means of colors was visible in ancient Rome. The purple stripe on the toga was a symbol of both sacerdotal status and political office.

The toga was used as outer wear in republican Rome. The early Roman toga was white, formed by a wide circle of about ten square yards of undyed wool. The Greeks, however, retained straight edges and right angles. While the toga was white, a dirty toga was a sign of mourning. In those times, color was not used, with the exception of a purple stripe along the edge—this was called the *toga praetexta*. This color had a twofold meaning: religious and political. The color was used by priests, senior magistrates performing sacrifices, and boys and girls. Thus, this symbolic color was indicative of sacerdotal status and of the sacred nature of childhood as well. At the same time it was indicative of *imperium*, of political power, since it was associated not only with ceremonial functions but also with higher political office.

Senatorial togas had a wide purple stripe, while the noble Equestrian order had the right to use a narrower one. Somewhat later, in imperial Rome, the tunic began to displace the toga, but senators retained a broad, vertical stripe on their tunics (*tunica laticlavia*)—a badge of status and political power. Hence this color, which was taken over by the church hierarchy, was symbolic of class status, saintliness, and political power all at once.[4]

In time the symbols of power and the color of power became tools in the control and exercise of power. The symbols or colors worn by the representatives of the king or a powerful prince called for submission and obedience. Those present at hearings or meetings responded to persons dignified by such symbols (coat of arms, crown, imperial colors) by the customary baring of the head, lowering of the head, or kneeling. The repetition of such ritual reinforced the established social relations of sub- and superordination between the ruled and the rulers.

Today in China the faithful pay homage to the portrait of Mao Tse-tung. Swimming in the Yangtse river to celebrate the leader's birthday, before Mao's portrait, is a novel and unusual form of symbolic behavior. Through the repetition of the political ritual, the collective pattern of obedience is reinforced. As symbolism develops, the control and manipulation of symbols gives the ruling elite power over man, who is a symbolic creature and whose social behavior to a certain extent depends on the established symbolism.

Every society creates certain patterns of subordination or conformance to institutions, to the law, to individuals or groups. Such patterns are usually identified by symbols or symbolic behavior. In American society, such relationships are expressed by restraint and reduced symbolism. On the other hand, in autocratic regimes the complicated symbols of sanctity or political power become the tools of a political and religious organization, instruments of worship and subordination.

In later historical periods of European culture, there was a discernible struggle between personal taste in dress, between individualism, also reflected in a spontaneous development of style, and symbols imposed by the state or Church. Even in Protestant countries, for example, Switzerland, there were strict regulations that forced certain types of

dress on the different social classes in the name of modesty or ascet-
ism dictated by religion. And here again dress or its symbolism fulfilled
many functions; it was a manifestation of a number of mutually contradictory systems of values. Taste, esthetic preference, and new
fashions slowly eroded the dictates of imposed uniformity. Efforts
in the direction of change and indivuality, rebellion against imposed
style were harbingers of approaching social changes. This rebellion was
also apparent in dress.

In the Middle Ages, during the early Renaissance, and even later, the
dress of a peasant, nobleman, or bourgeois was regulated by law in many
countries of continental Europe. A man's station in life could be judged
by his mode of dress. The individual's position in the class system or
system of political power could also be recognized by his shoes, gold,
silks or satins, family crest colors, or sword. Woe to him who dared
to cross these strict barriers. Even the great Molière mocks the bourgeois
who dresses like a nobleman, who "plays" nobleman.

A collection of the laws of three republican Swiss cities of that time
provides an illustration of the religious and state control over dress for
three hundred years.[5] In Bern, Basel, and Zurich, centers of urban liberty
of that time, there was no freedom of dress; first of all, the poor or
members of the lower classes who had "made good" and wanted to
indulge in some extravagance of dress to please some member of the
opposite sex could not dress as they wished. And the authorities imposed limits on the extravagance, rights, or licence of other estates as
well. So, for instance, the special decrees of 1375 forbade women to
wear embroidered gowns and pointed shoes. It would seem that the
world had no greater problems than the length of a dress, style of sleeve,
or type of decoration. And city clerks actually pursued these"criminals";
the court records show a great many cases of this kind. Although these
laws were eventually interpreted more liberally, it was the French Revolution that put an end to this special kind of cultural slavery. The
French Revolution abolished the privileged estates and granted equality
to all before the law. A striking or revolutionary change was reflected
in the style of dress and its symbolism. Attire changed; new styles as
new symbols of freedom and equality appeared. The symbolic costumes
of the magistrates, officers of the Republic, both civilian and military,
were sometimes very elaborate and ornate. Their attire symbolized
political, judicial, or military power, as did the attire of the rulers they
replaced. Thus social and political changes in Europe were apparent
on both city and country streets, in revolutionary caps and ribbons,

the freedom of dress, the change in fashions, as well as in verbal symbols of equality and liberty.

With the advent of totalitarianism, symbolism took on special significance. Just as once the Church for religious reasons, so now the party and the state came to impose symbols on the people by force and to dictate symbolic behavior in the form of demonstrations, political rituals, and even everyday behavior. The form of greeting is regimented; the proper salutation is proof of loyalty toward the party and the super-elite. The party imposes the type, style, and color of dress. Now the street becomes monotonous, filled with masses of people in one predominant color, almost military outfits, in shapeless caps, with the great leader's catechism book in hand. On orders from the state, all are now equal—with the exception of the superman, the "maximum leader." Everyone wears the same caps and carries the same booklet the "chairman" wrote for them. This means—of course, only symbolically—that now everyone thinks in the same way. A single, identical color of dress, the same quasimilitary shape of clothing, identical political catechism are in turn symptoms of regimentation and total power. The street and daily life become "gray," dull, and oppressive.

Color and attire have been used throughout history to mark social distance: social stratification, estates, classes, and power. The style or fashion regulated by law and imposed by the state was a tool in class domination and maintenance of privilege. Color and garb divided the sacred from the temporal; it was indicative of sacerdotal status and power. Freedom of choice, dress and symbols of freedom, the colors of the revolution and republic also marked the beginnings of social change that harbored both freedom and total power. When totalitarian states appeared, the dull uniform betrayed regimentation, often confused with equality. Freedom of choice in attire and change of style thus far have been symptomatic of free and dynamic societies, a phenomenon that can be observed on city streets in republican countries.

4. THE POLITICAL UNIFORM

The individual seldom realizes that he is being manipulated through the means of symbols by political groups or commercial concerns through advertising. The "projection" of dress or other symbols from one field of life to a different one, from one social system to another, can play a vital role in the process of consolidation and struggle for power. The projection of symbols or religious cults into political life facilitates the deification of political power and leaders.

After Austria was occupied by the Allies, Soviet units also entered Vienna. As the troops marched in, the likeness of Lenin could be seen on the banner of one of the Soviet units. On American, British, or French banners, there were no embroideries of presidents, premiers, or other dignitaries. The Soviets were following an established practice— that of embroidering on religious or military banners the likenesses of saints. People respect the flag and they respect the saints. In states which have gone through a revolution, some of the military banners were decorated with an embroidered likeness of the political leader, living or dead. In the categories of semantic terminology, the portrait of this leader on the banner is both a signal and a symbol. It is a signal because it conveys the information that this person should be given the same homage as that given to earlier banner portraits. It is a symbol because it represents a set of values, a new ideology. Religious symbolic techniques have been transferred to politics; the symbols are now controlled by political elites.

Now let us turn to the problem of the use of the military uniform in political action, to the projection of military behavior and action into the political arena.

The uniform, as every form of dress, fulfills many functions. The uniform of the French soldier of the Napoleonic army was probably esthetically pleasing to the eighteenth- or early nineteenth-century eye; it also gave the soldier a certain status, and thus importance, in society. Biologically, however, it was nonfunctional and did not provide needed warmth and comfort in, for instance, the bitter Russian climate. The uniform was also a symbol of the republic and empire—a symbol of power. What is more, for the soldier it was a symbol of discipline. The soldier, man in uniform, obeys orders issued by another man in uniform—a uniform decorated with the proper symbols of an officer. The relationship is impersonal. The soldier and the officer are often "nameless"; the soldier does not know the name of the officer, and the officer does not know the names of his soldiers. The symbols that differentiate them externalize their social and organizational relationship. The display of these symbols becomes a psychological stimulus.

In the continental European armies a soldier saluted at the sight of an officer. Here the military salute becomes a *response* to the *stimulus*: the display of symbols of rank and status. The uniform, with the aid of tough training and military drill, psychologically conditions the soldier to discipline. The soldier internalizes, subsconsciously adopting a certain mode of behavior associated with the uniform and the command (signal), so that after extensive training he responds to orders (signals). Here the signal-stimulus results in a quasiconditioned response. All this reminds us of Pavlov, but it is not quite as clear and simple.

Military organization is based on a chain of commands, orders, and obedience. There is no room for discussion, hesitation, or objections. Communication between an officer and his soldiers fits into a fixed mold. It is reduced and standardized. At the signal, the soldier immediately answers in the standardized way. His response is predictable. Disobedience is punished without delay. During his rookie period, the soldier learns through immediate experience that obedience is synonymous with avoidance of pain; this psychological mechanism in time recedes into the subconscious, somehow merging with the subtle, perhaps intuitive feeling we sense for avoidance of pain. The very sound of an order communicates alertness, awakening this entire psychological mechanism based on association of a certain sound with a specific kind of action.

But pain and reward is not the sole psychological mechanism or motive. Shared values, sentiments of identification, fidelity, even love supply additional, sometimes powerful support for the psychological mechanism of discipline. Among these is the ideological appeal characterizing what might be called ideological armies—whether revolutionary or democratic.

Many factors contribute to the efficient functioning of the mechanism of command-orders-obedience. However, for the sake of our discussion let us limit ourselves to a simplified model of discipline connected with the symbol of the uniform, since it is vital in the modern system of military structure. Naturally, discipline is different in the democratic Swiss army from that in Bismarck's Prussian army, different in the general sense of the soldier's rights, the length of time that the command relationship lasts, the soldier's independence off-duty, etc. Nonetheless, at the moment of military action or maneuvers, the uniform is a symbol of a certain way of behavior, which differs from behavior symbolized by clerical garb or a judge's robes. In uniform, a man obeys; he does not discuss. He becomes an obedient part of a whole which the commander must move quickly and methodically in a conflict situation.

The use of the military uniform by a political organization, such as the Fascists, projects the pattern of military behavior to a political organization. The projection of symbolic patterns from one sociological system or structure into another is often a spontaneous technique. Ideologists and leaders may institute in their party political uniforms for the militants not realizing the latent functions, the consequences of such an innovation. This may be a mechanical imitation of the army or another party. Such a step may also be simply a consequence of a routine or quest for establishment of rank and order. In human society the patterns of behavior are marked with symbols just as methods of procedure in arithmetic. The projection of the symbol of a military uniform to a political organization is the projection of military aggressiveness and disciplined behavior to political structure. Unlike members of a political club who carry on discussions, uniformed party soldiers obey the orders of their commander-leader. In our historical period, universal military service has familiarized people with military discipline, along with the pattern of symbolic behavior in uniform. The projection of military uniforms to the Nazi or Fascist organizations changed the type of traditional political party into an organization of political aggression and blind obedience to the leader. Private political armies, called party militia, have militarized political movements. This pattern developed during the period between the wars and has continued in altered form in various parts of the world (see Chapter III, "Dynamics of a Political Party").

But how to mobilize these uniformed masses of the political army, how to impose the military uniform and discipline on them? Generally people do not rush to join an army. Ideology has its basic appeal—to people's values, interests, prejudices, subconscious psychic needs, hidden emotions. Party militiamen are recruited for the cause. Totalitarian movements recruit their political soldiers by appealing to economic political values, to ideologies, as well as to racial or national hatred.

Man is by nature an aggressive creature, and it is through education, ethics, philosophy, religion, and culture that he learns to control his aggressive tendencies, pushes them back into subconsciousness, or else channels them in another direction, at best in the direction of creative action and effort. We also know that frustration—the feeling of anxiety and anger resulting from failure, obstacles, or injustice—although the actor may not be aware of it, manifests itself as aggression. These aggressions are channeled, modified, or controlled by the civilizing process, but the appeal to political hatred loosens these brakes, to some extent supplies ideological rationalization for man's natural aggressive tendencies; it could almost be called the awakening of primitive biological forces and instincts. Moreover, active aggression, even in verbal form, offers a release for these pressures and tensions, a welcomed psychological outlet. But that is not the whole story.

Against this background, it is not difficult to understand the ideological appeal of Nazism during a period of social crisis and disintegration. Fascism succeeded not only because of the crisis, but also because of the irresponsible tactics and lack of political wisdom of the left. It is often forgotten that irresponsible tactics of the progressive camp may lead to the victory of the far right. The man bogged down in everyday, uphill work values a promise of a national order that can ensure him a peaceful life.

After World War I the antimilitaristic, pacifist mood was a humane and understandable political response. That is true. But there was also another side to the postwar psychology other than antiwar feelings. These were the feelings of the demobilized army. The army is poeple who have fought, born a hard, inhuman fate, have gone through sufferings and mortal dangers. Now, after the war and in their own country they have come up against a wall of mistrust and hostility. There has been no reward for their sacrifice and suffering. An Italian officer or noncom, coming home after the triumphs of the Allies and festive parades, found his standard of living and class position deflated drastically. The former officer or noncom, who until recently had power, social status, and a modest but secure income, suddenly found himself in a new situation—often without work, sometimes as a belated student; in either case he lost his former superior position. In his appeal to the veterans, Mussolini restored to them their officer's uniform and former rank, promised work and status, and also appealed to their patriotism, the Italian traditions of Risorgimento, the glory of Garibaldi. The appeal was directed at the whole gamut of loyalty, emotions, and associations. While the party uniform imposed party discipline, it did so in the name of patriotic loyalty close to the hearts of some of the former soldiers. What is more, Mussolini formed a militia composed only of officers—all had officers' uniforms and insignia, everyone was given brass and illusion rank.

In their military role, identified by the symbol of the uniform, the party militiamen behaved not like members of an independent party but like military men, although people are usually reluctant to submit themselves to military discipline. Mussolini found a brilliant method here. A common private is something quite different from an officer. He gave all his militiamen well-cut officers' uniforms, in which his young followers looked better than in civilian clothes. He also appealed, as if pressing various buttons of the psychological machine, to other functions of the uniform: it was a symbol of superior status, gave a feeling of personal authority and social importance, provided a privileged position in a totalitarian society. A Fascist uniform was composed of an officer's tunic with a civilian type of shirt and tie. It was of a cut introduced by the then universally admired British only for their officers. This uniform also had a "Sam Brown" shoulder belt, used exclusively by the officers of the Allied armies after World War I, and of course high cavalry boots, most uncomfortable in the torrid climate of southern and central Italy, badly suited for riding a motorcycle, but how attractive to the ladies, and of course symbolically very manly. The head of the party and the state also showered them with an abundance of copper badges and medals, gave them new and fancy titles that concealed special privileges. Thus the political soldier of the twentieth century was given the feeling of importance, power, and special privilege because it was obvious, as it is obvious in all totalitarian states, that party members, and especially the political militia, enjoy special privileges in relation to the rest of society. Hitler built up his militia in a similar way—the difference was that the uniforms of the Nazi party were in much worse taste than the Italian ones. In this way the totalitarian militia forced democratic and republican parties to form their own defense apparatus—a democratic militia. The result was a general militarization of political life. Masses of thousands, when dressed in the symbolic party uniform, were marshalled into disciplined columns, responded with obedience and action to the command of the leader, and became the object of manipulation by the party super-elite.

When the drums began to beat, political commanders shouted their orders: flags were lifted, bands began to play, the political regiments marched like automata. Party members were now interested in keeping in step, jutting out their chins, looking properly martial while facing the stern countenance of the maximum leader. The music, the floodlights, screams, display of flags dulled their minds and controls. Now rampant emotions were released on command in a balanced dose of hatred and love—hate for the archenemies, the political demons, the opponents, and love for the maximum leader, the party, the chosen nation, the chosen class—expressed by rhythmical chants, slogans, screams intermixed with music and songs.

And do not forget the songs and music. Music also has a symbolic function and affects the emotions. The "Pariser Marsch" (The march of Paris) is associated with German victory over the French in 1871; "Die Wacht am Rhein" (The guards on the Rhine) reminds you of your archenemies, the French, and your moving fidelity to the Reich; "Horst Wessel" appeals to your hero complex and hero worship. Above all, the music affects your mind. These songs and marches are associated with a political content; many were socialized from childhood. When Hans or Guiseppe sings the party song in a political regiment, in uniform, watching for the next orders of his *Scharführer* or officer of the *Squadristi*, he cannot and does not think critically and politically. He is carried on a flood of emotions. The impact of all these media on a person is of a massive nature.

The political uniform worked of course only within this social and psychological context—the environment—of the political movement. It was combined with other ways of control. Take, for instance, goose-stepping. Once in a political uniform, a party member responds to the order; once the drum begins to beat, the goose-step ordered and slogans rhythmically shouted in a chorus, the will and mind of a national-socialist party member is under complete control and spell.

The excellent chronicler and penetrating observer of totalitarian Germany, William L. Shirer, records on 6 September 1934 the response of Hitler's *Arbeitsdienst,* the Labor Service Corps, to goose-stepping:

> Standing there in the early morning sunlight which sparkled on their shiny spades, fifty thousand of them, with the first thousand bared above the waist, suddenly made the German spectators go mad with joy when, without warning, they broke into a perfect goose-step. Now, the goose-step has always seemed to me to be an outlandish exhibition of the human being in the most undignified and stupid state, but I felt for the first time this morning what an inner chord it strikes in the strange soul of the German people. Spontaneously they jumped up and shouted their applause. There was a ritual even for the Labour Service boys. They formed an immense *Sprechchor*—

a chanting chorus—and with one voice intoned such words as these: "We want one Leader! Nothing for us! Everything for Germany! *Heil Hitler!*[6]

Of course, not at all times, in every situation, and not all Germans would respond that way. Only certain groups did. But, as Shirer's description suggests, manipulation works effectively when it has a psychological response among the manipulated; the values, the attitude were there. The interaction is essential, the interaction of the multitudes, the leadership, and the *manipulatives.* We shall use the latter term for technical devices, material and behavioral, applied by political actors to control and move multitudes.

Members of Hitler's Reichstag, in their party uniforms, did not discuss or disagree; they obeyed as soldiers are expected to do. Shirer describes such a Reichstag meeting on 7 March 1934: "Now six hundred deputies, personal appointees all of Hitler, little men with big bodies and bulging necks and cropped hair and pouched bellies and brown uniforms and heavy boots, little men of clay in his fine hands, leap to their feet like automatons, their right hand outstretched in the Nazi salute and scream "Heil Hitler.""[7]

Political decisions and activity turned into a military form. In place of free discussion by free people, the command of the leader became the basis for action and the mechanism of political decision. The symbolic character of the uniform created conditions for manipulating great masses; the application of military organization and symbols to political organizations, the projection of military patterns to political structure and symbolism contributed to the formation of new military-political structures and tactics of massive aggressive political action.

Sometime in 1944 in New York, during a long conversation over coffee, Friedrich Stampfer discussed with me Hitler's advent to power and his effective use of violence and mass appeal. Stampfer had been a prominent member of the Reichstag, representing the powerful Social-Democratic party of Germany (SPD). He had also been editor-in-chief of *Vorwärts*, an intellectual labor daily, the largest working-class newspaper in what was democratic Europe between the wars. I asked him suddenly: "But why didn't you use their methods for defense?" "We were not political jugglers," he replied calmly, "and politics for us was not a circus." Once politics was displaced into this new scenario, a novel political theater, democratic procedures ceased to work.

5. PROJECTION OF RELIGIOUS SYMBOLISM INTO POLITICAL BEHAVIOR

I hope that the reader will excuse a short digression here, nevertheless connected with the main topic.

In the 1930s, large masses of Europeans were swept up by the ardor of faith in totalitarian ideologies. It was a period of growth and triumph for Fascist parties and Nazism, a period of narrow, "zoological" nationalism. Today it is difficult to even comprehend these feelings. In countries that had no militaristic traditions, and in which Protestantism was the dominating religion (with some important exceptions, however), neither the Fascist party nor, at the other extreme, the Communist movement gained any great influence or organizational strength. Both of these movements of far right or left remained microparties, small, artificially nurtured political clubs. It is enough to add here the examples of England, Sweden, Holland, Denmark, and Switzerland. There were sympathies for these movements in these countries, but only small groups backed them. In countries of radical, sectarian Protestantism, to give the example of the United States, Fascist movements never flourished on the right. It is true that other forms of extreme reaction and racism, connected closely with certain forms of Protestantism and anti-Catholic in content, as for instance the Ku Klux Klan, existed there, but these were local or regional movements, limited to the South or a few Western states (such as Colorado), and had some spotty influence on the East Coast (e.g., New Jersey). Although these were movements of extreme racial and religious reaction that practiced terror tactics and had substantial support, they were never mass movements in the sense of European political movements and were never of comparable dimensions. Totalitarian movements found fertile ground in certain Catholic countries, countries where the Inquisition was once powerful, and countries of "marginal" Protestantism, Lutheran rather than Calvinist, colored with nationalism, as in Germany, and at the same time in countries with militaristic traditions and centristic institutions. This hypothesis, however, calls for a substantial qualification.

In Protestant sections of Germany, the Nazi party was powerful and influential. In a Catholic Poland, prior to 1939, the Fascist movement never gained an influence similar to the one in Italy, although there were some fascist groups and the extreme right was strong. In Catholic

Belgium, Social-Democrats were influential; the Fascist Rexists, however, had a powerful appeal. The militaristic tradition, so it seems, must be emphasized here, too. The combination of several "causes," determinants, as was mentioned, favored the appeal of fascist ideologies and the militaristic tradition belongs here. But, anti-Nazi conspiracies were primarily organized by army officers, one may argue. Yes. What is essential is the attitude of the masses, of the former soldiers and lower ranks of officers and noncoms, not the attitudes of aristocratic and high officers. The latter traditionally served in the army, but they were trained to command rather than to obey; furthermore, the opposition was not massive. Those dissenters were sensitive and educated men, strongly motivated by moral considerations, critical, trained since early years to apply their mind and their own judgment to matters of politics.

But we should not confuse the problems of the Catholic church with projection of rituals (ritualistic substitution) or political patterns influenced by church institutions and its religious customs, rituals, and dogma. This was an unintended influence. Religion has a variety of effects. Catholic laymen and Catholic priests offered heroic resistance to Nazism and Fascism. Many took grave risks to rescue victims of persecutions and paid with their life. In this short sketch, we cannot consider the entire syndrome of values and institutions which influenced behavior and political movements. We are concerned with a fragment and with attempting to understand only a segment of a complex problem.

The hierarchical structure of the church offers a certain pattern of organization. Religious customs and rituals give rise to festive processions in which tens of thousands of the faithful take part. The behavior of the faithful during the procession is controlled by religious symbolism. Ritual is primarily symbolic behavior. Spiritual meaning, internal emotions are externalized in symbolic behavior, for example, in the sacral movement of the hand indicative of the sign of the cross, folding the hands in prayer. The behavior of the faithful is controlled by symbolic signals—they genuflect at the sound of a bell or at the moment a priest raises his hands in the ritual of blessing. Ritual behavior has not one but several psychological and sociological functions. For many it is a deep psychic experience, for others a formal pattern that must be followed for one reason or another. Thus there are masses celebrated for the truly dear departed, for friends and family members, filled with sincere emotion and religious dedication; but there are also official, formal masses in which the ritual becomes a symbolic mechanism, during which those present go through symbolic motions—for business or social reasons—following commands and symbolic signals in order to carry out the accepted social patterns. Rituals are "multidimensional" and carry a number of functions, may respond to a variety of needs.

Catholicism is a ritualistic religion in which formalized, symbolic behavior and liturgy play a vital role. Solemn observances attract tens of thousands of people to one place, one square, or hundreds, even thousands, to the great cathedrals. In radical Protestantism or in numerous Protestant sects, religious gatherings tend to be small, Protestant churches are rather modest in comparison with large cathedrals. There are few, if any, processions; there is no complicated ritual. There are few symbolic signs, and those that do exist—for example, baptism and communion—are not generally practiced daily or weekly. The Quakers, at one extreme, have none in the generally accepted sense (unless silence is a symbolic sign). Nor is there mass or formal church service among the Quakers. The procedure is similar among Unitarians, some Congregationalists, and other sects. Mass religious meetings (frequently held in tents and large sports arenas) and simple symbolic behavior such as baptism can be found in the United States among evangelistic and the so-called chiliastic Protestant groups, sects that appeal primarily to the emotions, emotion that is expressed mainly in spontaneous song and in "witnessing," both informal and non-ritualistic behavior. In Protestant countries in which there exists something that we have named sectarian radicalism, man is not conditioned to frequent symbolic behavior. The common prayer, although frequent, is not formal; it may even be expressed in silence, which makes it personal, related to meditation. Songs and hymns, on the other hand, are a means of psychological communion. But here again Protestant hymns are not as strongly anchored in formalized behavior or rituals as are the hymns and music that accompany the Catholic mass (at least in the way the Catholic mass was conducted prior to recent changes).

The child absorbs the patterns of social and religious behavior early, and the pattern of behavior learned in childhood is usually lasting and difficult to change. In the Protestant society symbolic behavior is kept to a minimum in the child's upbringing. This society could be described as one with reduced symbolism and ritualism. In Catholic countries the faithful, from earliest childhood, are used to mass participation in formal and solemn religious rituals. The situation is similar, even more so, in rituals of the Greek Orthodox Church where there is even greater emphasis on the faithful execution of symbolic movements and formalism (strict adherence to established forms) of ritual.

The very architecture of towns reflects not only the social structure and economic activity of their inhabitants, but also their cultural needs, systems of values, esthetic sense, customs, and religious character. We shall return to a fuller discussion of this subject soon. Our concern at the moment is the town architecture of predominantly Catholic societies, where great cathedrals for mass services were erected, cathedrals with huge squares for religious but also secular (generally, political) manifestations. An example of this is St. Peter's Square in Rome, a vast square bordered with a circle of columns and walls, dotted with exquisite fountains and enclosed by the beautiful stone frames, *Il capolavoro*, of Bernini. Thousands of people are united here symbolically as one at the moment of benediction. For thousands this act of blessing is a profound inner experience, but it is also the act of subordination to authority, repeated down the centuries from childhood to old age. It is true there are no lay political gatherings in St. Peter's Square, but other great squares in Rome, as well as in other Italian towns, have been used effectively for political purposes.

During their historical development, individuals banded in societies have learned to separate different areas of life—religious behavior from the professional or political. This division is not sharp or precise, but is nevertheless reasonably followed in modern societies. We do not pay divine homage to our governments or political leaders, we do not kneel before the portraits of a cabinet member or prime minister, do not accept political speeches as revelation, theories as dogmas. We are aware of the difference between these areas. We know that the patterns of behavior are and should be different. The practicing or nominal Catholic in France or Italy knows that behavior in church is different from that at a political meeting—after all, these are simple matters. But this pattern of religious behavior may be cleverly shifted to political, ideological movements. Then the projected symbolic mechanism serves the purpose of consolidating power and spreading militant political ideology.

Under these conditions political ideology becomes a kind of religion. Even today political leaders in totalitarian systems (or those patterned after totalitarian systems) in Asia and Africa are paid religious homage. Such homage was paid to Hitler by party members. In this political cult the Führer was a superman.

In London or New York, despite the vast size of these cities, there are no vast squares that would hold mobilized masses which could be manipulated by means of symbols. Trafalgar Square or Time Square are quite small in comparison with the squares of large continental cities. In New York, for instance, there are few massive cathedrals and churches. Let me stress the point again—Protestantism knows no huge, mass rituals or complete symbolic subordination. Protestant countries are ones with reduced symbolic formalism, while Catholic countries have been in the past and still are countries of extensive symbolic expression.

The function of symbols and rituals is far broader than what we have discussed here. Religious ritual has its spiritual and emotional functions and significance; it is a formal expression of deep-seated sentiments and needs. For many it is a source of inner balance and spiritual renovation. It also has esthetic appeal. Moreover, it supplies continuity, integrating the faithful of the past and the present. Symbols and rituals have beauty, and their absence impoverishes our lives. Rituals are "multidimensional" since they affect not one, but several aspects of life and behavior. They are also "multifunctional," because they perform several functions at the same time, and some of the latter may be unintended by actors.

6. MANIPULATION OF SYMBOLS

Now let us return to our main topic. The projection of the military uniform to political activities and organizational structure has made it possible for the party super-elite to organize volatile multitudes that are aggressive and generally uncritically obedient. The symbolism of the uniform has integrated these men into "storm" or "shock" troops, into militant, well-disciplined organizations.

The general strategy of symbolic and ritual projection covered practically the entire nation of Germany. This was part of public policy, which was a technique of regimentation, called *Gleichschaltung*. This projection reached far, penetrating the entire social structure. Even nonparty people, even resisters were reached through the office, street, block organizations, schools, and factories. From schools the rituals and symbols moved to families. Those tired of continuous parading, who resented the brutal imposition on the mind of man, as well as those who resisted, went through the motions, just to survive, since symptoms of disloyalty to the system were severely punished.

These masses, for centuries conditioned by religious behavior, were now taught to respond to new symbolic signals, trained in new ritualistic behavior. Now this ritual became political in content. The homage once paid to saints and icons was now projected to the portraits of party leaders, martyrs of the movement, or even directors of the enterprises of mass terror. In periods of crisis and emotional stress, the leaders of totalitarian parties could now herd multitudes of many thousands to huge squares, manipulate them through symbols and uniformed political militia, create an emotional environment, an "atmosphere" by means of music, lights, and slogans. The frightened, submissive, or enthusiastic multitudes answered stimuli signals with signal responses, always in extremes of emotion, whether in love and loyalty for the tyrant or hatred for the enemies.

Manipulations of this kind were not unrelated to social-political processes. Movements such as Fascism appeared in a specific social, political, and economic situation, during a period of political crisis, a period of particular psychological stress, so that they must be viewed in this specific context. Nevertheless, the choice and success of this technique is a result of certain historical conditions, experiences, education or processes of learning (which begin in early childhood), systems of values, and cultural patterns. The emotional, psychological function of the ritual, the traditions of participating in an organized mass, must also be remembered. Man has an unconscious need for symbolic behavior, for ceremony and ritual, which in a certain sense and in certain situations is a formalization and channeling of emotion. Some people draw almost physical pleasure from participation in mass gatherings, in marches or military parades (similarly as from dancing), even from mixing in a crowd—but first of all from an identification of a show of strength.

* * *

The seminal problem is what effect symbols, rituals, and uniforms have on society, how they work as "antecedents" of collective behavior, of attitudes such as willingness to follow, to submit to the leader's will. Whether action is intended or planned is, of course, of significance. However, the effect symbols have on society, their "function" in the social process, whether intended or not, is our concern in this essay.

First of all, we should add that rituals and symbols may carry many functions; they are usually multifunctional. However, here we are concerned primarily with social control—the domination or manipulation of societies. The leadership of a movement may use symbolic "equipment" of many kinds: tradition, custom, sentiment, even love. Rituals can and do have a "manipulative" function, but it is a mistake to consider all rituals and symbolism at all times as solely technical devices for manipulation and subordination of multitudes. Religious rituals are not isolated, independent "blocs." They are simply a consequence of the entire outlook, of the acceptance of an entire belief system. In fact, rituals are part of the religious fabric. A Catholic procession in Seville is meaningful as an external expression of faith and acceptance of a theology. Here are external actions, which reflect and are the consequence of an "internalized" belief system. The ritual has a reinforcing quality; it reintegrates the religious groups and sentiments of identification and belonging. The ritualistic and symbolic motions, rooted in faith, meet some inner spiritual needs, which we call, in an empirical approach, psychological needs that are formalized, channeled expressions of emotions. They do have in many cases a profound impact on personality. Here is one dimension, one aspect of rituals.

The powerful social movements have grown in this initial religious environment. The new political belief systems created their own liturgy and rituals. The latter were also a consequence of the entire idea system, but their origin can be traced to the "antecedent," to the religious environment within which they appeared and grew. In Russia, in an Orthodox country, where the Czar was worshipped as head of the church and a saintly person, where dogmatism in religion bred dogmatism in political philosophy, the attitudes were transferred from one belief system to another by certain, perhaps even few, individuals. But once rituals are practiced, they may exercise a variety of effects even without any intentional manipulation.

However, a ritual may be also used by a religious or political hierarchy to control the multitudes. Political leadership, a group in command, may organize a political manifestation and use intentionally pictorial or musical devices, behavioral patterns to indicate or reinforce a new political stratification and consolidate power. What is of significance is the social function the ritual carries. In such a case, a religious behavioral pattern, custom, or even technique may be projected into political behavior. We have called this type of performance "ritualistic substitution." Here is an example; my observation of a political procession in 1939, a celebration of the October Revolution in a large town of what was once the Polish Republic after the occupation by the Soviet army and establishment of Soviet rule. Political power seized by conquest had to be reinforced and a new political stratification, the new elite, introduced to the local people. By means of this procession, personalities of the new ruling class had been communicated to the multitudes.

This was an orderly political procession, but I had an impression of a religious one. I could hear now familiar songs of the working class movements, known to the workers of this town, such as the "Red Banner," "Varsovienne," "The Internationale." They were sung one time in a brisk form, may I say *allegro con fuoco,* not unlike the "Marseillaise." Now, the rhythm was different; they were sung like religious chants while marchers were moving slowly, carrying large portraits of the party leaders. Men and women carried on wooden structures and sticks large pictures of Lenin and Stalin, and were followed by likenesses of other commissars: Molotov, Beria, Voroshilov, and still more. But those were conspicuously smaller, more modest in size. The likenesses of Lenin and Stalin were of a strikingly large size. Lenin's face was quite pale; after all, he was dead. Stalin looked healthy and vigorous on this picture. It was evident that here is the direct successor. Green garlands and red ribbons were attached on the top of Stalin's picture and were dropping down gracefully. The ends of those garlands and ribbons were carried by singing girls and women. The number of those portraits struck me; there were so many. Sections of marchers were identified (post office, railroad, utilities workers). The pictures were carried largely by women. Those smaller ones were decorated probably by some marchers as they best could. In Poland only the monuments and pictures of saints were decorated with ribbons and flowers; only in religious procession pictures were carried—pictures of the saints and of the Madonna. This was the master pattern imitated here, and this political manifestation had also an appearance of a religious procession. The way political leaders were honored here gave them an unusual and superior quality.

About eight months later, I saw a similar celebration in a northern town. But some of the marchers displayed a silent protest. Some of the pictures quite conspicuously were carried the reverse way with the likeness of the leaders turned back; some pictures were touched by mud.

The October Revolution was not celebrated before in those towns, and the Communist party had no significant influence prior to the occupation. The celebrations were organized by those in command, and required considerable equipment and expenditure. This was a carefully organized manipulation of multitudes, a way of reinforcing a new social system.

In certain environmental situations, as we have already indicated, it is relatively simple to manipulate assembled multitudes—to induce the people in such a gathering to simple actions. A theater offers an effective environment. A transient multitude is subject to an identical, powerful audiovisual experience within a closed, encircled place. The interplay of light and relative darkness facilitates manipulation, and the use of powerful searchlights permits a strong focusing of collective attention, and, consequently, control.

Years ago, I witnessed a performance called "Town Hall of the Air," which was a radio show of fine quality. But at certain moments, applause was initiated from the platform, with a convincing gesture to follow. The large audience followed easily and cheerfully. Such practice was at one time known in European theaters, when the applause was initiated by a small group (*die Klakke*) in Viennese theaters, or initiated as a response to flowers presented to an actor who played a major role. More than a hundred years ago, the French composer Hector Berlioz wittily described the many types of "professional applausers" known as *claquers,* Parisians hired to throw flowers and create enthusiasms.[8] The technique of inciting competitors and manipulating audiences was well known to the Romans. They employed the *iubilatores* in their circuses whose job was to encourage by exhortations the riders and excite the multitudes in harness racing. An intended manipulation of attitudes was and is, after all, generally known; there is no secret about it. It is practiced on a large scale in advertising.

There is evidence that the choice and use of political symbolism and formalized behavior by some of the modern totalitarian movements was not always spontaneous or accidental, but at times was planned and intended by the leadership. There is, for example, indication of it in *Mein Kampf,* where Hitler discusses the nature of the political multitude of reasons for the choice of colors of his flag. There is abundant evidence in the activities and publications of Goebbels' Ministry of Propaganda. Hitler's architect and minister Albert Speer was also a social engineer of those massive political circuses of the *Parteitag* in Nuremberg, where columns of flagbearers and music and floodlights were all used to elicit the expected response from uniformed and regimented multitudes. Practically all of the Luftwaffe's searchlights were requisitioned for this gigantic show of excitatory political behavior.[9]

Mussolini also had a remarkable understanding for the political theater. He played his political role like an actor in *commedia dell'arte,* changing costumes depending on the occasion and throwing up his arms in a variety of ways during his speeches. He ordered colorful parades

with elaborate marching steps and theatrical political rallies on the
Piazza Venezia. He probably enjoyed political pageants, but he was
also an intelligent leader who understood the effects of his theatricals
and party regalia.

Mussolini knew the work of Le Bon, the author of pioneering works
in the field of collective psychology. Le Bon expressed rather pessimistic
opinions and had little if any admiration for what we call today the
"common man" or "common people." Likewise, most of the totalitarian
leaders had contempt for the "masses" they tried to win and move; they
valued only the techniques of mastering them.

7. MYTH-MAKING AND PERSONALITY CULT (POLITICAL DEIFICATION)

Stalin

In a fascist system, elevation of a leader to superman status is related
to political philosophy of a hierarchical society. Creation of a legend
of a superman in a communistic society is contradictory to the philosophy of perfect equality, a classless society and final form of democracy.
But the elevation of Stalin to the status of genius, of a superman—we may
call this myth-making, deification, or caesarism in this case—has been
systematically followed in the U.S.S.R. Khrushchev later called it a
personality cult. Step by step a legend of his genius was created; slowly,
his name was to become a worshipped symbol, his person a legendary
superman, at least in the official lore.

The myth-making of Stalin was carried out under conditions of
extreme terror. Rules and techniques were used to elevate his name and
accord him the status of a superman. The emergence of a caesaristic
cult can be followed from a voluminous literature in tens of languages
of the various nations ruled by the Soviet government. This type of
writing and political worship appeared of course in Russian, but also
in Ukrainian, Byelorussian, Polish, Latvian, Lithuanian, Estonian, to
mention only a few languages., in addition to the voluntary English
and French sycophantism in New York or Paris. Pictures of Stalin were
displayed in gigantic sizes, and his monuments appeared in the streets
of Soviet cities in colossal sizes. By analogy his monumental physical

depiction symbolized his historical and political role.

During celebrations of the Soviet and Communist holy days, for example, the October Revolution, canvasses with pictures of Stalin and Lenin have covered three floors on main streets and public squares, whether in Moscow or in the provincial city of Minsk. Sometimes the portrait covered the front of a house. This made a striking impression. A visitor, a passerby, and of course a Soviet citizen realized immediately his status, power, and a suggestive historical role. Some would leave those pictures for a longer time as evidence of personal loyalty. Not unlike holy ikons, they protected against "evil," this time political evil—the risks of arrest or deportation. A number of articles were written and books published about the ways Stalin and Lenin (with Stalin being presented as Lenin's successor) were and should be painted.

Not unlike a medieval hagiology,[10] a political hagiology of approved Communist heroes, and especially the myth-making literature about Stalin, was encouraged. Together with this new hagiology, an iconography advanced, rules of presentation of heroes and supermen in plastic arts. The scholarly style of these writings and the fact that they were published by academies and authoritative party journals were indicative of the official policy, of the party line.

The work of Kravchenko can be mentioned here as one of many examples. In his article on representing Stalin in the pictorial arts, he writes: "The biography of Comrade Stalin is equal to a substantial part of the revolutionary movement in Russia. . . . The picture of the leader is a picture of the country and nation which he leads to victory." Kravchenko then gives suggestions concerning style and presentation. Stalin should be pictured "realistically" (according to the imperatives of socialist realism), and in any composition Stalin must be the center of the entire picture. Kravchenko also suggests some of the major themes: "Stalin with children," "Stalin presenting the project of the Constitution, November 1936," "Lenin and Stalin in Cracow, 1912," etc.[11]

Themes in paintings and sculptures were rigidly held to political subjects related to the history of Soviet rule and the Communist revolution. A theme was built around a central personality, Stalin or Lenin. Style had to conform to a photographic naturalism called realism. All these rules and manners remind us of iconic norms of medieval art, when saints were presented in an established way, accompanied by known symbols, always as central figures, and themes were reduced to religious subject matter.

By an elaborate procedure, step by step the name of the dictator
is elevated to "superhumanity." It thus becomes a caesaristic sanctified
symbol. On the other hand, the name must be repeated often, with
proper respect, and not in an arbitrary manner. Special permission has
to be granted to those who wish to honor Stalin's name with a project,
a factory, a town, a bridge, or a highway. Thus, by frequent repetition
of the name and by a special status of reverence accorded to the name,
the leader of the Communist state, of a state based on a philosophy of
perfect equality, is elevated to a superman, a god, superior to all others
who among themselves are, of course, equal. The difference between
the masses—the citizens—on the one hand, and the party elite on the
other, the far narrower super-elite, and finally the superman-leader is
accentuated that way. Thus I open at random the bound collection of
Pravda for 1940, the 6 August 1940 (no. 217) issue. On six pages of
Pravda the name of Stalin appears seventy-one times. Now I take the
issue of 23 July 1940 (no. 203) of this largest and most important
Communist daily. On the first page alone, his name appears twenty-six
times.

The name of the superman, the political god, must be revered,
respected, loved, adored. Thus, the name of Stalin in this country of
folklore and peasant lore will now appear, on party command, in
proverbs and adages.

Such a collection of proverbs and sayings has been presented in
(Ukrainian language in the present stage of development), a study
written by three Ukrainian scholars, I. Gubarevskyi, B. Masalski, and
M. Pilinski, and published by the Ukrainian Academy of Sciences in
1940.[12] We read in this article that "the name of the beloved leader of
the working class is remembered in popular, peasant proverbs and songs
with great love and gratitude, for example: 'The sun shines best—the word
of Stalin is wisest,' 'To live well Stalin says [teaches] to work honestly,'
'Little sun and all stars rise from little father Stalin [*batko*], from
Moscow, from the Kremlin.'" The image of the political deity of the communist world is even coquettish in an elementary school poem or song
from Poland: *Slodkie usta jak malina, u Marszalka, u Stalina* [Sweet is
the mouth, like a raspberry, the mouth of our Marshal, the mouth of
Stalin]. Imagine such a song about Queen Victoria or President
Coolidge. The rhyme *Malina* [raspberry] *dziewczyna* [a young maid, a
girl] usually appears in folk love poetry.

The *name* of the genius, like the genius or the political god, himself
should be loved and worshipped but also protected. It is a "sanctum"

which should be distinguished from all "profanum." Factories, bridges, highways, mines should carry his name, of course, but only by special decree, not by arbitrary decision. This permission can be granted by the Presidium of the Supreme Soviet of the U.S.S.R. Once permission is granted, it appears on the front page, in the most prominent and honorable place of *Pravda.* Again, we read in *Pravda* of 23 July 1940 (no. 203): "Decree of the Presidium of the Supreme Soviet of U.S.S.R., awarding the highway 'Eastern Circle' the name of comrade J. V. Stalin: Resolved, to comply with the request of the meeting of the workers employed at the construction of the highway 'Eastern Circle' and the request of the leadership and organs of the party and the Soviets of the Kazakstan Republik, it was resolved to award the highway 'Eastern Circle' the name of J. V. Stalin. The President of the Supreme Soviet, Moscow, Kremlin, July 22, 1940" (translation mine).

Are those acts evidence of flattery and fear, or part of a design? The answer is not a simple one. Of course, terror, fear, and flattery are related to these acts. But there is more to it. There is an attempt to create an image and a myth; also, whatever the motives, there is an attempt to build up the leader as a superman: a god of a monotheistic political creed. A perusal of the official publications and press suggests this. What the intentions were is not as relevant in this case as the seminal problem of what effect this type of activity has and how it works. The end result is that it leads to the elevation of the leader to a kind of political god, and creates a legend around him. The person, even the name, thus becomes a *symbol.* It is the way a modern caesaristic cult was advanced, later to be called, modestly, a "personality cult."[13]

Philosophers, men of politics, and simply careful observers, so it seems to me, saw the nature of these processes in the making of a legend, and they also understood the diverse functions a symbol or ritual may have: a profound emotional, even a religious one, and at the same time one of practical politics, influence, and domination.

We will now move to conversation and gossip.

Bonaparte

An old volume of the anti-Bonapartist Benjamin Constant, which I found in the Brooklyn College Library, had an unusual, handwritten addition. On the last printed page of *De L'Esprit De Conquête et De L'Usurpation*[14] begins a handwritten record (in quill) and exchange of views which carries dates from 1814 to 1846 and gives us a certain insight into the development of the social image of Napoleon at that time, and of the creation of the Napoleonic legend. The topic of the notes is a discussion evaluating the personality and historical role of Napoleon Bonaparte and the way he should be transmitted to history. The record reads like a fascinating discussion, written once by an anti-Bonapartist, another time by an ardent Bonapartist. This exchange of handwritten notes, buried for a century and a quarter in a library, are timely and have quite a modern tinge. They give us an idea of the process that produces a social myth. The handwritten comments show how differently the same historical actor and the same occurrences were perceived by different persons. As a consequence, not one, but several social images of Napoleon are formed.

A few dates are found on these pages: 1814, 1833, 1840, 1841, 1843, 1846. The notes with earlier dates suggest a decline of Bonapartist appeal. In a controversy, and in an ambivalent evaluation of facts and personality, the social myth begins to grow again stronger, and at that point it seems to me, it is crystallized, it is formed. The funeral of Napoleon Bonaparte in 1840 (when his remains were returned to France) forms a major focus of comments. This was the crucial event at the time in the "collective representation" of the social image of Napoleon, in the popular evaluation of his role, but also in a current controversy. The notes and comments, written and gathered by three or more different writers, or perhaps collected and copied by one unknown recorder (the handwritings differ, but graphology is here irrelevant), reflect three perceptions of the same personality. Thus, three images emerge.

The first view is "Napoleonic," a reflection of the style and perceptions of the romantic era. Napoleon is deified and glorified with a nostalgia characterstic of the times of greatness. It is primarily an emotional view, colored by such values as "gloire, l'honneur, liberté," as seen by an ardent Bonapartist. This is a view and an image opposite to one presented by the author of the book.

The second view is "cold," rational, and evaluative. The comment "character of Bonaparte" (1814) is representative of this more evaluative and rational view, written by someone without, or with a controlled, political or emotional commitment; the writer considers on one hand the deficiencies of Napoleon's personality and deeds but does not underestimate his contribution and his historical role. It is an image of Napoleon written by a moderate observer who exercises his critical qualities.

The third is critically anti-Bonapartist. Here Napoleon is seen as
a great general, but also as a man who destroyed democracy, and a very
different one from the leaders of democratic revolutions who strengthened
democratic institutions and then retired. Napoleon built a personal empire, and was worshipped by crowds. This anti-Bonapartist also expresses
a democratic outlook. In spite of all, the comments of the anti-Bonapartist writer of these notes do not reach the intensity of the powerful
condemnations of Benjamin Constant. Social images of Bonaparte are
formed through the controversy reflected in these notes, although not
without some manipulation of the myths. The trend toward glorification
and deification wins, and by the end of the notes an image of the hero
is formed for the "social memory," (memory transmitted in society) for
popular appeal and tradition. This discussion, written in longhand in
the margins of an anti-Bonapartist book, seems like a reflection of a
contemporary debate which may have psychologically prepared the
soil for the Second Empire.

Who wrote these comments? The author or authors of the notes are
unknown. Some essays and remarks are identified with prominent names:
Byron, Lamartine, Manzoni, Berlioz. One comment is signed with the name
of a certain Dr. Strauss. But the handwritten, unsigned, personal remarks
are incisive and penetrating. They reflect men of intellect, erudition, and
talent. Some are written on the stationery of the French Ministry of
Colonies and Marine "Dépot de Cartes et Plans." Perhaps a quiet and
intelligent observer of the world, unmolested and unsuspected by anybody, perfectly safe in his sheltered "Dépot" of maps, wrote his impressions, recording current comments and conversations? A one-time officer
of the glorious army? But it seems rather probable that the record was
written at least by two, possibly even more persons. Part of the material
has been copied from current publications, or recorded by a witness.

Differences of views appear at the very beginning. The handwritten
record begins with two comments:

Napoleon had only the courage of his will (courage de volonté) and
he wished always to live the role of a great military leader (en grand
General) instead of dying a great man. The posterity which was the
future of others had for him less importance than his life which was
his future: There was always egoism in his genius, because this was
a genius of selfish design (calculations; le génie de calcul).

This judgment is not one of justice. This is one of hatred.

Diverse comments, some of them copied from published remarks, follow:

He commenced his life a stranger by birth, a scholar by charity.

He conquered the world with no friend but his sword and no fortune but his talents.

He knew no motive but interest, he acknowledged no criterion but success, he worshipped no god but ambition.

That he has done much evil, there is little doubt, that he has been the origin of much good there is as little. . . . Through his means, intentional or no, in Spain, Portugal, and France have arisen the blessings of a free constitution.

Superstition has found her grave in the ruins of the inquisition, and the feudal system with his whole train of satellites, has fled forever.

The patient collectors and commentators give us a picture of conflicting views of contemporary public opinion of a hero. But the issue of Bonaparte was not dead. The symbols and ideology were alive, a part of daily conversations and intense emotional discussions. This is the picture which emerges from these notes, written and collected between 1814 and 1846. It is a kind of a public-opinion record written on the back pages of a controversial book.

There is, however, something more to it. The collector and author of most of the notes gives us an insight into the building of a social image and myth or the revival of it—a social myth of Bonaparte after his downfall. As Byron is quoted in these comments: "Depuis Lucifer, aucun mortel aucun ange n'était tombé de si haut." (Since the times of Lucifer, none of the mortals, none of the angels has fallen from such height.)

A sober, even a cold evaluation of Napoleon as a man (dated 1814) is followed by Byron's poetic comments, and then, in a continuous exchange of views, the story of myth-making and social image develops.

The main part deals with the problems of transporting his remains from St. Helena to France and discussion as to where to place the ashes, where to build his tomb, what to write on the stone, in order to produce for posterity the "right" kind of symbol, the right type of a legend.

A handwritten comment informs us that in the French parliament, on 26 May 1840, the poet Lamartine discussed the issue of where to place his remains: "Under the column of Place Vendôme? [No], the Place would become a center of all the seditious meetings . . . a robe of Caesar displayed before the city. At the Church of la Madeleine? too close to the crowds. At the Arc de Triomphe? This is too pagan. In St. Denis?— No, his is a symbol of Dynasties and Kings," thus argued Lamartine, and added: "I would vote gladly for St. Denis, "but one single reservation worries me: This is a kind of meeting which history, even stones should avoid (il est des rapprochement que l'histoire et les pierres mêmes doivent éviter)." Bonaparte was simultaneously a soldier, a consul, a legislator, an emperor. There is only one inscription for this unique man and difficult epoch: "Napoleon . . . alone," suggested Lamartine. "Napoléon . . . seul."

And here an earlier note on the inauguration of the monument of Napoleon (28 July 1833). Now, solitude, isolation of his person is emphasized as a symbol. The "*Lonely* Column" is a symbol of the imperial destiny, its greatness is in isolation (si grand dans son isolement).

A personal note dated "15.x.1840" follows. Here our Bonapartist commentator writes about the changing mood of the people he observed back in 1815, and ponders about the instability (mobilité) of popular passions: "I think about the passions of the people who enjoyed with the same enthusiasm his coming and going because it is a spectacle (qui se rejouit avec—un égal enthousiasme du retour de l'empereur parceque c'est un spectacle et de son départ)", and he ends, "Napoleon was a man of the south, he should be permitted to "dormir dans sa gloire d'exil africain."

A copied report of the abbé Coquereau, on exhumation of his remains in St. Helena on 15 August 1840, reinforces the myth and popular image with a new legend: "I have seen," reports the abbé, "after twenty years, his body as though it were intact," and our commentator writes in bold letters: "During twenty years, death has respected Napoleon."

A comment of 4 March 1841 tells us: "For sure, Napoleon is a myth" (Très assurement Napoleon est un myth); he is a "symbolic and mystical person (Un être symbolique mystique)," as contrasted with the "low" materialistic forces. After all by whom was he defeated—"par commerce c'est a dire par l'Angleterre"—by the merchants, by England. The collector or one of the authors of notes writes after the funeral of Napoleon (which he assisted personally and calls a pompous affair): "All poetry is sorrow or desire" (Toute poésie est un regret ou un désir). The proper thing to do was to leave his tomb at St. Helena: "Napoleon at St. Helena is so far from us and so deified, as if he were in heaven. It is in Jerusalem, on the road of his infamous torment and suffering, where the Christians, when there were still Christians, went to worship Christ." (C'est à Jérusalem sur le chemin de son supplice infâme que les chrétiens, quand il y avait de chrétiens, allaient adorer le Christ.) Again, in another note: "St. Helena should be *Le Tombeau* of Napoleon, after all grand and poetic, a resting place of a great history which made a god out of a mortal man. (Où l'homme était fait dieu.)" An accessible tomb, a visible monument, becomes natural, human— the distant unknown is superhuman, deified. And on 4 March 1841, Doctor Strauss, as was mentioned, writes about Napoleon as a "symbolic and mystic being," and ends, "very definitely—Napoleon is a myth."

These notes reflect the process of the decline and resurrection of a social myth and a social image. The defeat and exile of Napoleon, accompanied by the social fatigue of the people, a consequence of wars, results in a decline of the myth followed by rational, critical evaluation; but soon a renascence of the legend is noticeable, a nostalgia to the historical pageant of glory and success, of flags and armies, of intense passions and enthusiasm. There were substantial sections of the army, bureaucracy, and the former Bonapartist elite to whom these ideas and symbols would appeal to personal interest. However, among those who once served or supported the Bonapartist traditions, symbols also appealed to dominant values, to ideological convictions, to patriotism, or to identification with social significance of his rule and national success. Now was the time to carve again a hero into a demigod. Traits of character are emphasized, others erased in conscious or unconscious efforts to build up an image.

The *solitude* is emphasized. The solitude which is so much in accord with the romantic times and style and paves the way to a vision of tragedy, uniqueness, and suffering, a vision that generates sympathy. A demigod is *unique Napoleon seul*; he is superhuman—even death respects him for twenty years. *Physical distance* or *physical absence* comes next. This absence assists in deification—as the comments suggest; his qualities are now magnified, an appeal is directed toward imagination and emotion unchecked by such a shocking experience as: "He is no different from others, he died like anybody does, he was only human." With time the memory of the hero is dominated by symbols, by a symbolic trinity of "La gloire, l'honneur, et la liberté." The Person and Symbols merge into a myth, into an image.

The historical personality is transformed now into an "emotional category": the name of Napoleon is associated with values, symbols, historical reminiscences, it is a divisive category, appealing to emotions of Bonapartists and anti-Bonapartists. A social myth contains some facts which were experienced and recorded, fused with values, symbols, and emotional attitudes. The empirical part of it supplies qualities or a semblance of "historical truth," but there is no one perception of the past nor one social image or evaluation.

In a speech recorded on these pages, delivered on the occasion of "funeral honors," Monsieur de Lamartine said: "If the great general had been a completely great man, if he had been a citizen without 'reproche,' if—after defending the country against counter revolution he would have introduced democratic and liberal institutions, if instead of destroying representative institutions, he would have supported them with his military force, if he had become an architect of social progress and protection of the people, if he had allowed and supported like Solon or the Legislator of America, a stable and wise government, and afterwards retired, so that freedom and free institutions could grow, who knows whether all this homage would be given by a crowd which worships especially those who have oppressed it (*écrasé lui*)? He would probably sleep quietly if not neglected, in his tomb."

Reading the manuscript notes we can follow a process of development of two, perhaps three, different social images. Not all of them are simple symbolic and emotional images. We can see also opinions and views, a result of a critical and balanced view, integrated with moral judgment and political values. From the rich clay of history, various monuments of the past are made—some by the hands of critical and imaginative thinkers and historians, others by the fanatics of irresponsible imagination, some by manipulation, and still others by dedicated and loyal followers. Like ancient sculpture, some resemble reality, others are built for purposes of worship.

8. POLITICAL ARCHITECTURE AND THE POLITICAL THEATER

Architecture is a very human art; it reflects man's values, ideas, imagination, even his senses and his body. The size of doors, windows, the height of ceilings, even stairs, are determined by dimensions of our body, the needs of movement, air, and vision. Unlike nature, unlike caves, mountains, and valleys formed by powerful, independent, sometimes adverse forces of nature, man's artificial environment has been shaped and built by his fantasy, imagination, practical sense, with his hands or machines. He builds in response to his need and he does not imitate nature.

Churches, cathedrals, temples, and theaters are a consequence of his spiritual, emotional, and esthetic needs, and not necessarily of those basic biological needs for shelter. First, they were conceived in human imagination. Thus, man has created an "artificial" environment, within the conditions of a natural one.

Architecture is not detached from the social fabric, it is its consequence and part of it. The public buildings erected by democratic nations are different from those of a theocracy or a tyranny. The pyramids of Egypt and the circuses of Rome are products of two different social systems—as is the Agora, the great square of democratic Greece. The architecture of the circus or colosseum becomes understandable in the context of its social function, the psychological needs of its times, as an "architectural social artifact" of a political system.

The Roman circus had many functions. Entertainment—play—was of course a major one. But the cruel performances also channeled social tensions and emotions of the demanding and volatile Roman plebs. Both the spectators and the unlucky performers corralled with their emotions and bodies in a closed arena made life easier and safer for the Caesars. The circus was an emotional *cloaca maxima,* which helped to keep the existing social and political order, at least for short intervals. It was one, a minor one to be sure, device for stability.

Modern politics is also reflected in stony artifacts, and political systems leave their imprints on what they build and destroy. Emergence of new leadership, a revolutionary change of political elites may also call for the assistance of a "political architect." A coup of a revolutionary party succeeds, a party takes over political power, a new and unknown elite emerges. Seized political power must now be consolidated. In the process, the image of the change must be shown to the nation so that people know whom to obey. Mass media serve this purpose, of course. The new elites are presented in many ways. Their names appear in newspapers; they appear with the supreme leadership of the party at public meetings; their names are repeated on the radio. But a "real" image, a visual presentation of the new elite, is a powerful message and also a mechanism for consolidating power, a reinforcement of the new social structure. And mass meetings, mass manifestations practiced by totalitarian parties, serve these functions.

What interests us at this point is the architectural artifact, the special structures erected for displaying a new leadership and power structure. This is modern political architecture. One of its sociological functions is to communicate the change of elites or leadership and to reinforce the new political order.

The National Socialist party in Germany displayed its power and control over thousands of party members in a vast open-air political theater, a political stadium. The party multitude gathered for such meetings was obedient, followed orders, and expressed love and hate on command. At a grandstand of this stadium a "political proscenium" was built. It had two wide balconies, a lower and a higher one, and a protruding box. This stony political "artifact" was specially built for the great *Parteitag*—party meetings (see Model 11).

On top of this proscenium was the party symbol, a swastika of great proportions. It appears from photographic evidence, that during these massive political parades the party elite and the much more limited commanding super-elite were displayed on the balconies while the box was made for the maximum leader, Adolf Hitler.

In a photograph of a parade during such a *Parteitag*, we can see the *Arbeits Dienst* (labor organization) members, marching in party uniforms, with their spades on shoulders, carried in a military fashion, as one would carry a rifle. The balconies are filled with those who seem to represent the new ruling elite. The box is empty. Hitler stands, with his hand outstretched, in an automobile, in a gesture of proximity to and identification with the people. The scene is one of powerful political theater. The photograph shows all, or nearly all in political uniforms. They are an obedient political army, easily manipulated by their political commanders.

The powerful symbol in the middle and on top of the proscenium stresses common ideology, it integrates the multitudes with the distinctly visible elites and with their leader. The architectural device suggests clearly, in a visual, observable manner, the new power stratification: those who are "higher" and "lower," those closer to the centrum of power (maximum leader), and those more distant.

Franco's special status as maximum leader was suggested, during what seemed to be a military or political parade, by a somewhat different architectural device. It was far more modest, in better artistic taste, and also impressive. Model 12 suggests the shape of what might be called a *political rostrum*. We can see a kind of pyramid of power, composed of three steps—probably presenting different rank and status. The

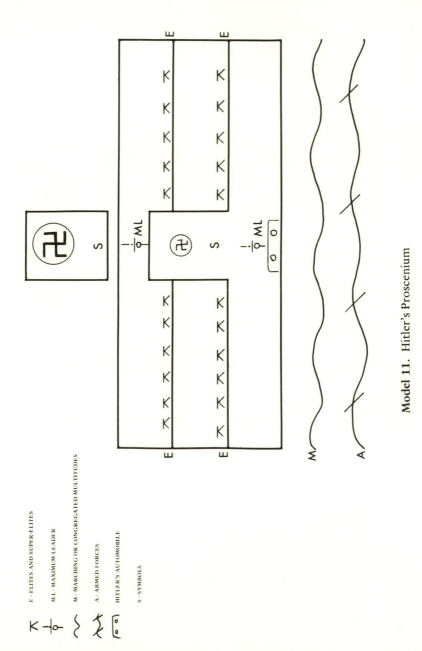

E - ELITES AND SUPER-ELITES

ML - MAXIMUM LEADER

M - MARCHING OR CONGREGATED MULTITUDES

A - ARMED FORCES

HITLER'S AUTOMOBILE

S - SYMBOLS

Model 11. Hitler's Proscenium

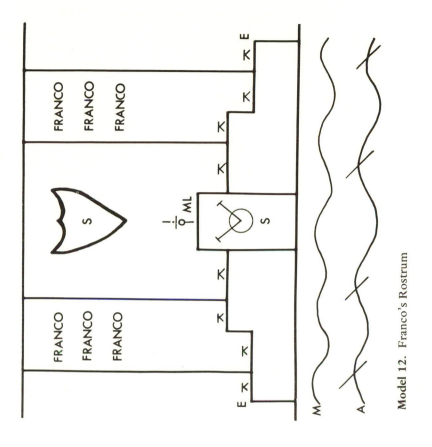

Model 12. Franco's Rostrum

E - ELITES AND SUPER-ELITES

M L - MAXIMUM LEADER

M - MARCHING OR CONGREGATED
MULTITUDES

A - ARMED FORCES

S - SYMBOLS

photograph displays primarily, but not exclusively, men in military uniforms. This rostrum has a clear shape of large steps. Again on top in the protruding box appears Franco. At the very bottom are a row of saluting soldiers in Moroccan outfits, impressive and colorful. In the center is an elaborate symbol of the party, on top of the coat of arms of Spain. On the wall, in the background, the inscription cut in stone: "Franco, Franco, Franco." I suppose the architect was aware of what he was doing. The plans of such a device were probably carefully discussed. The distribution of power, the difference in rank and status are again visually suggested by this pyramidal structure.

The Soviet architectural device, Lenin's Rock, has simplicity (see Model 13). It is a simple stone block, a square pedestal: the mausoleum of Lenin on the Red Square of Moscow. Stalin chose this as a receiving stand for the display of power and rank during the great parades, the processions of political holy days of the October Revolution, and of May Day. During those festive days the political super-elite appeared on top of this stone square under the massive inscription "Lenin." This burial place of Lenin is the *sanctissimum,* and the charisma of Lenin was "routinized," as Weber may have said—extended to the super-elite. The focus of power was in the center and it was occupied by Stalin. The distance from Stalin (the maximum leader) marked the distance from supreme power; those closest to him were the most powerful. Thus the spacial distance from Stalin on this sacred rock indicated rank and status. All were powerful, of course. The space was limited. This was the super-elite *Verkhushka* (the very top) as some Russian would call it. Any change of post, or disappearance from this symbolic rock was commented upon at home and abroad. A change in super-elite was (and is today) visible. Those in power appeared on the political altar. This way a simple, symbolic communication was made, and power structure was reinforced. The multitudes, marching and saluting, performed also an act of symbolic submission.

In all three examples the super-elite is on a pedestal. Precedence on the ladder of political power is expressed by distance and levels (higher or lower) in relation to the maximum leader. The symbolic equality of the multitude amounts only to regimentation: everybody is equally obedient to the political elite and super-elite.

But—one may object—Americans and Swiss also have their parades and receiving stands. Of course they do. However, an American presidential inauguration is similar to a grandiose and festive commencement in one of the large public universities. The elaborate play of rank and distance

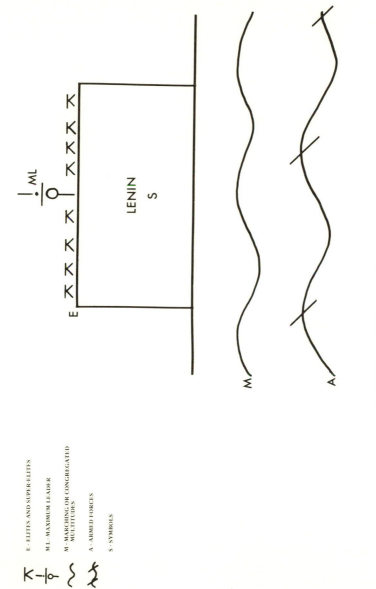

Model 13. Lenin's Rock (Mausoleum)

E - ELITES AND SUPER-ELITES

M L - MAXIMUM LEADER

M - MARCHING OR CONGREGATED
MULTITUDES

A - ARMED FORCES

S - SYMBOLS

is subtle and as a rule transient, or seldom repeated.

Of course, every political system produces a style, a political theater of its own. Thus there are various styles and ways of political acting, of dress and gesture; there is a variety of political scenery and architecture. But the drama and tragedy of democracy is different, quite different indeed, from those of tyranny, and democratic politics cannot be played with the gestures, equipment, costumes, and artifacts of a dictatorship.

In politics, architecture has its function, although political actors are not always conscious of the consequences of their own building and doing. In science fiction, I suppose, a successful dictator, once in power and fully cognizant of the political potentialities architecture offers, could advance grandiose urban plans which would facilitate processes of myth-making, caesaristic cults, as well as periodic control of large crowds summoned to mass meetings and political celebrations. The techniques of projecting uniforms, party symbols, and flags, and the interplay of floodlights and use of music and symbolic fires would create an artificial environment within which will and judgment were dulled. Such a depersonalized, militarily structured mass becomes submissive, obedient, and predictable. Is this solely fantasy? The experience of National Socialism has been recorded on films. Cinematic evidence suggests that planned physical environment is important to the political manipulation of people.

Man can create an architectural technical environment which may influence his emotions and behavior once it is well integrated into the social fabric and relates to his psychological needs. An artificial environment may regulate an orderly democratic process or foster reverse tendencies. Even the simple interior design of an American court room organizes, structures the contending parties, the judge and the jury, and facilitates orderly legal proceedings. The shape of the British House of Commons facilitates the display of a clear division of the party in power and the opposition. Architecture does not create the social processes or institutions, but it fosters or facilitates their working.

It may also affect our sentiments and emotions. Many years ago, in my student years, I visited the cathedral of Cologne. The simple bare walls, the tall gothic ceiling, the powerful pillars led to a sudden reflection on the smallness of man, his insignificance. It brought to my mind thoughts on moral and human issues. Church architecture was and is closely integrated with religious sentiments, emotions, deeper needs. Powerful religious architecture can appeal to our imagination and sentiments, affect our attitudes and emotions, and move us to contemplation.

The Austrian art historian Dvorák has pointed to the spiritual relationship of the medieval man to gothic art and architecture.[15] But in turn the art and architecture affected his emotions and appealed to his religious imagination. A humble peasant who attended church service was impressed by the view of the saints painted on stained glass windows. They were seen as real, observable beings hovering in the air, in unusual lights and colors. His religious beliefs found here a visual expression, a kind of reality.

Architecture can encourage a gamut of attitudes and emotions, and can also affect our behavior. A gifted French architect, Claude Nicolas Ledoux, published in 1804 a large volume on the relation of architecture to art, customs, and laws.[16] Ledoux was not a Montesquieu, he was not a rigorous student of human society. He was primarily an architect. But, in his poetic and romantic treatise, profusely illustrated with plans of a perfect industrial city, one can easily discover his major thesis: a perfect architectural environment created by man may create the foundation for a better, if not perfect society. Montesquieu suggested a close relationship between natural environment and society. Ledoux, in a vague and poetic way, suggests the relationship between an artificial, architectural environment and man's social behavior. He lacks the clarity of Montesquieu's argument, he lacks his erudition, philosophy, and talent, but the concept, the approach, is striking. He explains his plans for a variety of buildings. Their architecture, Ledoux believed, would foster certain sentiments and thus shape human behavior. He designed a special building which he called Pacifière or Conciliateur. Its architecture, he believed, would encourage reconciliation. Another, Maison d'Union, was designed to emphasize harmony and encourage discussion.

Ledoux points to a paramount problem: the potentialty of the relationship between architecture—the artificial environment man creates—and man's emotions and behavior. He is a poetic forerunner of environmental psychology and sociology.

Architecture by itself will not, however, create values and attitudes, or effect, as a necessary antecedent, a definite type of behavior. There is an interplay between man's values, attitudes, and sentiments and the artificial environment he creates. This is true also for political architecture. Its function and significance is anchored in social relations and psychological attitudes. Once these are present, the artificial environment man creates fosters the tendencies. It may also be designed in order to manipulate, control the multitudes, to reinforce and above all

consolidate a new political power structure. At such time, the ideology
of the major actors, the elites, affects the design of a new "political
theater."

9. ANTI-MYTH AND DEMONIZATION
OF POLITICAL OPPONENTS

What may be called "demonization" and "anti-myth" is a reverse
process of myth-making political deification or cultism. Once power is
seized, a totalitarian rule established, selected political opponents are
presented by the new ruling group as symbols of evil and national or
social danger. Step by step, the leading opponent becomes synonymous
with a political antichrist. He is elevated to the magnitude of a satan
who threatens the chosen nation, the chosen class or party, above all
the "humane and good maximum leader." The image is developed by
means of negative cartoons and word associations; finally, as the face
of this "antihero" becomes a symbol of political evil, so does his name.
In this dialectics the superman and the antihero become antinomic. A
Soviet poet, Demian Biednyi, wrote in his poem "My Report to the
XVIII Congress" [Moy Report XVIII Sézdu Partii] : "Trotskisms evil-
emigrant cadaver . . . and gigantic picture of Stalin against a background
of fabulous victories."[17] The symbol of evil is built up systematically.
The famous purge trials Stalin initiated against dedicated communists,
to mention only Bukharin, Rykov, and Piatakov, were part of this
process of demonization. They were accused inter alia of spying and
helping to prepare the German invasion. Once opponents became
symbols of evil and were morally destroyed, the next step followed:
biological destruction. Mass executions followed demonization.

Such a process involves a sharp division of the world into friend
and foe, red and green, good and evil. It harbors a subconscious belief
in and fear of forces of evil, an orthodox hatred of difference, a dogmatic approach to ideological differences. Heresy was one time the
hateful term for religious dissent. Now the concept and symbols of
heresy have been projected into political ideologies. Stalin's formative
and adolescent years probably made a strong impression on his
personality. A theology student in an orthodox seminary, he perceived
politics like a theologian. He created political devils and antichrists. His

attitudes, perception, and modes of thought formed in a religious
orthodox milieu were displaced to his new political creed. But Stalin's
demonization was of a political nature, seldom ethnic, when compared
with Hitler's campaign against Jews. (A specialized publication, *Der
Stürmer*, was dedicated to developing a satanic image of the Jews.)

The process of demonization has its political utility. It creates an
outside, clear target for release of hostility. It permits the channeling
of aggressions outside the party, outside a nation against a political
opponent. At the same time it supplies legitimacy for consolidating
the power of the maximum leader.

We will list here some of its major functions:

1. Consolidation and strengthening of the power of the maximum
   leader.
2. Destruction of opposition.
3. Outside channeling of inner tensions.
4. Tightening of social control over the nation.
5. Integration of a society or a nation.
6. Displacement of mass politics from rational to emotional experience,
   which permits easier control and manipulation.
7. Emotional preparation of a nation or party for aggression and
   violence, although this is not always the case (see below).

The demonization of a whole nation in international politics has
frequently been practiced. Today, the government of Communist China
promotes, through propaganda, the demonization of the United States,
reducing it to a symbol of imperialism and exploitation. During President
Nixon's visit in China (1972), the American guests were treated with
courtesy and attended a number of theatrical, especially ballet, performances. In turn, the American public was able to see the dances on
their television sets. Personae dramatis were of course soldiers and
workers, peasants. With their guns and sickles in hand, they were trying
to expel the bad demon of imperialism. From time to time they were
raising their hands in proud triumph over the deadly, though unseen,
enemy. The dances were repetitive, whatever their artistic value; they
were primarily politico-religious rituals. It was a struggle between good
and evil, a fight against unseen demons of evil imperialism and probably
Kuogmintang. Looking at a television screen, not in the milieu of Peking
and diplomatic guests, one had an impression of a ritual dance of fighting of a demon. But formally this was an artistic and political
performance.

At this point, however, a distinction must be made between a process

of political demonization and political criticism. It could be argued
that the former is a result of a shift of the latter into symbolism and
emotionalism. The two processes are not identical. Facts about politics
are often cruel. The German concentration and death camps are true
data, and criticism during World War II of German rule and moral
protest and indignation over the government's actions, accompanied by
massive presentation of data, were not tantamount to making a government politically evil through symbols. Here facts were used, not
symbols. Churchill criticized Chamberlain in 1938, and de Gaulle Pétain
in 1942. Facts were used and policies were criticized, sometimes
violently. The weaknesses and mental limitations of Pétain could be
stressed and ridiculed; but there is a difference between criticism, contempt, insult—on one hand (contempt may be based on moral judgment
and rational evaluation of data)—and on the other, a deliberate, propagandistic activity with an emphasis on symbol-building and maximizing
hostility. I must admit that it is not simple to draw sharp lines between
the two. Political criticism is, however, an essential component not
solely of a democratic process, but of any sound political judgment.

Negative symbol-building means, as was said before, constructing
clear targets for hostilities. A social movement with an aggressive
orientation may widen its appeal to certain persons, by impressive
symbols associated with the political target. In the late 1960s in the
United States, minor but vocal student groups selected a general symbol
of a pig—at first for whites associated with a certain political creed and
social status and specifically for the police—to express a distaste for and
opposition to certain social and political attitudes and, with regard to
authorities. The symbol was used in other ways also. A negative, cruel,
even repulsive "antisymbol" is developed and at the same time associated
with the political opponent. By this association a single psychological
category, a negative mental image, is created.

Here are my random notes from the Brooklyn College campus during
student unrest. It is not my purpose here to argue whether student
demands were right and justified. I am here a "secretary of nature," to
use Bacon's dictum; my interest at this moment is in nascent political
rituals and antisymbol-making:

6 April 1969, Thursday. A small group of 40 to 50 students gathered
in a circle at the quadrangle at the Brooklyn College campus. One of
the students carried a bloody, real head of a pig mounted on a stick
(which made an impression of a spear). Blood was dry (the head was

probably purchased in a butcher store). The mounted pig's head was
in the center of a circle of 12 to 15 feet diameter of laughing, insult-
ing students. The student carrying the head was hitting the beat with
the stick, while the head was shaking. Rhythmical chants against
"the pigs" were improvised and sung spontaneously. The chants or
songs grew louder, and it seems to me they intensified the group's
emotions. The beat became stronger, voices more excited, more
heated. I could see changing facial expressions (although hard to
describe specifically), feet beating the rhythm, hands clapping. They
were not chanting songs against white pigs. (There were also white
students standing around.) These boys and girls were excited and
emotional. Their message—it seems to me—has an appeal, since it
is being communicated to emotions, not to controlled, cognitive
qualities. The medieval monks, moving crowds against Jews and
heretics, must have also been emotional, excited, aggressive and
violent. . . . When A. S., my colleague, and I approached, observing
intensely, the cheerleader became embarrassed. One of the demon-
strators, neatly dressed, approached him rapidly, whispered something
in his ear. Another fetched a paper bag and put the pig's head in the
bag. The small crowd began to move now toward Whitehead Hall,
chants became lower and quieter.[18]

The war in Vietnam, the draft, and civil rights was the political
"scenario" of this demonstration. But what interests us here is only
the political ethnology, the rituals and antisymbols which are instrumental and serve various objectives.

The ritual and symbolism of demonization may serve as an emotional
buildup and preparation for violence, similar to a war dance or to those
insults Homeric heroes hurled at their enemies before battle. Rituliza-
tion of hostility and development of enemy symbols reflect and reinforce polarization, which in turn facilitates the precipitation of aggression.

But symbolic or verbal aggression or various kinds of insults (which
the American psychologist Gordon Allport has called *antilocution*) may
also have the entirely opposite function of channeling aggression into
nonviolence. In Bonagente, an Italian village I studied in during 1957-
1958 and in 1969, verbal, but not physical, aggression was frequent.
Verbal hostility was usually expressed within a group of friends against
enemies who were not present, but who got the news by grapevine and
kept at a distance. A violent struggle within a species—as Konrad Lorenz

so well describes—frequently ends among animals with symbolic submission.[19]

Symbols and anti-symbols are also "indicators" of hostility. They are signals of growing tensions. In international politics, a government agency may communicate the official attitudes or intentions of its country by symbolic behavior. The purpose of such behavior is to challenge the adversary into a desired action; such behavior may result in a more conciliatory change or intensification of tensions. Those signals may indicate displeasure and warning, or approval. We frequently read in the papers that an ambassador from country A has shown a warm reception to an ambassador of country B, or that the reception was cool and halted. In turn, we might read that ambassador A was not invited to the reception celebrating the national holiday. For a hard-working man, all those whims and formalities seem somewhat silly and unusually expensive. Their function, however, is to communicate by indirect means a government's political attitudes. Man has developed subtle symbols to express his intent. The intention may be cruel and brutal, but in international relations good table manners are functional. They help negotiations, even when business is "dirty." Sometimes however, those "indicators" of attitudes toward actions of another government are direct, even brutal. This small, though cruel tableau is quoted here, but responsiblity for its veracity is referred entirely to the editors of *Time* (21 March 1969).

> Until recently, the Amur-Ussuri area has been the site of the most spectacular provocations. On several occasions, the Chinese made a practice of marching prisoners to the center of the river, accusing them of being pro-Soviet traitors, and then beheading them. Another favorite habit was forming up on the river ice, sticking out tongues in unison at the Soviet troopers, and then turning and dropping trousers to the Russians in an ancient gesture of contempt. That tactic stopped when Soviet troops took refuge behind large portraits of Chairman Mao.

10. THE RAPE OF SYMBOLS AND SEMANTIC CONFUSION

Once power is seized and consolidated in a dictatorial way, symbols of leading ideas and norms share the fate of men. They are worshipped and sanctified, and showing offense towards them is subject to punishment. Socialism, Communism, the German Nation, Italy, the Soviet Union, National Socialism, above all the people, the nation—all these word-symbols displace the cross and religious chants. A dictatorship needs symbols to rationalize and justify its power and legitimacy. The *sign*, the outside shell of the word, remains, and the *content*, the *meaning* is subject to rapid change. Social change and facts contradict the old meaning of symbols. Forced labor and mass deportation do not agree with socialism, but still, all this is done in order to accomplish what is called the "socialist plan" and in the interest of distant generations. Purge trials and executions contradict the very appellation of "People's Republic." Concentration camps and mass executions hardly agree with the dream and utopia of "socialism," even if this is only "national socialism."

The *ideal* meaning of democracy and socialism, of early nationalism is now the opposite of the *real*. The hiatus between "what is" and what certain symbols "should" represent is obvious. They have or had an appeal to individuals, to social groups, to multitudes, to a nation, and their symbolic appeal is still used. It is used because it is needed and so many are emotionally committed, attached to the very sound. The symbol, although reduced to its sound, is still seminal. It has appeal—if not within the country, then possibly still to political adherents abroad. The faith of possible allies has to be maintained. Furthermore, symbols and ideology supply legitimacy to acts of violence. They also give consolation to the uneasy conscience of the super-elite.

They now have the hold on these symbols; it gives them a comfortable position in political tactics. A super-elite of a "republic" expels a minority. It is an ethnic, perhaps a racial minority, but its expulsion is rationalized and legitimized in terms of the interests of the nation and nationalism. A representative of the same super-elite protests violation of the rights of minorities in other countries, usually far more liberal and tolerant, in the name of human rights and "anti-imperialism," at a United Nations meeting, and he wins new allies. Now, personal autocracy is called a republic, dictatorship is represented as democracy, war and invasion of foreign and weak countries as preservation of peace or "a new socialist doctrine." Those who are not subject to direct experience still believe in the old meaning of the symbols. They support those who carry the name, who use it in daily speeches and official statements.

Experience is, however, stronger than symbols are, and step by step "liberation" begins also to mean "conquest." The term, however, also keeps its old meaning; it has now a double and contradictory meaning. The same signs harbors now the two opposites. This linguistic confusion reinforces the intellectual one. It is as if we had one single word, one single symbol, for green and red, good and bad. Every time such a word is used, what it means must be explained.

This semantic confusion begins to be part of a political scenario in the struggle for power. Combined with the massive processes of myth-making and demonization of enemies, it reaches the universities. By deductive and logical inferences, by selecting data and authorities, by omissions of data, easily rejecting contrary evidence as "unscholarly," "unprofessional," and emphasis on"where this leads in the future," the confused picture is again reinforced by those who are ideologically committed. The transition from "temporary dictatorship" to withering away of the state, a theory that total, unlimited dictatorship is necessary and the beginning of total, unlimited freedom of an individual is by now logically plausible. The highest form of freedom and toleration will be achieved by intolerance toward those who by benevolent tolerance destroy the chance of perfect tolerance and freedom. This is also logical. In their time the sages of the Inquisition were theologically convincing in their pious arguments.

At such a time, for judgment and guidance, not a few return to simple commitments toward fellow men, to basic ethics, to common sense and careful observation of social change. Sometimes, they are only hermits amidst an agitated multitude.

11. HYPOTHESES

A major purpose of this chapter was to develop a general hypothesis concerning symbolic behavior and the technique of manipulating multi-tudes. We have concentrated on the symbolic meaning and functions of dress, on the projection of symbols (and so also of dress, of the uniform) from one social system into another. Finally, we discussed the projection of religious symbolism into political symbolism, myth-making (personal-ity cult), use of political architecture and semantics. The displacement or projection of behavioral patterns and symbols has been and continues to be a powerful technique for the manipulation of the multitude. Here is our major hypothesis. But in such a short essay it is easy to create misunderstandings.

After the downfall of Rome, the church rebuilt European civilization. It built schools, universities, cathedrals, and around these sprang up marketplaces and towns. Wherever the missions from Rome, the capital of Christianity, reached, culture flourished: music, art, intellectual life. Hospitals and foundling homes, help for the poor, though primitive and imperfect, were still the portents of future social welfare.

Thus the role and contribution of the church in building great European civilizations, in the development of science and the humanities was paramount. Nevertheless, the Church has created certain patterns of ritual and symbolic behavior which make possible control of great masses of people. This psychological, symbolic mechanism facilitates an ideological mobilization of multitudes. These patterns orginated as a consequence of religious life and also satisfied profound inner religious and psychological needs. At the same time, the control of symbols and rituals fostered the consolidation of ecclesiastical power. The projection (or displacement) of this symbolic pattern into the political structure created completely new potentialities for the political and authoritarian superelite to manipulate great masses of people. In the Inquisition, the church also created the first systematic ideological terror in the history of mass terror and manipulation of fear.

In Protestant countries political mass meetings numbering tens of thousands are fairly rare, with the exception of national elections. But even during pre-election days in the United States, electioneering is frequently confined to the street and small neighborhood meetings. The candidates hand out election leaflets, shake the voters' hands, walk through the parks and streets talking to passersby, and hand out printed election programs. Automobiles with loudspeakers, television, and radio are powerful media of political advertising. On the whole Americans are suspicious of political crowds.

But even some of the large meetings, including the presidential conventions and primaries, resemble a picnic rather than a political brawl. Cheerful clothing, frankfurters and softdrinks, friendly songs (not pompous and threatening), contribute to relaxed human relations, reducing the tensions and animosities. There is something of a Broadway show—of a traveling circus as some said in 1972—in those meetings, but never a replica of a church sermon or military parade. A European observer may end with an impression that some of the meetings are "not serious." But serious business is discussed and sometimes decided.

Neither are the Protestant countries fond of dogma; as a rule, Prot-

estants avoid religious and political dogma, along with orthodox
ideologies. In the Protestant religous approach, the individual communicates with his maker directly. The intermediary of priesthood is not
necessary and formal services are few, replaced by informal religious
meetings and prayers. Neither is there a superior church hierarchy.
Protestant clergymen are under the control of their congregation.
Protestant sects, as previously mentioned, do not make use of complicated symbolism.

But there is more to it. The modern concept of religious toleration
was born in those religious struggles of sectarian protestantism against
the powerful church hierarchy and the monopoly of religious power.
Man's struggle for the right to religious dissent logically led to his
struggle for the right to political dissent, to respect for his political and
religious liberty, since it was not possible to separate one from the other.
"The liberal ideas bred in sectarian circles, here and in America, did not
become the common property of mankind until they were detached
from their theological root, and became a creed of a party," wrote a
prominent Catholic, the English historian Lord Acton. "In 1644 we
are told: 'Godwin . . . is openly for a full liberty of conscience, to all
sects, even Turks, Jews, Papists.'" "The author of the tract, *What the
Independents Would Have* . . ., reckons liberty of conscience to be
England's chiefest good," continues Acton.[20] Thus, protestantism
(but not all the movements of the Reformation) was one of the major
carriers of the modern institutions of political rights and respect for
political difference. Those were also the principles advanced by some of
the influential sects and the values the young generations were now
educated into. And religion affected political creeds even, as Acton
states, when it was separated from the theological fabric.

On the other hand, Protestantism has not produced great church
art, as did Catholicism. It has not created such paintings or magnificent
church architecture, cathedrals, sculpture, or stained glass windows.
Protestant churches are for the most part modest. The clergy is dedicated
more to religious philosophy and social work than to liturgy. Neither
do the radical, sectarian Protestant churches know any special ecclesiastical garb or ornament—with the exception of a simple black toga.

I end these random remarks on this note. These are just hypotheses
that occur to me in light of contemporary—or today already historical—
experiences. Manipulation and the techniques of manipulation are still
practiced in many parts of our little globe. The quasireligious cult of

the leaders of totalitarian political movements is an indication of this.

The great, unsolved social problems of our globe require rational thought, experience, thorough knowledge of the subject, talent, imagination, and ethics—and not political magic. The way to the humanization of political activity, to enlightened policies, leads through dialogue and search for intelligent alternatives. Rational political activity, to enlightened policies, leads through dialogue and search for intelligent alternatives. Rational political decisions have no need for manipulation. On the contrary, an appeal to emotion, appeal to aggression, can break down, and thus delay any rational and enlightened social change.

NOTES

1. Vilhjalmur Stefansson, "The Colonization of Northern Lands," *Climate and Man* (Washington, D.C.: U.S. Department of Agriculture, 1941), pp. 206-209.

2. Thucydides, *The Peloponnesian War,* trans. Crawley (New York: Modern Library, 1934), pp. 6ff. For a somewhat different translation, see *Thucidides,* trans. B. Jowett (Boston: D. Lothrop & Co., 1883), pp. 4ff.

According to Jacob Burckhardt, early Athenian attire (about 500 B.C.) was resplendent and colorful. Athenians even used gold jewelry. In the times of Pericles, however, Athenian clothing became simple and modest. Jacob Burckhardt, *Griechische Kulturgeschichte* (1902; reprint ed., Basel: Schwabe & Co., 1957), pp. 197ff., notes 117, 118. Greek attire remained the same from 480-450 B.C. and changed little until 330 B.C. In times of Alexander, with the hellenistic trend a change did appear, but, typically, change in material, only the form remained practically the same. The new materials came from India, China and Egypt: cotton, silk and linen. For details see: Margarete Bieber, *Entwicklungsgeschichte der Griechischen Tracht von vorgeschichtlichen Zeit zum Ausgang der Antike* [History of development of the Greek attire from prehistory to the decline of antiquity] Berlin: Geb. Mann, 1967), pp. 25ff., 32.

3. George Simmel writes about this in his essay "Individualismus" in a collection *Brücke und Tür* [The bridge and the door] (Stuttgart: Kohler, 1957), pp. 251ff.

4. F. R. Cowell, *Cicero and the Roman Republic* (London: Pitman, 1948), pp. 72, 137; Jerome Carcopino, *Daily Life in Ancient Rome* (New Haven: Yale University Press, 1960), pp. 153-155; Moses Hadas and the editors of Time-Life Books, *Imperial Rome* (New York: Time-LIfe, 1965), p. 86.

5. J. M. Vincent, *Costume and Conduct in the Laws of Basel, Bern, and Zurich, 1370-1800* (Baltimore: Johns Hopkins Press, 1945), pp. 42-130. A relatively rapid change of costumes with the appearance of certain fashions and styles has been recorded during the Renaissance (fifteenth and sixteenth centuries). Fashions of various nations spread through paintings, dance troupes, diplomatic contact, and, above, all, by trading. Thus, at times Saracen, Spanish, and Hungarian dress appeared in distant towns. Regional differences were also noticeable in the dress in Italy. At this time, so it seems, the frequent and seasonal rhythm of changing styles made its appearance. See J. R. Hale, *Renaissance in Europe* (London: Collins, 1971), pp. 113ff.

6. William L. Shirer, *Berlin Diary* (New York: Alfred A. Knopf, 1941), p. 20.

7. Ibid., p. 52.

8. Hector Berlioz, *Tales of the Orchestra,* trans. C. R. Fortesque (Baltimore: Penguin Books, 1963).

9. Mass manipulation of multitudes was carefully planned and designed with an assistance of a staff of architects. Albert Speer made his personal career in this manipulative enterprise. His designs of party celebrations won Hitler's approval and support. See Albert Speer, *Inside the Third Reich,* trans. Richard and Clara Winston (New York: Avon Books, 1971), pp. 57ff., 96ff. See also *New York Times,* 11 May 1971.

10. For the definition of *hagiography* and *hagiology,* see *The American Heritage Dictionary of the English Language* (New York: American Heritage Publishing Co., 1969).

11. J. N. Kravchenko, "Obraz Stalina v Sovetskom Izobrazitel 'nom iskusstve" [J. V. Stalin in Soviet painting and sculpture], *Architektura* (January 1938); also J. Rabinovich, "Obraz Stalina v Zhivopisi i Skul'pture" [Pictures of Stalin in painting and sculpture], ibid. (January 1939); "Obrazy Lenina i Stalina v Kinô", [Pictures of Lenin and Stalin in cinema] Sbornik Statei, Gozkinoizdat, 1939; J. Rabinovich, *Lenin v Izobrazitel'nom Iskusstve* [Lenin in plastic arts] (Moscow-Leningrad: Gos. Izd. Iskusstvo, 1939). See also F. Gross, ed., *European Ideologies* (New York: Philosophical Library, 1948), pp. 38-40.

12. "Ukrain'ska Mova Na Suchasnoii Stadii Rozvytku." This study appeared in a collection, *J. V. Stalinu,* Akademia Nauk, Sbirnik Prac (Kiev, 1940), pp. 88ff. (Translation mine with the assistance of N. N.)

From their early school years, children were taught about his manifold talents; thus, he grew to a size of a superman. In a textbook on social science for a fifth grade, we find the following sections. (I quote only part of table of contents, as an example):

"40. Lenin's legacy in trustworthy hands.

"41. Stalin the best disciple and adherent of Lenin.

"42. Stalin and the Red Army.

"43. Stalin and the National question.

"44. Stalin and the industrialization of USSR.

"45. Stalin and the collectivization of agriculture.

"46. Stalin and the cultural construction.

"47. Stalin the leader of Communism."

And so it goes. Quoted from M. Ovsyannikova, B. Levitan, and V. Nekrasova, *Social Science, Textbook for Elementary and Middle Schools,* trans. I. Levin, ed. by B. Perel (Moscow, 1933), pt. 3. A patient reader may find also some rather modest comments. Wrote D. Zaslavskii in an essay on the famous Russian writer M. E. Saltykov-Shchedryn: "Stalin had quoted Shchedryn, and such a quotation elevates a man above criticism, it shows [the greatness of] the writer. "Shchedryn's types in Lenin's and Stalin's speeches," in *God Dvadsat Vtoroi, 1939.*

13. This analysis of the cult centered around Stalin is based on an unpublished study by the author written in 1941.

14. Benjamin Constant, *De L'Esprit De Conquête et De L'Usurpation,* 3d ed. (Paris: Chez le Normant, 1814).

15. Medieval architecture and art was a part, a consequence of the entire religious idea system (Weltanschauung). The Christian view affected almost the entire individual and social life. Dvorák follows the German philosopher and historian Wilhelm Dilthey in his comprehensive evaluation of the totality of a historical period. The medieval art—he writes—sought to give form to the invisible and what is immortal. Dvorák stresses the powerful impact of stained glass windows

in cathedrals (he quotes here extensively the art historian Julius Lange), which creates the mood impressions. Lange, quoted by Dvořák, emphasizes further that the genius of the stained glass art was in its function as a means of producing an impression of supernatural, "a means based on the prevailing spiritual orientation of the times." Dvořák, and especially the author of introduction, Karl Maria Svoboda, advance a strongly idealistic viewpoint. Their emphasis is "Dilteyan," the stress on the idea system, Weltanschauung. See: Max Dvořák, *Idealism and Naturalism in Gothic Art*, trans. Randolph J. Klawiter, (Notre Dame, Indiana: University of Notre Dame Press, 1967), pp. xxv, 33, 75. But the two art historians seem to overlook some of the sociological consequence. Man creates art, but once an art environment is created, such as the environment of churches, and cathedrals, it does affect in turn the individual perception and may reinforce the existing social and political order, rooted in religious beliefs and philosophy.

16. Claude Nicholas Ledoux, *L'Architecture Considérée Sous le Rapport de l'Art, des Moeurs et de la Législation* (Paris: By the author, 1804). Ledoux must have spent a substantial sum of money to have published this unusual and richly illustrated volume. This rare publication can be found in the New York Public Library's Art History Collection. See also *Visionary Architects,* Metropolitan Museum of Art, New York (April 15-May 13, 1968), especially an informative introduction on Ledoux by J. C. Lemagny, pp. 66ff.

17. In W. Muselian, ed., *Stalinskaya Konstytutsia V Poesii Narodov S. S. R.* (Moscow, 1937), p. 24. (Translation mine.)

18. Recorded on 6 April 1969 from my observations. This text is shorter than the original notes.

19. Konrad Lorenz, *On Aggression* (New York: Bantam Books, 1967), pp. 72ff. Gordon W. Allport, *The Nature of Prejudice* (Boston: Addison-Wesley, 1954), pp. 14, 49-51, 57ff.

20. Lord Acton, *Lectures on Modern History,* (Cleveland and New York: Meridian Books, The World Publishing Company, 1967), pp. 198ff.

VII

Notes on Command and Consensus Structures

1. COMMAND STRUCTURE

Man exists only as a member of human society. His existence and survival are determined by his ability to act together in an organized and coordinated manner with other members of society toward a definite end. He works and acts together, either under coercion and fear of punishment, or he cooperates in a voluntary, often spontaneous manner; he acts either on command or by consensus. In consequence social structures and institutional behavior can be reduced to two, perhaps three ideal types: 1) those based on consensus, 2) those on command, and 3) a combination of both.

There is a fundamental difference between the group action of a consensus structure and that of a command structure. The command structure operates by means of a latent system of rewards and punishments, and any member of the intermediary and obedient subgroups is directly involved in it. Consensus, on the other hand, requires common values (norms) and the conscious or customary acceptance of common rules, which, in turn, are based upon common interest.

Now, to begin with a general principle of the command structure, the functioning of a command-type institution is based on orders and obedience (also called submission or subordination), and the personnel active within a simple command-type structure are in positions of either command or obedience. Hence, the individuals or subgroups within them can be divided into positions of command and positions of obedience or subordination, the individuals in the latter accepting and executing the orders of the former. Their response to orders is submission.

A more complex command structure is known as hierarchy. Any hierarchy has at least three subgroups or links:

1. *The command subgroup.* This subgroup at the top makes decisions and issues commands and does not take any orders. It may also be called the sovereign subgroup.

2. *The intermediary subgroup.* Members of this group accept and obey orders, and they issue orders to the subordinate group. They also make certain decisions within the orders issued by the top subgroup. But while the sovereign group can always change the decisions of the "intermediaries," the latter have no power over the former.

3. *The subordinate or obedient subgroup.* Its members—at the bottom—accept, obey, and execute orders.

The above is the scheme of the simplest type of hierarchy, which we shall call a three-link hierarchy.

The members of the command subgroup enjoy all the pleasures of power. They are the decision makers. The members of the last group have no share in the decision making. They are subjected to the continuous repression of their wishes and are trained, through long experience, to become a subgroup with a submissive pattern of behavior.

In countries with a long history of feudalism, where the peasants or subordinate groups have had a long experience of oppressive servitude, the behaviorial patterns of passive and symbolic submission may often survive long after the original social system has disappeared. This phenomenon can be observed, for example, in Latin America and South Italy.

Army structure serves well as a general example of a hierarchy. We may demonstrate with an imaginary army of a state like Monaco to illustrate the simple three-link hierarchy. Let us assume that the ruler of Monaco is also the top officer of the army. He represents the command element and issues orders. Then, the noncommissioned officers form the intermediary group, while the military band and the few soldiers belong to the subordinate or obedient group.

However, a military organization has, as a rule, many more steps or links in its hierarchy. There are many intermediary links between the command group and the subordinate one—we may say that there are many levels of subordination. Men like the late Generalissimo Trujillo in the Dominican Republic or the top leader Fidel Castro in Cuba are in

command posts. They make the army's basic decisions. Between them
and their respective private soldiers or militarymen there exists a "chain
of command" with various levels of subordination and obedience.

How does a hierarchy work?

In a totalitarian army, the private is a member of a hierarchical
"command structure." He belongs to the bottom or obedient subgroup.
Should he refuse an order, he is punished, perhaps by the administration
of corporal punishment. On the other hand, if he executes orders well,
he expects to be "out of trouble"—meaning there is, for him, the
immediate prospect of punishment. And if he shows an outstanding
loyalty or dedication, he may obtain some suitable reward, such as
decoration with a military order.

This basic system of rewards and punishments, even in such forms
as decoration with military orders, is the underlying element of
military discipline. The behavioral patterns of the military are closely
connected with this system of rewards and punishments through
military drill. Through years of continuous training, the soldier psychologically associates command with two elements: 1) an immediate and
standardized behavioral response, and 2) a "recall" system which makes
him remember that a refusal of the proper behavioral response or even
its absence is associated with pain or other predicament.

The modernization of the Western armies in the eighteenth century
introduced mechanical discipline and rigor. Discipline, in the military
sense of this word, meant an unconditional submission to orders and
an immediate formalized and standardized behavioral response to an
order. From saluting, marching, firing, attacking, parading, all the way
down to heel-clicking, the behavioral patterns were formalized and
standardized—just as weapons and other instruments of war were.

In this way, the organizers of armies and the command subgroup
of the military hierarchy achieved both the maximum enforcement of
their orders and the maximum predictability of their effects. The
behavior of the army could be predicted, at least *rebus sic stantibus,*
provided the remaining factors of the situation remained the same.
The command would be followed by the appropriate response unless
outside pressures produced a breakdown in the army's hierarchical
system. To prevent this from happening, the armies had to be given a
stronger firepower and a better discipline than the enemy armies.

Military discipline is behavior based on immediate and standardized
responses to commands. It was reinforced by the development of a
specifically military symbolic behavior and the creation of a system of

rewards and punishments. The symbolic behavior was influenced by earlier medieval feudal patterns and consisted, above all, of repetitive symbols of submission. Some examples are the saluting of officers and imperial symbols like flags and coats-of-arms, as well as standing at attention while addressing one's superiors. A daily repetition of such symbolic submission reinforces the association between such symbols and the obedience to orders and their execution. Moreover, the "modernized" armies of the eighteenth century made a very wide use of corporal punishment for the smallest infraction of the rules of formalized behavior (i.e., response to commands).

The military training of the obedient subgroup was in fact a process of conditioning through the association of punishment and reward with definite types of behavior. This is not unlike the training of animals. A rigorous training of this type produced a higher, "operational" type of social mechanism, which responded to commands instantly and with a predictable and coordinated aggressive group action.

This is, of course, a simplified generalization. Military discipline is also built with ideology, values, symbolism, esprit de corps. The morale of an army, the basic ingredient of solidarity and dedication, is developed with this variety of "bricks." In addition, armies of democratic countries give greater recognition to civic duties toward soldiers, to the need for partial or latent consent, and to the soldier's support for wider areas of activities such as college education. Discipline is anchored in a different social fabric; it is also more limited and checked. The basic mechanism of command remains, however, and when the moments of high risks arrive orders are expected to be obeyed or else. In daily military life in the barracks, order and submission operate too.

There are social groups of "pure" or integral command relationships. Here belong slave gangs, in some cases a work gang of prisoners. This type of hierarchical social machine proves highly effective in totalitarian control. Also, in certain historical periods, this type of social organization, associated with slave or forced labor on a large scale, proved efficient for such uses as large-scale hydraulic schemes, road-building, and the erection of public buildings. The colossal architecture of antiquity was built largely—though not entirely—by the great "tyrannies" or hierarchical social structures based on the command mechanism. The Egyptian pyramids represent this class of architecture.[1]

Neither the seventeenth-century English and Scottish settlers in America nor their independent and democratic descendants of the next century produced a colossal type of architecture. Instead, they built modest houses, even where, as in Vermont, marble for colossal structures was abundant. The consensus structure of early American institutions and values favored modesty. Also, unlike in the South, where slaves were used to a far greater extent, the Northern settlers did most of the work themselves. And the Southern states differed substantially from the North.

In the Spanish colonies further south, the conquistadors employed the command system of group action. And so, while they left imposing cathedrals and other buildings, they also left their command-based institutions and social system which, in turn, influenced the historical development of that area and its present-day state.

2. CONSENSUS

The consensus type of group action requires for its functioning the existence of common values (norms), customary rules, or folkways, as well as common interest. Cooperation and mutual aid are generally found in small communities, as they were in the early primitive communities or folk cultures.

In a long historical perspective, simple and less complicated communities have, as a rule, acted efficiently through the operation of such a consensus-based system. A group action based on consensus may be a customary one, a kind of folkway: in this case, it does not require specific and clear decisions. Thus, in Trapetto, a Sicilian fishing village, I observed fishermen in 1958 repairing their nets on the beach. When, at evening time, some boats approached the shore, they quietly left their work, and, barefoot, in their trousers pulled up, moved into the water, got hold of the towing ropes, and silently hauled the boats to shore. The boats were rather flat, and waters close to shore were very shallow. Those incoming large boats, or *barcas*, were towed in by a cooperative effort without orders or exhortations. This type of cooperation is called spontaneous. However, in most cases cooperation requires decision making; such decisions are based on motions as explained below.

A typical South Italian neighborhood or *contrada* of the rural community of Fumone in the province of Frosinone is largely operated on the basis of customary consensus. When the time comes for such special tasks as sheep-shearing or wool-cleaning, neighbors help each other without any pay or compensation. The host just offers some food, and another neighbor comes in with a musical instrument. The work is done as part of a *festa,* and labor is not separated from leisure. I witnessed this type of communal work in Fumone as late as 1958.

On the other hand, a Grange of fishermen in the state of Maine is an institution based on common values. At the end of every meeting, the question is asked: "Is any member in need or in distress?". The action to assist is the result of consensus. A motion is made and voted upon—and thus it becomes a decision. Contrary to the command system, its execution is not based upon an expectation of a punishment or reward. When the money is collected to aid the needy or distressed member, no one is forced to give, and no one is rewarded for his generosity.

American society has developed its own traditional approach to group action. It is called "team work," a phrase that has no accurate equivalent in the continental European languages. Its essence lies in the cooperative voluntary action of a small group, oriented toward a definitely attainable and visible goal to be reached within a limited time span.

The team work involved in scientific research may serve as an example. It involves two or more people in small groups who act through consensus and consciously avoids tensions and arguments. This attitude is verbalized into such norm-phrases as "keep smiling" or "take it easy." The emphasis is on small, informal ties and friendships, which transforms what would otherwise be chores into a sport-type endeavor in a relaxed atmosphere, indicated by opinions like "we had a lot of fun doing it."

Team work is an essential part of the American style and of American strength and efficiency. It often appears in the process of a spontaneous formation of informal and highly efficient work groups.

3. COMPLEMENTARY STRUCTURES

A more complex social organism, an integral institution, like a state or even a large business corporation, usually has a complementary system of mutually interdependent command and consensus structures. In fact, any modern state must have its command institutions. For without such a system it is impossible to arrest a killer, to stop a reckless driver, to disarm and immobilize gangsters. Again, a democratic army has some elements of consensus; but to operate effectively it must also have a chain of command.

During the Congo revolution of 1960-1961, the command system of the Congolese army, the former Force Publique, broke down. Armed soldiers were on the loose and refused to obey anyone. In one particular case, representatives of the United Nations requested the release of some Canadian officers of the U.N. forces. The Congolese officer gave the order to his soldiers. These, in turn, went into a huddle to decide through a meeting whether or not to release the Canadians.

The total absence of a command system in an army or armed police force would put the citizen—in most cases—at the mercy of an armed soldiery. However, the Swiss militia system is a combination of the command and consensus systems, and other democratic armies contain larger or smaller doses of consensus.

The army is part of a war machine geared for defense or aggression. Tactical movements, let alone combat situations, require swift decisions and their rapid exeuction. There is often no time for the mechanism of motion-and-resolution. But a military unit which has common values, such as an ideology, and which is used to team work, may often show resilience and determination, while its command structure requires swift action.

A primitive society is based, above all, on consensus structures. War, at an early stage of social development, is part of other occupational activities and the warrior, when not engaged in it, is a hunter or food-gatherer. And even in war the discipline is not rigid.

Command institutions and the command structure develop with the appearance of a military establishment as a specialized institution and the military professional as a social class, and with the development of the state, which from its beginning has a tendency toward a monopoly of physical power and means of violence. A command structure and its attendant discipline supply the state with elements of power and control over its own subjects and with protection against aggressors and competitors for power.

4. DEMOCRACY AND
INSTITUTIONAL STRUCTURE

As has already been pointed out, any state usually possesses both consensus and command types of institutional structures. The problem is to determine their relative proportion and strength. The strength and amount of one or the other cannot, it seems to me, be measured in a quantitative manner. Still, even if the quantity cannot be measured, its distribution determines the quality of the state. Even if the quantity cannot be measured, it still exists, and as Hegel pointed out long ago, quantity determines quality. In fact, the two are, in a sense, identical.

The proportion, distribution, and intensity of the command structure determine whether a state is authoritarian or democratic. A state which is based primarily on a command structure and which extends this structure to such areas as legislation and judiciary is an authoritarian state. Contrariwise, a state whose structure rigorously limits the area and functions of its command system is basically a democratic state.

In a democratic state, the command institutions have their share of the common values and consensus. Hence, the quality of its discipline or command-submission mechanism is different and is based in part upon self-discipline or an execution of decisions based on common values. The intensity of the system is also different, as are its symbolism and the meaning of its symbolic behavior. And so the values and even the command system of a democratic army are, to a high degree, different from those of an authoritarian army. A democratic army relies more on team work and informal structures, and has a stronger tendency towards a mixed command-consensus structure.

The command structure in many cases is also combined with a spontaneous, consensus-like cooperative pattern. The command lines are advanced to a certain organizational point, e.g., to the level of a small "nuclear" group consisting of a few individuals. But once orders are given, a teamwork pattern rooted in consensus follows. Here is a case:

> March 11, 1972. A fire of a New York brownstone house at West 83 Street. A five story brownstone house was on fire just after 7 A.M., and I could observe the work of firemen on the terrace of the burning house. The number of the firemen varied. At the beginning there were two, later four, and eventually there were

seven men, including the commanding officer. [This was what has been called in this essay "a command structure."] The chief decision maker, the commanding offier, could be easily identified. All firemen had black helmets, the commanding officer a white one. He stood somewhat in the back, as if he tried to observe the entire "scenario." He had a microphone or radio in his hand. He evidently gave orders, to which the firemen in black helmets responded. But it was also easily observable that within this command, to a certain degree, the action of the firemen was "independent," their cooperation being spontaneous. They acted now on their own, within the situation to which they were ordered. It was a command "to a point," and from there on it was a cooperative and rather spontaneous action of the black-helmeted men.

It was striking behavior. From a distance of only four or five feet, they were directly facing an open fire and clouds of dense smoke. It was indeed a disaster situation. The men were calm, moved slowly, without nervousness and unnecessary agitation. While I observed them, the white-helmeted man never gave loud or irate orders. His arms seldom moved; there was nothing uncontrolled in his behavior. Dangerous and threatening big red flames were jumping from the windows, and smoke sometimes covered the entire scene. While two or three black-helmeted men were cutting the burning wood, pouring water, others stood by silently and moved in only when obviously needed.

As I understood the pattern, the white-helmeted man gave the orders, but within these orders the black-helmeted men made individual decisions, always demonstrating calm and spontaneous cooperative action.

This type of command structure provided the black-helmeted men on the front line with high flexibility and freedom of choice in the immediate situation. This was a strikingly intelligent and efficient performance.

In a complex society, an individual usually belongs to both types of institutional structure and takes part in both types of social relations. He is, therefore, subject to both types of influence. He learns early by experience what he is "permitted to do," and he learns the symbolism of both command and consensus situations through such respective symbols as standing at attention and shaking hands. Symbols are associated with behavior. They contain both values and information. In the latter sense, they are signals. A symbol used in group behavior is a message through which an individual communicates a social relationship and indicates the response he expects.

Thus, in Czarist Russia, a young male peasant was a member of a village community which exhibited a certain degree of mutual aid and group action based on consensus. But he also belonged to a subordinate subgroup—as a "subject" of the Czar and as a private in the Czarist army.

The modern state commands the monopoly of physical power; in addition, it controls a number of other instruments of power and influences and controls ideologies through symbolism and the media of mass communication. A democratic state emphasizes the symbolism and ideologies of consensus and supports institutions based on grass-roots movements. Its group action is based on consensus. Autocratic or authoritarian states, on the other hand, stress the values and symbols connected with command action and, therefore, prefer command-based institutions.

The state, acting through both a formal and an informal educational agency and also through its fundamental institutions, influences the future personality development of its citizens. It shapes their attitudes and behavior. But the state is not the only active agency in this connection. Other institutions and social values are also at work, and at certain historical moments their influence may be more powerful than that of the state. In such moments, when the balance between the dynamic forces of public institutions and values is upset, a fundamental change may occur.

NOTES

1. Back in 1853, Karl Marx noted the fundamental difference between the occidental state and what he called oriental despotism. While large hydraulic projects (control of water systems or irrigation projects) in Flanders and Italy led to voluntary associations and enterprise, in the Orient "where civilization was too low and the territorial extent too vast to call to life voluntary association [led to] the interference of centralizing power of government" and eventually to the extreme forms of despotism. Similarly Friedrich Engels writes in his article "On Social Relations in Russia" about oriental despotism which spreads from India to Russia. Karl Marx, "The British Rule in India," *New York Daily Tribune,* June 25, 1853 and Friedrich Engels, "On Social Relations in Russia," *Volkstaat,* 1875, both reprinted in Karl Marx and Friedrich Engels, *Selected Works,* Foreign Language Publishing House, Moscow, 1958, vol. I, p. 344ff., vol. II, p. 57.

Marx's articles on India were a starting point for the pioneering work of Karl A. Wittfogel on despotism and oriental state (*Oriental Despotism, A Comparative*

Study of Total Power, Yale University Press, 1957). This is, I suppose, the most important and original single volume on origin of states since Ludwik Gumplovich's publication of the well known theory of conquest. Wittfogel traces the origin of the total power and totalitarian state, based on what we have defined here as command lines to the great hydraulic projects of the Orient. He analyzes in a penetrating way the working and structure of total power.

VIII

Approaches to a Sociology
of International Relations

1. STUDY OF WAR AND PEACE

Elimination of war is certainly the most fundamental challenge facing
us today. It heads the long list of unsolved contemporary social and
political problems. The fact that this has been said so many times that
it now sounds like a weary platitude does not make war any less the
key problem, any less deserving of the best efforts of scholars as well
as of statesmen and men of good will.

It is, then, important to emphasize that maintenance of peace is no
longer the sole concern of pacifistic ideologists and theorists; and that
a passive solution of abstention from action or perhaps verbal renuncia-
tion of war is no longer sufficient. This was the creed of a large group
of pacifists throughout the nineteenth century and later after World
War I. But present and recent experience indicates that maintenance
of peace requires an active and dynamic policy, not solely abstention
from certain acts. Positive and constructive policies, in turn, require
understanding of ways to eliminate war, tensions, and conflict, and
these must be based on study of the nature of these phenomena. Peace
is not the absence of war, but a complex system of social and human
relations which must be sustained by international operations founded
on a solid structure of sound scholarship.

How much have the contemporary social sciences contributed as a
basis for the studies that are needed? And how much can they contrib-

ute? Especially, what has sociology to contribute to the cause of
world peace?

The question of war and peace is an ancient subject of study. But
for a long time this area was the property of historians, jurists, and
philosophers. Then, in the nineteenth century, students of economics,
sociology, and political science began to extend our knowledge of it.
Theories of conflict dominated sociological theory, and consequently
international conflicts were explored and became an important field
for sociology and economics. Then theories of social cooperation
began to develop. Studies of war and of the elimination of violence
from international relations were continued throughout the period
between the two world wars. Today this area of research belongs to no
less than four major fields—political science, economics, sociology, and
psychology (including social psychology and psychiatry).

The present tendency of the social sciences, however, is not what is
called in professional parlance "problem-centered." In other words, the
dominant attitude of social scientists in the West is that the objective
of the social sciences is to study social phenomena, interpret them, and
advance research that will contribute to an understanding of them.
According to this philosophy, the social sciences should not be chained
to a value or to a normative objective. (Of course, not all social scientists adhere to this viewpoint.) The approach is "method-centered" and
predominantly quantitative.

Yet, in sociology this attitude has led to the development of methods,
techniques, and theories which can be effective in limited, empirical
studies, though unable to embrace broad phenomena. The dominant
methods are analytical and lack the qualities needed for broad synthesis;
the functional approach (which is useful and important, even for studies
that will be suggested here) is far more relevant to the study of a well-
working society than to the problems of social change. In sum, current
sociology may not offer as much as it might to the problems of international relations, but its contribution is not at all inconsiderable.
Neither is the contribution of political science, which has considerably
advanced our knowledge of the broad field of international relations;
nor is that of history, the mother of the social sciences, which has continued the process of recording and interpreting the single unique
occurrences of conflict or cooperation.

It seems, however, that something more is needed today: a specialized field of social sciences, devoted entirely to the study of war and
peace, and oriented normatively toward the definite purpose of

eliminating war and violence between nations. Such a field requires an interdisciplinary approach, similar to the approach used today in the United States in the new field of area studies.

What should be the scope of such a field? It should include the study of those social relations and social conditions that are conducive to the use of force and violence between nations, and those that facilitate the elimination of force and violence between nations. These studies could be labelled the "Sociology of International Relations."

2. INTERPOLITICAL AND INTERETHNIC RELATIONS

What might be the major divisions of the proposed field? What direction can be suggested for studies within that field?

International relations can be divided into interpolitical and interethnic relations. Interpolitical relations occur between governments and, more broadly, between nation-states. Interethnic relations occur between cultural or ethnic groups. Tensions between states may be interpolitical and not interethnic; while interethnic tensions are not necessarily interpolitical. Before the war of 1914, the Czech nation was under Austro-Hungarian rule. Tension between Serbia and Austria-Hungary, as far as the Czech ethnic group was concerned, was at that time interpolitical but not interethnic. Again, the 1960-1970 tensions in Alto Adige are interethnic and not interpolitical—neither the Italian nor the Austrian governments encourage the conflict, indeed both are inclined rather to try to lessen it. The tension exists between the German ethnic group and the Italian ethnic group. Finally, in Kashmir the tensions between Pakistan and India are both interpolitical and interethnic. Interethnic relations, then, concern relations between nation-cultures, between certain cultural (in a cultural anthropological sense) or linguistic groups, each of which has a common cultural and historical tradition and, as a philosopher once put it, is "a community of fate."

We may distinguish, then, the following groups of relations: a) interpolitical (between governments and states); b) interethnic (between nations as ethnic groups); c) combined (involving simultaneously interethnic and interpolitical relations).

The state has the instruments of power, whereas the ethnic group is above all a community of common culture. The government and the state may reinforce or lessen tension by its policies. Therefore a tension which is only interethnic, with a state attempting to lessen tension, is less dangerous than one which is interpolitical while the ethnic groups are indifferent. Only governments have power to use force and violence on the grand scale through their military establishments. As long as conflicts are solely interethnic, while governments do not reinforce the tensions, the danger of war is not imminent. Such is the character of tensions in so-called tension areas, in definite geographical regions, where group tensions have a historical background. The 1959 tension over Berlin was of an interpolitical nature solely. Tension existed and exists between the governments, but the East and West Berliners do not show ethnic hostilities.

This division has its practical significance. Lessening of interpolitical tensions requires entirely different means from those required to lessen interethnic tensions. Interpolitical tensions are often falsely identified with interethnic ones for reasons of propaganda; still, interpolitical tensions can be solved on the level of governments and political action. Interethnic tensions, though, are a problem to the understanding of which sociology can make a contribution. And this, perhaps, may be the first field of exploration.

Extensive study of intergroup relations in the United States, the extensive research and consequent legislation in northern and western states in the area of interracial and interethnic relations—these are little known outside the United States. American scholars have carefully probed the social origin of prejudice, the role of the formative years in prejudice formation, the early childhood influence of family and peer group, significance of ethnic and ideological values in prejudice formation. This and similar research has profoundly influenced the public policies of cities and states, schools and universities. Mayors' committees on intergroup (or human) relations (such as in New York or Cincinnati), which are in charge of fostering cooperation and lessening tension between various racial and ethnic groups; states commissions against discrimination (like the one in New York), which represent public policy and enforce laws against discrimination in housing, employment, and other areas; school boards and teachers—all apply today many of the findings of sociology and social psychology and education toward the end of lessening tensions and breaking down prejudices.

Interethnic relations within a state are of course different from inter-

ethnic relations in an international context. Nevertheless the nature of
the tensions is the same. Ethnic prejudice, race prejudice, the values
of prejudice, its stereotypes and attitudes, the origin of prejudice, on
whatever level they occur, are identical in nature. An attempt to lessen
interethnic tensions on an international scale may use many of the
findings and methods already advanced by sociologists in this field.
There is a possibility here, then, of a fruitful extension of the field of
intergroup relations, ethnic and race problems, into the realm of
international relations.

3. CONFLICT AND COOPERATION

Two types of human relations (or, as they are called today, "interactions") are used as guideposts in sociological studies: association and
dissociation; that is, processes which lead to social integration and those
which are divisive and result in social disintegration. This useful
polarization has led to the classification of a great array of relationships, according to whether they lead to cooperation or conflict.
Sociology of international relations, then, would incorporate research
and study subdivided as follows: a) international cooperation; b) international conflict, i) techniques of lessening tensions, ii) techniques of
fostering cooperation. The social processes and techniques grouped
under each of these headings may belong to one of three classes: interethnic, interpolitical, or combined.

The study of international cooperation involves discussion of common
interests, common values, and common institutions. In the systematic
study of international cooperation emphasis has heretofore been put on
institutions. Political science and international law emphasize the
structure and form of international organization. The economist has
focused on the common economic interest. Nevertheless, the institutions will not work unless there is a certain amount of common, shared
values, which may or may not be economic in nature. Peace, as a value,
and the elimination of violence, are not necessarily economic. Still
other elements are essential in a process of cooperation; a certain amount
of shared interest (not solely economic interest) is of basic importance if
international organizations are to work.

The two paramount sources of interpolitical conflict are conflicts of

economic interests and conflicts of ideologies (values). Interethnic
conflicts may in addition stem from conflicts between and misunderstandings of cultural patterns and values, and from social-psychological
conflicts. The study of conflicts, then, should be centered on: a) conflicts of interests; b) conflicts of ideologies; c) conflicts due to misunderstandings of ethnic-cultural patterns and values; d) conflicts due to social-
psychological problems. All these processes may be interrelated. Therefore
their interrelationship is also a subject that must be explored.

4. PERSONALITY AND
INSTITUTIONS

The study of social processes between ethnic groups and between
states leads, of course, to the study of groups and their behavior. The
more important elements in the development of intergroup conflicts
include the political ideologies of extreme nationalism, racism, ethnic
values connected with hostile attitudes toward neighbors, and similar
group values. Head-hunting by primitive tribes, which is only part of a
culture of a given tribe, involves hostilities toward neighboring groups.
Head-hunting is not necessarily an economic phenomenon; it is, however,
closely connected with group values and symbols of status. What we call
advanced civilizations have head-hunting customs of a different kind, and
likewise they may be closely related to questions of status and class and
the symbols of status and privilege.

How should we approach the study of groups?

Social anthropology, as well as modern sociology, has developed a
method generally known as the "culture and personality approach."
Its core is the study of learned behavior and behavioral patterns, their
function and their influence on personality formation, and the consequent interaction between personality and social environment (the latter
being analyzed in terms of culture). Time and space do not permit a more
extensive discussion of this approach, save in connection with the study
of groups from the vantage-point of the sociology of international
relations.

From such a viewpoint it appears that values and institutions are of
primary significance (though of course other elements of group culture

should not be omitted). Values, of course, are closely related to the sum total of the culture. Ethnic values may contain elements of hostility toward definite groups. This may be a result of socioeconomic conditions and of historical experience. History and literature, as taught in the schools, may both serve to reinforce hostile attitudes. It seems to me that the antagonisms between the Poles and the Germans and between the French and the Germans were nourished in this fashion. Later experiences with Nazi Germany naturally reinforced the antagonisms, since the experience of Nazi occupation and the true facts connected with it were indicative of potential dangers which the future might harbor. Lessening of such interethnic tensions and hostilities cannot be successful without such changes and provisions on the interpolitical level as give real protection to the victim nations against the repetition of acts of violence.

Analysis of values may permit us to identify and understand the nature of interethnic conflicts; and it may also help us to discover such values as may help to foster cooperation.

Social values, or group values, are usually closely related to social institutions and socioeconomic conditions. They are transmitted by such institutions as family and school, or by a "super institution" which integrates many institutions and sets directions—the state. Antagonistic values and ethnic prejudices may be a result of learning in the formative years in the family, as perhaps reinforced by the school, and later by the state. This was the case with attitudes of hostility toward certain ethnic groups among European nations, as no doubt can be empirically proved.

Violence and force in international relations require a decision and a locus for such a decision in those who control the instruments of power. This implies a need for studying the institutions of power and its administration, the way in which power is attained, and the decision-making machinery. This leads us in turn to personality study, to the study of those who make decisions. This area belongs to the field of psychology—but it is still essential to our discipline.

The special approach of the sociology of international relations to the personality of leaders, of men in positions of power and decision, may be illustrated with Hitler as an example. A historian is primarily interested in his biographical data, as related to great historical events. A sociologist and psychologist studies the social conditions and primary groups (such as family) which produced him. Hitler and his movement cannot be explained solely by economics; a psychiatrist is needed to contribute to full understanding of Nazi personalities and the mass psychosis of a large portion of a nation.

While a number of useful personality studies exist, more and better ones are required. What is perhaps most needed is an interdisciplinary approach to biography.

Thus the second section of the sociology of international relations embraces study of: a) cultural and ethnic patterns and ideologies (values), especially those conducive to conflict or cooperation; b) institutions; c) personality types. This, we repeat, is by no means a new and unexplored field. An extensive literature is available, the product of wide research, which can supply a wealth of material and a foundation for further work. The sociology of international relations, though, suggests a definite focus and directon for this work, toward integration of related disciplines with the emphasis on a sociological approach.

5. CAUSATION

The third section of the suggested discipline deals with the problems of causation. The study of causation is fundamental to any social study oriented toward problem-solving. It should be said here that no study so oriented can function on the basis of any theory or method that abandons causation. Causality was first disputed in antiquity by the sceptics; later, from the eighteenth to the twentieth centuries, from Hume to Mach, it was challenged; and in the social sciences the concept of interaction or function, as suggested by Pareto, is in part an attempt to replace the concept of causation by a new, more precise theorem. Yet even Pareto in his later years (for instance in his well-known introduction to *Systèmes Socialistes*) applied the concepts of causation. Robert MacIver rightly indicated that a causal approach is of fundamental significance in the social sciences, and that causation as such is not an a priori theorem as some of the great philosophers (including Kant) argued, but a sequence of phenomena which can be observed. Whenever the social sciences face an issue of practical significance, such as delinquency, the concept of causality becomes an obvious and essential element of theory. Thus, it is an essential and important part of modern criminology. Neither an effective policy of crime prevention nor a rehabilitation policy can be developed without understanding of causation. Likewise, the study of methods of prevention of interethnic or interpolitical conflicts must be based on an understanding of causes. Only such an approach can suggest answers.

In regard to causation, the social sciences, like other disciplines, have a strong tendency toward "reductionism"—toward reducing the variables to a single one, which is regarded as the primary causal element. This is true, at least in part, of certain Marxist interpretations of war; and at the other pole it may be true of certain psychoanalytical or geopolitical interpretations of international relations. The tendency toward reduction was especially characteristic of the social sciences at the turn of the century; and it has, of course, its methodological merits. Such an approach narrows the investigation to a single variable, which can then be thoroughly examined. This approach also has some practical merit since situations do exist that monocausal theories seem to explain adequately.

Unfortunately no monocausal theory explains every situation. The economic factor may seem sufficient in one instance; ideological factors in another; the drive for power of certain human beings may explain a third. The sociology of international relations must find a more realistic and less simple approach to causation. We must not limit ourselves a priori to one causal approach. Or to put it more tentatively, we cannot exclude a priori the possibility that a number of causal factors may operate in the variety of social situations embraced by the vast field of international relations. We shall call the former a monocausal, the latter, a multicausal approach.

Ideally, the sociology of international relations should investigate each problem from a variety of monocausal approaches and also from a multicausal approach. Monocausal studies have, after all, contributed a great deal to our understanding of imperialism, war, and conflict.

Perhaps a modest beginning for causal studies would be a survey of sociological theories of international conflict and cooperation. Extensive and important work has been done in this area. Such a review should be useful for educational purposes and should provide a useful starting point for studies aimed at a more profound understanding of the social causality of war.

6. PLURALISM AND ELIMINATION
OF VIOLENCE

The purpose of a synthetical approach to international relations, as
was mentioned before, is to find alternative solutions to the problems of
eliminating force and violence from international relations, and to provide a basis for constructive solutions of the problems of peaceful coexistence and cooperation.

Any coexistence or cooperation requires two or more parties; a uni-
lateral desire will not suffice. It requires also definite actions—deeds,
not words. Adolf Hitler spoke about his desire for peace. Coexistence
can be established on the basis of fear and a common biological value
of survival; wider forms of international cooperation, mutual aid,
organized and continuous international interactions require a wider set
of common values in addition to common interests.

The present coexistence of the large blocs is based on fear: fear of
total destruction; and on a minimum biological set of values: survival.
Total destruction has become a deterrent to total war. This is surely
one of the weakest varieties of coexistence, and tensions are one of its
characteristics.

Pluralism is one of the alternatives which a sociologist of international
relations may find as a useful field for discussion and further exploration.
Pluralism in the field of religion was very successful in the development
of the United States. It was and is based on a minimum set of shared
common values and respect for differences. There is a common set of
values in the Judeo-Christian ethic in all the religions, and respect for
differences became part of the national cultural pattern. Pluralism
as a method of continuous and organized peacefulness, and as a means
of reducing tensions and perhaps eliminating force and violence between
nations and ethnic groups, suggests a minimum set of conditions: a) a
minimum set of common values shared by the governments; b) respect
for differences in values, ideologies, and interests which are not vital to
the quest for peace; c) respect for differences of values and ideologies
within the state and protection of the basic individual freedoms, human
rights, and civil liberties; d) a set of common interests—these, in a sense,
to be determined by the common set of values. Social welfare, a more

advanced standard of living for workers and peasants, control of natural catastrophes such as floods and hurricanes, control of epidemics, an increased supply of food—these are all common interests and common values too; and they require peace and international cooperation. There is a strong bond of common interest in favor of the achievement of logical objectives of social welfare and the social advancement of the people.

Do we have a common set of values? We do have a statement of such common values—the Universal Declaration of Human Rights, adopted by the General Assembly of the United Nations on 10 December, 1948. Not all member states really observe this bill, respect or enforce or even agree with its tenets. Nevertheless, the declaration expresses the desires of a sizeable part of mankind. Perhaps a public opinion study, using an adequate sample, could be made to explore the degree to which this declaration represents a set of common values of the peoples of the world. Naturally, as long as any government cleaves to the objectives of continuous expansion and ideological domination, pluralism will not work.

We may find alternatives other than pluralism. In fact, there is probably an arc of possibilities and degrees of international system which may work in exclusion of the use of force and violence. We may even venture to suggest that new forms of conflict, short of force and violence may be possible.

The difference between research and education and practical politics should not be forgotten. Science is not self-enforcing, especially social and political science. Change and practical policy require power. However, a better understanding of relations between states and ethnic groups, understanding of the causes of conflict and the conditions of peace, should give us a better chance to select the proper means for achieving the desired ends. It may, that is, help us in developing better policies.

Here, then is a suggested outline for a sociology of international relations, a general framework for research, study, and education. War to date has been almost a continuous phenomenon; the study of it must be attacked massively and in all possible ways. The sociology of international relations should be part of a general college education, as well as a field for theoretical approach, in order to create more enlightened public opinion and more general interest in the area. In this way, indirectly as well as more directly, it can give us some practical results. A naive propagandistic program that overlooks the realities of the present world, is not the best type of education for peace. Education for peace requires rigorous thinking and methods, scientific inquiry, and, above all, truth.

IX

Independence
and Interdependence

1. THE NEW HISTORICAL STAGE:
FROM EUROPEAN TO WORLD POLITICS

The problem of independence and autonomy in international relations cannot be explained, understood, or even discussed in an abstract way, out of the context of our political and geographical environment. This is a problem which has to be considered against the background of the entire globe and our recent technological developments. Only then can we see the seminal issue of cultural, national, and political independence or autonomy in a process of integration of states into a single association of nations (e.g., the European community). In such a macro-sociological, global approach, we do see perhaps more clearly not only the dialectics but also the complementarity of independence and interdependence.

It seems to me that our perception of the globe is changing, and perhaps changing rapidly. Man's exploration of space has given us different dimensions and different perceptions of the planet earth. We suddenly saw on our television screens a lonely sphere isolated in space. Thus far, scientists have not received any signals from space which could be identified as initiated by distant "kin." The regular emissions received seem to be pulses from other galaxies. Thus far we and our globe are

(Introductory address of the Round Table on Independence and Interdependence in International Relations at the XXII Congress of the International Institute of Sociology, Rome, 1969).

alone, suspended in a vast desert of distance. In this perspective our conflicts, wars, and ideological fanaticism have been reduced to human, or
perhaps, let me say, to proper proportions. They are irresponsible,
often silly, in this small and lonely house; they are frequently absurd
with regard to human survival. The advancing knowledge and understanding of our environment impose upon us a concept of life based on
the perception of an entire humanity, a concept of existence in which
peoples who are different, have different cultures and different political
institutions can and must live together in peace.

Almost in the same historical time, the discovery of nuclear weapons
and missiles also imposes on us new imperatives, forces us into rational
reflections and discussions, calls for prudent actions. There is not enough
space on this earth to fight wars with modern weapons. Indeed, it does
not make any sense to fight a war without victory, to fight and destroy
everything and everybody. This is one aspect of our international reality
which seems at first so obvious. The perception of our globe as a "whole"
sooner or later will have an impact on our understanding and our concepts of international relations. I hope I am not too optimistic. The
educational gap between societies, dogmatic and fanatical indoctrination
of totalitarian systems, totalitarian societies dedicated to war and conflict, may, however, endanger the rational and humane outlook, and the
entire system of international relations. Here is an area worth discussion
and calling for mass education. The perception of mankind and present
political realities are, however, two different things.

In the meantime, since World War II the system of international relations has changed profoundly. Until World War II any change of the
so-called European balance of power meant war or peace for the entire
world. In the not-so-distant past, conflicts on the Franco-German border,
although local at first glance, ignited wars not only in Europe but also in
Asia and Africa. In consequence, changes in these sensitive areas in
Europe resulted in territorial changes in distant lands, destruction and
death, exchanges of territories and population. This was one of several
sensitive contact lines of European politics. In south and east Europe,
changes and tensions on the Balkan borders or along the German-
Polish boundary line again had impact on world politics.

Now, the balance of power has shifted from the relationship of the
European powers to the relationship of the continents. From the past
stage of intra-European balance of power and relations crucial in world
politics, we have moved after World War II to an era of intercontinental
balance of power and relations. The Soviet Union and the Soviet Bloc;

the United States and Europe; the Atlantic Community; China; perhaps the "uncommitted countries"—these form the major elements of world politics. Basically, of course, the power resides with the superpowers. The major continental blocs now have the power to decide about world politics which at one time resided with the major European states.
But even the decision-makers of the superpowers are not fully independent in their actions. Even they are caught in the dialectics of interdependence (dependence on their minor allies) within their own system and in the world system of international politics.

Thus, a number of reasons—technological development, economic but above all political changes (distribution of political power and international threats)—set into motion the formation of large continental and subcontinental systems after World War II. Outside threats and loss of colonies also prompted tendencies toward a European Community. But the process is doubly a dialectical one. At the same time that tendencies toward Continental units or aggregates appeared, when the internal and external interdependence of the Continental blocs could be sensed, social and political trends toward national independence and autonomy also appeared; leaders and partisans became more vocal, audible, and visible by means of official statements, discussions, manifestations, and even conflicts. Even within blocs based on free association of nations and strong interdependence, as is the European Community (which is still in its initial stage), problems of national independence began to be of significance.

2. VOLUNTARY AND COERCIVE INTEGRATION OF NATIONS

The cohesion of the European Community is based, however, on free, voluntary agreements of the governments involved. The unity has been achieved with a simultaneous strengthening of individual, even national, political, and civil rights. The problem of independence and interpendence here is rather the issue of a hopeful future than solely a dilemma of today.

The Soviet Bloc, however, is based on a coercive unity with the consequence of war, conquest, and distribution of "influences" by the victors. This kind of unity comes into frequent conflict with national tendencies toward independence, autonomy, or even simple demands for individual and cultural freedom. Problems here are different. The nations of the Soviet Bloc, true, have become more and more economically interdependent. The Soviet Bloc moves slowly to a more integrated economic system. The tendencies toward national and political freedom and independence appear within this process of economic integration and coercive imposition of a single economic system.

But let us return to the Western European Community. The problem of independence and autonomy in international relations, as was suggested, is a dialectic one, and dialectical in many particular aspects.

On one hand, the process of voluntary association, of international integration (e.g., Europe), calls for safeguards which would also secure a continuation of national and cultural historical entities and differences. On the other hand, tendencies toward integration and interdependence, in which seasonal or semipermanent migrations of labor plays a part lead toward "Europeanization" of the population—emergence of a common, European cultural pattern in a more explicit, stronger form than exists today. In addition to local, regional, and national loyalty, a new kind of European consciousness and identity seems to be slowly emerging. An Italian *manovale* or *bracciante* who has spent five or ten years in France or Germany is not the same person he was when he worked only in Calabria or Campagna. The way of life is changing, and in certain areas moves toward a standardized European pattern. It is changing also because of technological progress and general improvement of living standards. Nonetheless, the abstract concept of political independence on one hand and cultural tendencies on the other may not necessarily move in the same direction.

In the meantime, nations are more dependent on each other—so are even the major blocs, though frequently opposed and antagonistic. In addition to world politics and world economics, in addition to raw materials, tools, and machines, we are more and more dependent on each other in our scientific efforts, which require cooperation, access to areas where research is conducted, and also access to information and sources. Even modern leisure involves an international exchange of population. Tourism, at one time a luxury of a small elite, has become a kind of mass movement, a social phenomenon international in its quality, important also as a source of national revenue. Economic development has led practically to a mutual almost global interdependence of nations. Technical assistance has even drawn one-time remote islands into this circle. Interdependence of nations is continually increasing.

In certain areas it has led to functional arrangements which sometimes pave the way toward a limited but constructive cooperation and initiate the road toward permanent forms of cooperation.

3. THE CHANGING ROLE OF THE EUROPEAN COMMUNITY OF NATIONS

Europe, however, does not play today the role which it deserves, to which it is called. Not only the economic resources of Europe, but above all the genius of European peoples—the great cultures the European Community has inherited—should have a much greater part in building a new and peaceful world system today.

For the first time in modern European history, the governments of the Mediterranean states of Europe have not indicated any clear and active interest in major changes in the distribution of political power in their neighboring waters, in changes in international politics in this vital area, especially in the eastern Mediterranean. European representatives did not voice any definite opinions on those changes; moreover, they did not advance any peaceful, constructive plans, did not take any initiative. Today the situation in this area calls for wise, peaceful, and constructive solutions. I have mentioned one area, but there are many more which call for new and constructive approaches. This area, however, is indicative that conflicts have not disappeared in spite of the United Nations, in spite of the sentiments of peace which seem to prevail in the simple desires of the peoples of the world. The conflicts all over the globe appear, however, in a new and different form. Limited but devastating conflicts continue in strategically important areas, to mention only southeast Asia. Armed intervention as a means of "pacification" in Hungary, indirect pressure in Czechoslovakia, are evidence of protest, discontent, and hidden conflicts. Even belief in an identical or similar political doctrine may not secure peace.

States of similar dominant ideologies may move, and in fact do move into conflict situations. The examples of Yugoslavia and the Soviet Union during Stalin's dictatorship, and China and the Soviet Union today, may serve as a reminder. The Soviet-Chinese "contradictions," to use Mao's term, are in fact moving into a variety of conflict situations. This is a process which has a long-range tendency. The Chinese government today claims Soviet territory, and the perception of this entire boundary situation is quite different on both sides. In addition, certain areas under dispute are inhabited neither by the Chinese nor the Russians. It is a long-range antagonism which can be answered by statesmanship and generosity on both sides or by protracted antagonism. History also offers examples of centuries-long cruel antagonisms and conflicts within "systems" of similar or even identical religious denominations and in historical periods when religion played a decisive role in group identification as ideology and nationality do today.

The nuclear weapons and missiles of immense power of destruction are, on one hand, as I said before, a threat to the very existence of mankind, but on the other hand, this same threat imposes an imperative of moderation, restraint, and cautiousness. It forces us to more rational and de-emotionalized thinking on and acting in international politics. The presence of these weapons has already imposed on the Soviet Union and the United States an imperative of limited cooperation, at least in the realm of arms limitation. There is one strong and common value shared at least by the decision-makers of the two powerful blocs: biological survival. But conflicts, as I have said, have not disappeared, tensions and antagonisms are with us and affect our daily life. However, because of the change of our technological environment, because of the destructive weapons we have produced, the forms of conflict are altered, they are limited in scope and in the use of resources. In short, they are limited conflicts and tensions.

In these new types of antagonisms and warfare, symbols and psychological appeals have been used as a modern technique to move people to antagonistic action. New forms of protracted wars have been applied in various areas of the globe, protracted wars which do not end, which stretch the conflict over years. New semantics are applied to them, and our values are eroded step by step by applying symbols and names to the opposites.

4. IN QUEST OF A SCIENCE
OF PEACEFARE

The science of warfare and strategy is an ancient and respected discipline. Our times call for a new discipline and a new scholarly approch to international relations, especially in this field which we may call "peacefare" as contrasted to "warfare." An attempt toward establishing a cooperative, global international system, a system of association of nations, which in the remote future may be able to eliminate physical violence from the field of international politics, calls for understanding of human and international society and for rational, scholarly, and constructive inquiry. Here is a task for a new field, a field of sociology of international relations, a field vital to our times. Of course, science or scientific inquiry, even a scientific discovery—as social scientists have said many times before—is not self-enforcing. But scholarly inquiry may suggest a direction for future constructive action. Again, let us return to the problem of independence in international politics. We may approach the same problem from a vantage point of social philosophy, its history or international law, but we may also study the international relations equipped with a sociological outlook, trying to explore international relations or processes as a result of political, but also social, economic, and cultural determinants. In addition to social relations and processes in this area, we may explore institutions and ways in which they really function, values which are emphasized, legitimacies applied, their social origin and function, the interests and conditions they may reflect. Furthermore, we may simulate or identify such pattern of international relations or integration which may secure the proper or desired balance of national independence, autonomy on one hand and integration on the other.

Thus, here is a broad field of sociology of international relations. We should start above all with the *structure* of these relations. In the general structure of international relations, two classes can be distinguished: 1) relations between governments and states—formal international relations, or we may call them "interpolitical"; and 2) the informal relations, or intergroup relations. The latter are relations between ethnic, ideological, or economic groups. Thus, conduct of policies of the German government vis-à-vis the French government in matters of their borders belongs to interpolitical relations. Relations between German and French ethnic groups in border areas, cooperation or antagonisms between these groups belong to the latter. Both are mutually interacting. The government to an extent may influence ethnic relations; on the other hand, ethnic pressures may also prompt government actions. The area of intergroup relations, so it seems to me, is an important area of sociology of international relations; but the former lends itself also to an interdisciplinary approach. Roughly we may suggest within the province of the discipline:

1. The study of international institutions, of social processes, and of relationships of cooperation, conflict, and neutrality.

2. Identifying and studying values (their origin) within their sociological context: values and ideologies that foster separation and independence and those that foster association, integration, and unity.

3. The relationship of ideologies, attitudes, and international institutions to interests and social-economic conditions; social and economic conditions, psychological determinants, and ethnic attitudes that foster cooperation and, on the other hand, those that generate antagonism and conflict.

4. And, to emphasize: the study of the origin, development, and reinforcement of ethnic values, attitudes, and changes in values and attitudes belongs here. This would broaden the methods or approaches in this field.

International sociology might favor an interdisciplinary approach. The term itself is somewhat misleading, meaning different things to different people. Generally it suggests a problem-oriented approach, as contrasted to a method-oriented one; it means also an attempt to understand the entire phenomenon instead of certain aspects. "Interdisciplinary approach" means a unified method and a single approach, a kind of synthetic "picture" in contrast to a "multidisciplinary," which suggests several segmented studies, corresponding to several disciplines. One does not necessarily exclude the other.

I have mentioned here a few of the general areas of such an inquiry— an inventory rather than a frame of reference.

Let us move to more concrete examples. The experiment in the reduction of tensions in the Saarland belongs to one of the more impressive experiences in the area of international relations and it is inspiring and hopeful. The generosity and wisdom of the French government and French people, who were the victors in the war, was a major contributing cause of this success. But now, after years, a psychological and sociological study of interethnic relations in this area is of great interest. Did the attitudes, ethnic prejudices, and hostilities of German and French ethnic groups toward each other change? Are the attitudes of antagonism and prejudice still strong? Is the overt behavior solely repressed by the government or other institutions? What are the attitudes of the younger generation of Germans, of children and adolescents toward Frenchmen (and vice versa) in the Saarland as compared with the attitudes of their parents? Now let us move to another field. The borders at one time were strongly divisive, fortified, and controlled. What is the nature of the French-German boundary now? How far does the present arrangement foster mutual interdependence and cooperation, how far does it preserve difference and independence? Here comes the entire area of the sociological influence of international borders.

We do know that ethnic and race prejudices develop in the early stages of socialization, during early childhood, and are later shaped or reinforced by peer groups and by the secondary environment—the community, the state. Ethnic attitudes still influence the evaluation of a situation; they do color the perception of international relations. This area of attitudes, values, and behavior vis-à-vis other national or ethnic groups belongs also to the field of international relations. Let us take another example. In almost every European nation a stereotype of the "Erbfeind," hereditary enemy, is well established. Prior to World War II, any high school student in many European countries could immediately identify the "enemy." A Bulgarian would probably name the Greeks and tell you the story of the emperor who blinded thousands of Bulgarians. The same emperor who was a tormentor of Bulgarians is a hero for the Greeks. Again, formation of stereotypes of neighboring nations, images of other ethnic groups, attitudes toward others is a seminal area of sociology of international relations.

Let us continue: Under what conditions do the attitudes of various ethnic groups change? For example, the people of Kossovo in the Balkans and those of Gorizia in Italy—what are the ethnic attitudes in these areas? What are their historical and sociological origins? Do they change?

Saar and the other areas mentioned were suggested here solely as examples. Such explanation is neither a new approach nor a new field. Research in fields mentioned here has already been advanced. Examples are Professor Jacques Freymond's study of Saar as an area of conflict (1950), the study of ethnic tensions in India conducted and written by Professor Gardner Murphy and sponsored by UNESCO (*In the Minds of Man*, 1953), Gordon Allport's work (*The Nature of Prejudice*, 1954), and Otto Klineberg's contributions in the social psychology of international relations (*The Human Dimensions of International Relations*, 1964). Those are well-known books. I shall also refer the reader to UNESCO's extensive bibliography, *La Nature de Conflits* (1957). The study of international conflicts has been extensively discussed in specialized journals and in the interdisciplinary areas of the behavioral sciences. We have mentioned here contributions in various fields of social sciences and not necessarily in the definite discipline of sociology. Disciplines here are largely overlapping; it is difficult to draw a sharp and dividing line. In addition, in a problem-oriented approach, the nature of the problem determines the choice of methods and approaches. Perhaps the field is broader than sociological; perhaps it is a social science field, which would suggest an interdisciplinary approach, which, in turn, is not a clear-cut concept either. We should be conscious of the limitations and problems of our scholarly interest.

I do not want to extend my discussion of concrete examples here. Work in interethnic and race relations forms a substantial area of American sociology. It seems to me that the still modest advance in this area could be fruitfully applied to the field of international relations.

The identification of this discipline requires extensive discussion. My identification of the subject matter is tentative; I am seeking to establish the limits of the field. The problem of method and the application of sociological methods to the universe of facts called international relations is of course essential.

We have learned in our century that contrary to the late nineteenth-century apperception, peace is not a simple absence of war; it calls for continuous and constructive action, but it also involves anticipation and the forecast of possible alternative courses of actions, and developments. This suggests a need for new methods, even new approaches, and also the development of applied disciplines.

Let me make here an additional point about training, education, and thinking in this area. Until very recently, I would say until 1945, what might be called the professional study of international relations was primarily a juridical and historical one. Schools which did prepare for professions in this field put the emphasis primarily on international law, organization, and diplomatic history. What was called political geography was an additional and necessary, descriptive discipline. Other subjects were rather ancillary; economics also played a role, sometimes a major one. Today, social sciences, especially behavioral sciences, have a powerful influence in the field of international relations in American universities and colleges.

I shall not question here the significance of juridical or historical approach. Both are important. But knowledge solely of those fields, and chaining our minds solely to the past, may not inspire us with solutions for times to come. I would be the last to promote an "ahistorical" education, or some kind of ahistoricism. Our culture is historical in terms of values and apperceptions of the present, and

historicism was and is creative and dynamic as a mode of thought in
sciences and humanities. Historicism is the closest kin of empiricism
and theory. Future problems and sometimes future solutions appear in
nucleus form in the past and present. They do not come from nowhere
or from nothingness. But it is not enough today to limit ourselves to the
traditional disciplines. To answer the problem of independence and
interdependence, the problem which is so vital to the hopeful association
of free nations, may need new solutions which do not yet exist, or
appear only in their nuclear form, or were not fully practiced in the
past. New problems and new perspectives call for new approaches to
the future organization and structure of international cooperation, and
such approaches may not have any historical parallel. Our thinking is
largely historical and empirical. What *ought to be*—what kind of
organization or social relations *should* be projected into the future—
suggests a departure from this pattern. Such thinking suggests, on one
hand, empirical exploration of things as they are, but it also asks for
projecting our minds into the future exploration of future solutions.
This calls for a more generous place for creative imagination, and
implies also the application of planning and policy sciences in the area
of international relations. We move here into the area of applied social
sciences, into explorations of possible alternatives which could be
envisaged by means of simulation of future developments.

5. RESPECT FOR NATIONAL
DIFFERENCE AND PRIVACY

This brings us to the problem of pluralism. It seems to me that one
of the alternative answers to the crucial issue of independence and interdependence in international relations is the theory and practice of
pluralism, based on one hand on unity, and on the other on respect
of difference. In other fields—for example, religion—the practice of
pluralism evolved out of the tragic European experience. The idea of
pluralism appeared during the Italian Renaissance (although the term
was not yet coined), when Pico de la Mirandola searched for a common
denomination of religions. Pluralism has developed as an answer on
one hand to religious persecution, on the other to politics of tolerance.
With all their weaknesses and prejudices, American colonists on the

whole were tolerant people in matters of religion. Of course, there were
congregations of bigots and Puritan dogmatists among them. Still, by
the eighteenth century, with all the oppressions of the social economic
slave system of the South, the North by and large practiced religious
tolerance which evolved toward pluralism, especially in certain colonies
(e.g., Rhode Island). Tolerance denotes a dominant religion but
respect for and toleration of others. Pluralism suggests no dominant
creed—at least in theory. It suggests equality of religions and unity
based on common values, common to all—and on the other hand respect
for difference. This is an ideal model, which of course does not fully
coincide with real conditions. Pluralism in international relations, as a
theory of unity and independence, suggests unity in certain political
and economic matters and respect for difference in other fields. Of
course, pluralism requires some basic shared values. It suggests also—
at least in the case of international relations—institutions which on one
hand would function as an instrument of integration, and on the other
as a device which would also protect and safeguard the differences,
"national privacy."

Let me suggest that as we respect personal, individual privacy in a
modern society, we may have to learn in the future, as a step toward
interdependence and autonomy, to respect national privacy, the right
of a nation to live its own life in terms of national culture, religion,
values, or political institutions. Invasion of individual privacy is in many
countries regarded as an unlawful act. Similarly, invasion of national
privacy may require international protection. Of course, there are limits
of such "privacy." But—within the principle of international protection
of human rights—one may suggest this most modest step toward establishing independence as one of the core values of international
relations.

Pluralism means that nations have the right to cherish their cultural
heritage and also choose their own way of life. On the other hand, there
are limits of pluralism. At a certain point pluralism has a tendency
toward separation, and the entire institutional system, as well as the
community, begins to disintegrate and break up. The process of pluralism
may also serve as a policy of liberalization of relationships between
ruling and subject nations, an evolutionary transition to a new order
between those nations.

Perhaps in the cntinuum that moves from cooperation through
neutrality to conflict begins the study of sociology of international
relations. George Simmel, and later Leopold W. Wiese, at one time

identified the classes of formal relations between groups.[1] Identification
of formal types of relations is relevant as an initial step. Study of those
relations must, however, move further and explore social and economic
conditions and values which generate such processes, social structures,
and relationships—interests which favor one or another.

Sociology of international relations is by no means an entirely new
area. Space does not permit mentioning the many earlier studies,
especially studies of what might be rightly called the sociology of
war, which go back a century. These were studies that explored mainly
the social economic conditions that generate war. In recent times,
interest in social psychology and sociology of war has resulted in
numerous and often pioneering volumes and studies.

It seems to me that especially today the emphasis of our inquiry
should be in the field of international cooperation. The nature of
conflict has been studied extensively and for a long time. Conditions
and behavioral patterns of cooperation in the field of international
relations, and various types and intensities of cooperation deserve
our full attention. Of course, this area has not remained entirely
uncharted, and political scientists, applying behavioral and sociological methods, have also advanced in this field.

We cannot change the political realities by research, but our findings
may suggest roads and solutions and may indicate alternative courses
of action open to man. Thus, our outlook extends slowly: historicism,
the interest in the past, is necessary to and complementary with the
inquiry into the problems of the present; but today our research must
also extend to the exploration of possibilities of the future.

NOTES

1. Kurt Wolff, trans. and ed., *The Sociology of George Simmel* (Glencoe:
Free Press, 1950); Leopold M. W. Wiese, *Allgemeine Soziologie als Lehre von
Beziehungen und Beziehungsgebilden der Menschen* (Munich-Duncker und
Humboldt, 1924-29); also see Howard Becker, ed., *Sociology* (New York:
John Wiley and Sons, 1932).

Index

ABOUT THE AUTHOR

Feliks Gross received his doctorate from the University of Cracow. He is professor of sociology at Brooklyn College and at the Graduate School, University Center, City University of New York. He has lectured widely in the United States and in Europe.